# MAHATMA GANDHI

Few men in their lifetime aroused stronger emotions or touched deeper chords of humanity than Gandhi. 'Generations to come, it may be,' wrote Einstein, 'will scarcely believe that such a one as this ever in flesh and blood walked upon this earth.' Yet it is important that the image of Gandhi does not become that of a divinity in the Hindu pantheon, but remains that of a man who schooled himself in self-discipline, made his life a continual process of growth, and tenaciously adhered to certain values to which humanity pays lip-service while flouting them in practice.

This revised and abridged biography is both chronological and analytical. Chapters are devoted to the background of Indian nationalism, the political scene, Gandhi's own religious evolution, his ethics and economics and his attitudes towards war and untouchability. But here also is the fullest account of one of the most eventful and moving lives in modern times.

# B. R. NANDA

# MAHATMA GANDHI

## A BIOGRAPHY

*m. K. Gandhi*

BARRON'S EDUCATIONAL SERIES, INC.

WOODBURY, NEW YORK

*Library of Congress Catalog Card Number: 65-22230*

*Printed in the United States of America*


EXCLUSIVE DISTRIBUTION RIGHTS IN
THE UNITED STATES AND CANADA
BY BARRON'S EDUCATIONAL SERIES, INC.

*To the memory of*
*my mother*
*and*
*my brother A.P.*

# CONTENTS

# Preface

FEW men in their lifetime aroused stronger emotions or touched deeper chords of humanity than Gandhi. 'Generations to come, it may be,' wrote Einstein of Gandhi in July 1944, 'will scarcely believe that such a one as this ever in flesh and blood walked upon this earth.' While millions venerated Gandhi as the Mahatma, the great soul, his political opponents saw in him only an astute politician. Not until 1946-7, when the transfer of power enabled them in their minds to disengage Mr Gandhi the man from Mr Gandhi the arch-rebel, were the British able to see him in a gentler light. And it was his tragic death which finally convinced his Pakistani detractors that his humanity encompassed and transcended his loyalty to Hinduism.

It is not easy to write the life-story of a man who made such a strong impact on his contemporaries. Yet it is important that the image of Gandhi does not become that of a divinity in the Hindu pantheon, but remains that of a man who schooled himself in self-discipline, who made of his life a continual process of growth, who shaped his environment as much as he was shaped by it, and who tenaciously adhered to certain values to which civilized humanity pays lip-service while flouting them in practice.

Though the arrangement of this biography is necessarily chronological, I have attempted at appropriate points to analyse Gandhi's attitude to important issues. The background of Indian nationalism, the Indian political scene when Gandhi returned from South Africa, his religious evolution, the transformation in his mode of life and acquisition of new values, his ethics, economics, and political movements, his attitude to war and untouchability—all these have been treated in separate chapters. This combination of the chronological and the analytical methods has facilitated the discussion in a single volume of Gandhi's long and many-sided life in some detail, and the correlation of the story of his life with the evolution of his ideas. Gandhi was no theorist; his principles evolved in response to his own needs, and the environment in which he found himself. In fact, it is as difficult to assess the events of his life without understanding the ideas which inspired him, as it is to interpret his ideas on religion, morals, politics, or economics without reference to the context of his own life.

I know how hard it is for one who has lived through the last forty years to be completely objective about the events of which Gandhi was the centre, but in assessing and reassessing events and personalities, it has been my endeavour to understand and to interpret in the historical perspective, rather than to uphold or to condemn. How far I have succeeded in this endeavour it is for the reader to judge.

I am grateful to the Government of India and the Director of the National Archives for permission to examine and use material from contemporary records, which have enabled me to present, for the first time I believe, a two-dimensional story of Gandhi's relations with the government. Any account of Gandhi's struggles which is wholly, or even largely based on official sources is, however, apt to be lopsided. I have therefore used these sources only to illuminate some of the obscurer spots, and to see events in their proper perspective.

The material for a biography of Gandhi is enormous. It is no easy task to try to sum up his long, rich and varied life in a single volume. I owe a heavy debt of gratitude to authors of numerous works on Gandhi and on the Indian national movement; acknowledgements have been duly made in the text, and in the footnotes. I am grateful to the Navajivan Trust for permission to quote from Mahatma Gandhi's writings. I would also like to thank the following for according permission to reproduce brief extracts, Messrs Victor Gollancz Ltd, from W. C. Smith's *Modern Islam in India*; Messrs Cassell and Company, from Vincent Sheean's *Lead Kindly Light*; Messrs Curtis Brown Ltd, from *Nine Troubled Years* by Lord Temple-wood; Oxford University Press, from *India: A Re-statement* by Reginald Coupland; and Messrs Jonathan Cape Ltd, and Philip Mason, from *The Guardians* by Philip Woodruff.

For assistance given to me in the preparation of this book my thanks are due to the Gandhi Memorial Museum Library, New Delhi, particularly to Mr Avanibhai Mehta; to Mr Girja Kumar, Librarian, and his assistants in the Indian Council of World Affairs Library; and to the staff of the Central Secretariat Library.

I am grateful to Mr V. K. Krishna Menon, Mr Pyarelal and Kaka Seheb Kalelkar, who were good enough to discuss and elucidate certain points. Among those who evinced keen interest in the progress of this book I must mention Mr Devadas Gandhi, who unfortunately did not live to see it; and Mr N. C.

Chaudhuri, Mr K. P. Mushran and Mr M. K. Kaul gave me much encouragement.

Mr B. N. Khosla read the entire book in manuscript and made useful suggestions. I alone, however, bear responsibility for the views expressed in the book and for its shortcomings.

I am indebted to my wife for her encouragement and patience during the long hours of silence in which this book was composed.

B. R. NANDA

# CHAPTER I

# Childhood

---

'WHY were you absent from the gymnastics class on Saturday?' asked the headmaster, as he looked severely from the attendance register to the fourteen-year-old boy who had been brought before him.

'I was nursing my father,' replied the boy, 'I had no watch and the clouds deceived me. When I arrived all the boys had gone.'

'You are lying,' said the headmaster curtly.

The year was 1883. The place was Rajkot, a small princely state in Western India. Dorabji Edulji Gimi, the headmaster of the Alfred High School, was a strict disciplinarian; he had made games compulsory for the students of the upper forms and accepted no excuses from those who failed to attend. The boy was Mohandas Gandhi. That he should have been convicted of lying was more than he could bear. He cried helplessly. He knew he was right but he did not know how to convince the headmaster. He brooded on the incident until he came to the conclusion that 'a man of truth must also be a man of care'. Never again, he said to himself, would he put himself in a position in which his explanations would be dismissed as lies.

He shone neither in the classroom nor in the playground. Quiet, shy and retiring, he was tongue-tied in company. He did not mind being rated as a mediocre student, but he was jealous of his reputation. He was proud of the fact that he had never told a lie to his teachers or classmates; the slightest aspersion on his character drew his tears.

This moral sensitiveness may seem precocious in a boy of fourteen, but it was part of the tradition of the Gandhi family. Mohan's father Karamchand and grandfather Uttamchand had been known for their integrity and for the courage of their convictions.

*Bania* by caste, the Gandhis were grocers and hailed from Kutiyana in Junagadh State. An enterprising member of the Gandhi clan, Harjivan Gandhi, bought a house in the year 1777 in Porbandar, where he and his children set up as small traders.

The family, however, came into prominence when Uttamchand, a son of Harjivan Gandhi, made such a striking impression on Rana Khimaji, ruler of Porbandar, that he was appointed as the *Diwan.*

Porbandar was one of some 300 states of Kathiawar Gujerat which were ruled by princes whom the accident of birth and the support of the suzerain power kept on the throne. Kathiawar, though feudal in structure and politically backward, had not remained impervious to currents of social reform which have given India her fundamental unity over the centuries. Some of the famous places of Hindu pilgrimages are situated in Gujerat: Dwarka in the extreme west, hallowed by association with the life and death of Lord Krishna, and the historic temple of Somnath. The teachings of Buddha, Mahavira and Vallabhacharya, have mingled in common emphasis on the sacredness of all that lives, and the songs of Mirabai and the poems of Narsinh Mehta have inspired the people. Gujerat has been noted for its enterprising businessmen, but it has also produced religious and social reformers; one of them Swami Dayananda, an apostle of reformed Hinduism, was a contemporary of Karamchand Gandhi. There is a certain tenacity in the Gujerati character which, when allied to a sense of mission, can sweep everything before it. Perhaps it was not an accident that Gandhi and Jinnah, the two men who in different ways most influenced the history of India in this century, had Gujerati blood in their veins.

To be a Diwan of one of the princely states was no sinecure in those days. To steer one's course safely between the wayward Indian princes, the overbearing British Political Agents of the suzerain power, and the long-suffering subjects required a high degree of diplomatic skill and practical sense. Uttamchand Gandhi proved a brilliant administrator and rescued Porbandar from the mismanagement and insolvency into which the state had drifted. Unfortunately for him, Rana Khimaji died young, and the Queen Regent, into whose hands the reins of administration fell, did not appreciate the virtues of integrity and independence in her Diwan. The inevitable clash came when Uttamchand gave his personal protection to Kothari, a minor but honest official of the state treasury, who had refused to oblige the Queen Regent's maid servants. The enraged Queen sent a contingent of troops to surround and shell the house of her chief minister; for long the ancestral house of the Gandhis bore the marks. Luckily the British Political Agent heard of these operations and had them stopped. Uttamchand left Porbandar for his native village in Junagadh, where he was kindly received by the *Nawab*. Observers noted, however, that the fugitive minister saluted the *Nawab* with his left hand. Questioned on this discourtesy, he replied that, in spite of all that had happened, his right hand was pledged to Porbandar. Uttamchand had to atone for this breach of court etiquette by standing barefoot in the sun for ten minutes; but the *Nawab* was chivalrous enough to commend his loyalty by exempting him and his descendants from payment of customs duty if they traded in their native village.

When the Queen Regent's rule came to an end and Rana Vikramjit came to the throne, efforts were made to get Uttamchand Gandhi back to Porbandar as the *Diwan*. He declined, and the post was given in 1847 to his twenty-five-year-old son Karamchand Gandhi, who served as *Diwan* for twenty-eight years. Like his father, Karamchand was an upright and fearless minister; in due course, he too incurred the displeasure of the ruling prince, and leaving the ministership to his brother Tulsidas, moved to Rajkot, where he became the *Diwan*. It was in this capacity that he had the temerity to reprimand the Assistant British Political Agent for speaking insultingly of the ruler of Rajkot; he was arrested, but refused to apologize to the British officer who, though taken aback by the intrepidity of a native minister, thought better of it, and let him go.

Karamchand Gandhi married four times, death having claimed three wives in succession. Putlibai, the fourth wife, was nearly twenty years younger than her husband. She bore him three sons, Lakshmidas (Kala), Karsandas (Karsania) and Mohandas (Mohania) and a daughter Ralitabehn (Goki), who survived all the brothers. Karamchand had also two daughters from his earlier marriages.

Mohandas, the youngest child and the future Mahatma, was born on October 2, 1869.

Even as the chief minister of Porbandar, Karamchand continued to share the three-storeyed ancestral house with his five brothers and their families. The suite allotted to him was on the ground floor and had, besides a tiny kitchen and veranda, two rooms, one of which was 20 feet long and 13 feet wide, and the other 13 feet long and 12 feet wide. It was in this house, with his brothers and sisters, and numerous uncles and cousins that Mohandas Gandhi grew up. The town of Porbandar, with its narrow lanes and crowded bazaars, surrounded by massive walls which have since been largely demolished, is no more than a

stone's throw from the Arabian Sea. The buildings, though by
no means architecturally distinguished, are built of a white
soft stone which hardens with the years, shines like marble in
the sunlight, and has given to the town the romantic name of
the 'White City'. The streets are dotted with temples; the
ancestral house of the Gandhis was itself built around two
temples. But the life of this port was and is necessarily centred
on the sea. Even in the latter half of the nineteenth century
there were scores of families with business contacts overseas, and it was to one of these contacts that M. K. Gandhi
owed his introduction to South Africa.

When he was seven Mohan's parents moved 120 miles east
to Rajkot; though the family link with Porbandar remained,
Rajkot became henceforth the Gandhis' second home.
Rajkot had no sea-beach where the children could play; it lacked
the picturesque panorama of the 'White City', but politically
and socially it was less of a backwater and had better facilities
for education. In Porbandar, Mohan had attended a primary
school where the children wrote the alphabet in dust with their
fingers. Rajkot boasted of a high school.

Mohan's mother Putlibai was a capable woman who made herself felt in court circles through her friendship with the ladies of
the palace. But her chief interest was in the home. When there
was sickness in the family she wore herself out in days and
nights of nursing. She had little of the weakness, common
to women of her age and class, for finery or jewellery. Her life
was an endless chain of fasts and vows through which her
frail frame seemed to be borne only by the strength of her
faith. The children clung to her as she divided her day between
her home and the temple; her fasts and vows puzzled and fascinated them. She was not versed in the Scriptures. Except for a
smattering of Gujerati, she was practically unlettered; her knowledge of religion was acquired at home or from discourses heard
at religious gatherings. She was orthodox, even superstitious.
She would not let the children touch an 'untouchable' or look
at the lunar eclipse. Mohan was more curious than the other
children and asked searching questions. How did contact with
Uka, the household sweeper, contaminate? How could the
eclipse harm the onlooker? Her explanations did not always
carry conviction. But for all this scepticism he was bound to her
by bonds the strength of which he felt throughout his life. 'His
voice softens when he speaks of his mother,' wrote an observer
in 1908, when Mohan was thirty-nine years old, 'and the light

of love is in his eyes'. She could not satisfy his curiosity nor stop him from rushing headlong into the secret atheism of his adolescence, but her abounding love, her endless austerities and her iron will left a permanent impression upon him. These qualities proved an undying source of inspiration for one whose life was to be one long struggle for self-mastery, and whose battles were to be waged and won in the hearts of men. The image of woman he imbibed from Putlibai was that of love and sacrifice. Something of her maternal love he came to possess himself, and as he grew it flowed out in ever increasing measure, bursting the bonds of family and community until it embraced the whole of humanity. He owed to his mother not only a passion for nursing, which made him wash lepers' sores in his *ashram*, but also an impetus for his technique of appealing to the heart through self-suffering—a technique which wives and mothers have practised from time immemorial.

Mohan's father Karamchand Gandhi was a man of little academic education but rich in experience of men and affairs. He was, in the words of his son, 'a lover of his clan, truthful, brave, generous'. He had little interest in piling up money and left hardly any property for his children. The epics, the *Rama-yana* and the *Mahabharata*, were recited in the house, and occasionally there were discussions with Jain monks and Parsi and Muslim divines. But religion was for Karamchand mostly a matter of ritual. 'Whatever purity you see in me,' recalled his son at the age of sixty-two, 'is derived from my mother, not from my father.'[1]

The half-century which divided Karamchand from his youngest son made the father not so much an affectionate companion as an object of reverence. It was a child thus predisposed who read the ancient play *Shravan Pitribhakta* portraying the boundless love of the mythical boy Shravan for his parents. The picture of Shravan carrying his blind parents on a pilgrimage by means of slings fitted to his shoulders was indelibly printed on Mohan's mind. The story moved him deeply and Shravan became his model. Obedience to parents became his motto. The rule of implicit obedience was extended from the parents to teachers, and from teachers to all 'elders'. This surrender of the privileges of childhood may have contributed to an excessive passivity, passing into a morbid diffidence and preventing him from playing with, and even speaking to, other children. If a prize or a medal came his way at school, he took it to be beyond his deserts;

[1] *The Diaries of Mahadev Desai*, Vol I, entry dated March 31, 1932.

he carried the distinction in his inner pocket, as it were, lest others should discover his poor worth.

And as if this were not sufficient handicap for a boy in his teens, he was married at the age of thirteen. For the greater economy and convenience of the parents, it was a triple wedding in which Mohan, his brother Karsandas and an elder cousin were married off. Mohan's bride, Kasturbai, was the daughter of Gokaldass Makanji, a merchant of Porbandar and a friend of the Gandhi family. Love came to these children, and more so to Mohan, with the hurricane force of adolescent awakening. From a Gujerati pamphlet he had imbibed the ideal of life-long fidelity from her and to exercise a surveillance over her movements. To visit friends or the temple, she had to have his permission. The fact that he was under the influence of a vicious companion who fanned his jealousy made matters worse. Kasturbai, the proud little girl, chafed under these arbitrary restrictions, and in her own quiet and determined way resisted them. These 'dark days of doubts and suspicions' proved to be a useful education to the young husband. 'I learnt,' he told John S. Hoyland many years later, 'the lesson of non-violence from my wife when I tried to bend her to my will. Her determined resistance to my will on the one hand, and her quiet submission to the suffering my stupidity involved on the other, ultimately made me ashamed of myself and cured me of my stupidity in thinking that I was born to rule over her; and in the end she became my teacher in non-violence.' The immediate effect of the marriage was that Mohan lost a year at school, though he made it up later by skipping a class. Luckily for him marriage did not mean, as it meant for his elder brother and cousin who had been married at the same time, the end of his education.

Mohan had secretly prided himself on being an obedient child. He had learnt 'to carry out the orders of the elders, not to scan them'. But there came a time when this want of independence began to hurt. The form which adolescent revolt takes depends upon the strength of the taboos which are broken. In the Vaishnava community in which the Gandhis lived meat-eating and smoking were horrible sins. There is little wonder, therefore, that Mohan should in this rebellious phase have been enticed into them. Mehtab, one of his schoolmates, filled the role of Machiavellian tempter. He argued in favour of meat-eating. He claimed that many people in the town, including the teachers in the school, secretly took meat in spite of their pretence to the contrary; that the British, being meat-eaters, were hardy and could not be overthrown by the vegetarian Indians. Meat was in fact a cure-all; it could prevent boils and tumours and drive off the ghosts which troubled little Mohan in his sleep.

The subtle sophistry of this friend overthrew Mohan's last defences and he consented to a meat feast, at a lonely spot by the river in order to spare his parents a shock. He had a bad night after the first feast, 'the goat bleating inside me'. The dinners were repeated at suitable intervals and gradually he overcame his early disgust. One complication, however, remained: after joining in these furtive feasts, he had to invent apologies to his mother for lack of appetite at mealtime. Since lying went against the grain, he was driven to the conclusion that the change in his diet would have to wait until he grew up and became accountable to no one except himself.

Smoking was another transgression of this period. With another boy Mohan began to pilfer stumps of cigarettes thrown away by his uncle. This was of course unsatisfactory. As the children had no money to buy cigarettes, they began to steal the servants' coppers, but that did not take them far. Then they started smoking the stalks of a wild plant. Their young spirits at last felt thwarted. One evening, in sheer despair, they slipped into a temple for a final ceremony to cut the Gordian knot by committing suicide. Their courage failed them at the critical moment; rather than quit the world, they decided to give up smoking.

Another escapade of the period was the theft of a bit of gold to pay off a debt incurred by his brother. The guilt weighed upon him until he could bear it no longer. He wrote out a confession and presented it to his father; their simultaneous tears at once marked the atonement by the son and forgiveness by the father.

The adolescence of Mohan was no stormier than that of many of his contemporaries; adventures into the forbidden land of meat-eating and smoking and petty pilfering were, and are, not uncommon among boys of his age. What was extraordinary was the way his adventures ended. In every case he posed for himself a problem for which he sought a solution by framing a proposition in moral algebra. 'Never again' was his promise to himself after each escapade. And he kept the promise.

There was nothing to mark him off from other boys of his age except perhaps an unnatural seriousness and passivity. He did not seem to be a child who could elbow his way forward. But under his cold unprepossessing exterior there was a burning passion for self-improvement. It was his habit 'to forget what he did not like and to carry out what he liked'. What others read for pleasure he read for instruction. Millions of children—and adults—in India have heard the stories of Prahlad and Harishchandra. The boy Prahlad, who suffered untold hardships without faltering in his faith in God, and King Harishchandra, who sacrificed all he had for the sake of truth, are heroes of Hindu mythology, the creatures of poetic imagination, and have been treated as such. But for Mohan they became living models. History or literature were for him not merely an un-minted mine of wonder, but an inspiration for a better and purer life. While children of his age competed for the conventional prizes and trophies in the school, this sensitive child posed and puzzled out moral problems for himself.

# CHAPTER II

# Off To England

MOHAN passed the matriculation examination in 1887. His father's death a year earlier had strained the means of the family. Being the only boy in the family who had persevered in his studies, its hopes rested on him and he was sent to Bhavnagar, the nearest town with a college. Unfortunately for Mohan, the teaching in the college was in English. He was unable to follow the lectures and despaired of making any progress.

Meanwhile, Mavji Dave, a friend of the family, suggested that Mohan should go to England to qualify at the bar. It was easy enough to become a barrister; in contrast, the degrees of Indian universities consumed more time, energy and money and had less value in the market. A Bombay degree was likely to produce nothing better than a clerical post. Mavji Dave argued that if Mohan aspired like his father and grandfather to be the *Diwan* in one of the states of Kathiawar, he needed a foreign degree. Karamchand and Uttamchand Gandhi had held high posts and managed with very little education, but times had changed. The universities were now producing Bachelors of Arts and Law by the thousand, products of the English education for which Macaulay had planned. There were, however, too many of them. It was, therefore, a definite advantage in the competition for the plums of public service to be able to sport a foreign degree.

Mohan jumped at the idea of going abroad. Not only was he anxious to see England, 'the land of philosophers and poets, the very centre of civilization', but also because it offered him an immediate escape from the agony of attending the classes in Bhavnagar College, where the teachers seemed to be talking over his head. His elder brother had no doubt that the proposal was attractive but wondered how they could afford it. Mother Putlibai felt lost. How could she let her youngest boy sail to an alien land to face unknown temptations and dangers? She wished her husband had been living to take a decision to which she felt unequal. She asked Mohan to seek the advice of his uncle, who was the eldest member of the Gandhi family. Mohan trekked by cart and camel to Porbandar to see his uncle, who was courteous but visibly reluctant to bless the unholy trip across the seas. Another disappointment was in store for him when he approached Mr Lely, the British Administrator of Porbandar, a state which the Gandhis had served so well, to grant him a scholarship for studies in England. The British officer treated him with scant courtesy, asked him to take a degree at Bombay University and then ask for a scholarship. All this was depressing enough, but Mohan did not lose heart. He knew that if the trip to England fell through, he would have to return to the classrooms of Bhavnagar, a none too pleasant prospect. He thought of selling his wife's jewellery. This desperate course was rendered unnecessary when his generous brother undertook to find funds. The misgivings of the mother were set at rest when a Jain monk, Becharji Swami, made the boy take a solemn vow that he would not touch wine, woman or meat while he was away from the shores of India.

A fresh hurdle appeared just when Mohan was about to sail. The elders of the Modh Bania caste to which the Gandhis belonged summoned him before the caste tribunal and declared that the trip to England was a violation of the Hindu religion. The nineteen-year-old boy, who had been unable to stammer a few words of thanks at a farewell party at his school, mustered the courage to resist the browbeating of the bearded leaders of his caste. Infuriated at this defiance, the caste tribunal issued a fiat of excommunication against Mohan. But before this order could become a real nuisance, he sailed from Bombay on September 4, 1888.

From the rural surroundings of Rajkot to the cosmopolitan atmosphere of a steamship was a tremendous change for Mohan. Adaptation to Western food, dress and etiquette was a painful process. He felt tongue-tied when accosted by fellow-passengers. The slender hold on the English language which he had acquired in school and college nearly gave way. He could hardly speak without being weighed down with a feeling that he was making a fool of himself. The vegetarian vow added to his embarrassment. Afraid to question the waiters on the composition of the menu, he lived on the fruits and sweets he had brought with him. He received much gratuitous advice. One passenger told him that he would not be able to do without meat after leaving Aden. When Aden had been safely passed, he was warned that meat would be indispensable after crossing the Red Sea. In the

Mediterranean, a prophet of doom announced grimly that in the Bay of Biscay he would have to choose between death on the one hand and meat and wine on the other.

His sense of isolation increased after he landed in England. A terrible feeling of loneliness gripped him. It was partly the usual nostalgia of the Indian student as he begins his self-imposed exile. To it were added the misgivings of an exceedingly diffident and sensitive boy. His thoughts wandered back to his home in Rajkot, his beloved mother, his wife, his baby boy. The prospects before him appeared to be bleak. He had to acclimatize himself to another climate, strange surroundings and a new mode of living. Vegetarianism, to which he was vowed, seemed to condemn him not only to perpetual semi-starvation, but also to public ridicule. Indescribably lonely, he wept as he lay awake in bed, and thought of the three long years which must run their weary course before he could return home.

The vegetarian vow became a continual source of embarrassment to him. Friends in England feared that his food fads would ruin his health, and make of him, socially, a square peg. He could not rebut the arguments of advocates of meat-eating; secretly he had always wanted to take meat but felt bound by the vow. When he felt puzzled or weak he went on his knees and prayed to God to help him keep the word he had given to his mother.

One day, while roaming about in London, he stumbled upon a vegetarian restaurant in Farringdon Street. 'The sight of this restaurant,' he recorded later, 'filled me with the same joy that a child feels on getting a thing after its own heart.' He had his first hearty meal since he had sailed from India. In the restaurant he also bought a book entitled *Plea for Vegetarianism* by Salt, whose arguments went home. A meatless diet had been hitherto a matter of sentiment to him; henceforth it was one of reasoned conviction. Vegetarianism, adopted out of deference to his parents, had been an inconvenient obligation, but before long it became a mission, the starting point of a unique discipline of body and mind, which transformed his life. The discovery of this restaurant was an event more significant than he could see at the moment. There was a long and hard but sure road which led from Farringdon Street in London to the Phoenix and Tolstoy Settlements in South Africa, and to the Sabarmati and Sevagram Ashrams in India.

The conversion to vegetarianism brought a new self-assurance to Gandhi. Henceforth he might appear a crank, but he did not feel like one. His friends, however, feared that by insisting on meatless meals he would make a mess of his health as well as his studies. To disarm his critics, and to prove that, vegetarianism apart, he was not impervious to the new environment, he began to put on a thick veneer of 'English culture'. There was a lot he had to cover up. Used to his native Kathiawari costume in school and college, he had felt palpably awkward in English dress while travelling aboard ship and stepping ashore. His hold on the English language was tenuous and even ordinary conversation entailed a laborious mental rehearsal from his mother tongue.

Having made up his mind to become an 'English Gentleman', he spared neither time nor money. Whatever the cost, the veneer had to be the best in the market. New suits were ordered from the most fashionable tailors in London; the watch was adorned with a double gold chain from India; under expert tuition lessons began in elocution, dancing, and music. The product of these sartorial and cultural exercises was later described by a contemporary. This is how the twenty-year-old M. K. Gandhi struck Sachchidanand Sinha in February 1890, when he saw him in Piccadilly Circus: 'He was wearing a high silk top hat burnished bright, a Gladstonian collar, stiff and starched; a rather flashy tie displaying almost all the colours of the rainbow, under which there was a fine striped silk shirt. He wore as his outer clothes a morning coat, a double-breasted vest, and dark striped trousers to match and not only patent leather boots but spats over them. He carried leather gloves and a silver-mounted stick, but wore no spectacles. He was, to use the contemporary slang, a nut, a masher, a blood—a student more interested in fashion and frivolities than in his studies.'[1]

Gandhi could not, however, throw himself into this experiment with complete self-abandon. The habit of introspection had never deserted him. English dancing and music did not come easy to him. Drapers and dance halls could turn him into an English gentleman, but only an English gentleman about town. His brother was straining the slender resources of the family, perhaps incurring debts to enable him to continue his studies in England. As he brooded over it all, he realized the folly of chasing the will-o'-the-wisp of an English gentleman.

After a brief three months' excursion, the introvert returned to his shell. There was a rebound from extreme extravagance

[1] Article in the *Amrit Bazar Patrika* (Republic Day Souvenir), January 26, 1950.

to meticulous economy. He kept an account of every farthing he spent. He changed his rooms, cooked his own breakfast, and to save bus fares walked 8 to 10 miles daily. He was able to pare down his expenses to £2 a month. He began to feel keenly the obligations to his family and was glad that he had reduced the calls on his brother for funds. Simplicity harmonized his inward and outward life; the dandyism of the first three months had been only a defensive armour against those who considered him a misfit in English society.

The connection between dietetics and religion may seem far-fetched, but the two were intimately related in the evolution of M. K. Gandhi. His early vegetarianism was part of his Vaishnava heritage; he had abstained from meat because it was repugnant to his parents. Sheikh Mehtab, a clever schoolmate, had coaxed him into meat-eating for a while; but he had given it up when obliged to tell lies to his parents to ward off their suspicions, and decided to defer the enjoyment of this delicacy till he was old enough to be independent of parental authority. In England he scrupulously observed the promise he had given to his mother not to touch meat, but he was conscious all the time that sentiment rather than reason was on his side. Not until he read Salt's book did he discover the virtues of vegetarianism. With the zeal of a new convert he devoured books on dietetics, developed an interest in cooking, outgrew the taste for condiments, and came to the sensible conclusion that the seat of taste is not in the tongue but in the mind. The control of the palate was one of the first steps in that discipline which was to culminate many years later in total sublimation. The dietary experiments, dictated by considerations of health and economy, were to become a part of his religious and spiritual evolution.

The immediate effect of vegetarianism was to give a new poise to him in England, and to draw him out of his shell. He made his first venture into journalism by contributing nine articles to the *Vegetarian*. These articles, largely descriptive, dealt with the diet and habits of the Indian people, their social system and festivals, and had occasional flashes of humour. That he should have sent these articles for publication is a notable achievement, if we recall that in Bhavnagar College he had been unable to follow lectures in English. He became a member of the executive committee of the London Vegetarian Society and took an interest in designing its badge. In Bayswater, where he stayed for a

short time, he founded a vegetarian club. He came into contact
with at least one eminent vegetarian, Sir Edwin Arnold, the
author of *The Light of Asia* and *The Song Celestial*, two books
which moved him deeply. In the vegetarian restaurants and
boarding-houses of London he came across not only food faddists
but also a few devout men of religion. He owed his introduction to the Bible to one such contact.

His excessive shyness was not, however, shaken off by three
years in England. Apart from the Vegetarian Society, the only
organization which drew him was the *Anjuman Islamia*, an
organization of Indian Muslims, mostly students, who debated
political and social questions over light refreshments. Non-
Muslim students were permitted to join these discussions, which
brought together a number of Indian students in England who
were later to make their mark in India's public life. Among these
were Gandhi, Abdur Rahim, Mazharul Haq, Muhammad
Shafi, Sachchidanand Sinha and Harkishan Lal Gaub. Gandhi
(along with Sinha and Harkishan Lal) held nationalist views on
political questions, but he spoke little and unlike some others,
lacked the faculty for vehement assertion.

New literary, social and political forces were stirring in the
England of the eighties and nineties but there is little evidence
of Gandhi having been susceptible to them. He does not refer in
the course of the forty-page account of his stay in England to
Karl Marx, Darwin or Huxley. Science, literature and politics
did not excite him. He was wholly preoccupied with personal
and moral issues. The crucial problem for him was how to marshal his inner resources in order to keep the promise he had
given to his mother, to fight the recurring temptations of 'meat,
wine and woman', and to inject into his daily life simplicity,
economy and purpose. His efforts at journalism were confined to
the columns of the *Vegetarian* and his reading to religious texts
such as the *Gita* and the New Testament. If any subject seemed
to strike a vital chord in him, it was religion. Nevertheless, at this
stage his acquaintance with religion, even with Hinduism, was
quite elementary.

In an article in the *Vegetarian* of June 20, 1891, Gandhi gave
his own assessment of what the stay in England had meant to
him: 'In conclusion I am bound to say that during my nearly
three years' stay in England I have left many things undone . . .
yet I carry one great consolation with me, that I shall go back
without having taken meat or wine, and that I know from personal experience that there are so many vegetarians.'

Here was an earnest but diffident young man with a definite but limited range of interests. Not even the most partial observer could have detected in this young barrister-at-law any promise of distinction when he sailed for India. He did not seem to be cut out for a brilliant career, least of all in law or politics.

# CHAPTER III

# Briefless Barrister

As Gandhi gave up the cultivation of the social graces and turned his attention to his studies, he felt that the law course could not engage him fully and that he had time to improve his basic education. His high school training had been indifferent; the lack of fluency in English troubled him in particular. Since he could spare neither the time nor the funds to go to Cambridge or Oxford, he decided to prepare for the matriculation examination of the London University. Undismayed by the first attempt, in which he was ploughed in Latin, he passed the examination. Knowledge of Latin proved useful to him in the study of law; it was an asset to him when he practised in South African courts where Roman Dutch was the Common law. Latin also helped to fashion his simple and crisp English prose.

Law Examinations at this time were not difficult; the examiners were generous and the percentage of successes was high. Most law students crammed summaries of their text-books for the examination; but Gandhi was too conscientious to use these short cuts. He read the Roman Law in Latin, and laboriously studied Broom's *Common Law*, Snell's *Equity*, Tudor's *Leading Cases*, William's and Edward's *Real Property*. Thanks to his conscientiousness and diffidence he turned even the bar examination into an arduous affair; when he got through it, he was assailed by fresh doubts and anxieties. He had read the law, but could he practise it? He found it hard enough to speak to strangers even in a small party. How would he be able to cross swords with his rivals in the court room? He had heard of legal luminaries like Sir Pherozeshah Mehta, and could well imagine the sorry figure he would cut in comparison. Frantically, he looked for advice. He could not venture to meet the great Indian lawyer and statesman Dadabhai Naoroji, who was in England at the time. An English lawyer, however, advised the Indian youth to widen his reading, to improve his knowledge of history, and to study human nature. Naïvely, Gandhi hastened to buy a book on physiognomy and to equip himself for the difficult role of a practising lawyer. He distilled what consolation he could from the opinion of this English lawyer that exceptional acumen, memory and ability were not the only prerequisities for success at the bar, that honesty and industry could also go far. Thus, 'with just a little leaven of hope mixed with despair', he sailed for India.

A great shock lay in store for him when he landed at Bombay. His mother had died while he was in England. The news of the tragedy had been deliberately withheld from him. It was a cruel blow. Many years later, he recorded in his autobiography, that 'most of my cherished hopes were shattered'. The austere life, the immutable faith and the abounding love of his mother were, nevertheless, indelibly imprinted on him. She was perhaps the biggest single influence in shaping the Mahatma of the future, the man in the loincloth, vowed to days of silence and fasts, waiting upon God for guidance, and answering hate with love.

He had now to reckon with the Modh Bania caste which had excommunicated him when he had sailed for England. As a sop to orthodoxy, he was persuaded by his brother to visit Nashik to wash off his transgression with a dip in the holy waters of the Godavari. This atonement appeased only one section of the Modh Banias; the other section stubbornly declined to lift the ban. Gandhi met this tyranny in an unorthodox manner. He did not protest nor betray any rancour against his opponents; indeed he co-operated in the enforcement of the boycott against himself. This attitude blunted the edge of caste-tyranny; the appeal to the heart went home. Many of his critics among Modh Banias later whole-heartedly supported his social and political movements. These early experiences did not sour him. He continued to defend the institution of caste, 'the Varnashramdharma', without, of course, its later incrustations.

Gandhi was anxious to justify the hopes of his family which had invested so much in his foreign education. His brother expected rich dividends in the form of 'wealth, and name and fame'. The barrister's degree, however, was not an open sesame to the top of the bar. The law course in England had not included Hindu or Muslim law; Gandhi noticed that the home-bred *vakils* of Rajkot knew more of Indian law and charged lower fees than barristers. To practise in Rajkot was thus to invite sure ridicule; Gandhi therefore accepted the advice of his friends that he should go to Bombay to study Indian law, to gain experience of the High Court and to secure what briefs he could. He threw himself with gusto into legal studies, digested the Evidence Act, skimmed Mayne's *Hindu Law* and grappled with the Civil Procedure Code.

His knowledge of Indian law began to grow but not his income. Brokerage to 'touts' for briefs secured through them was an accepted mode of building up practice, but to Gandhi it was something beneath the dignity of his profession. Briefs were slow in coming. After waiting an unconscionable time, he got his first brief from Mamibai, a poor woman whom he charged thirty rupees. As he rose in the small-causes court to cross-examine a witness, he was unable to collect his thoughts, collapsed into his chair and refunded the fee to his client. This was a disgraceful *début*, which filled the young barrister with black despair as to his future in a profession he had entered at such a heavy cost.

The straits to which he had been reduced may be surmised from the fact that he applied for a part time job as teacher in a Bombay High School with the modest salary of seventy rupees a month. He had passed the London matriculation examination with Latin as his second language. But he lacked what the school wanted, an Indian university degree. London matriculation could not secure him a teacher's post, but it had given him a command of English. It was with some relief that he discovered that he had a flair for drafting memorials and petitions, and that he could make a living out of it. To set up as a petition writer it was not necessary to prolong his stay in Bombay. He wound up his little establishment and returned to Rajkot, where petition writing brought him in an income of 300 rupees a month.

He might have settled down as a barrister scribe but for a predicament into which he was pitchforked. His elder brother, Lakshmidas, who had once held a political appointment, was under a cloud and persuaded him to see the Political Agent, whom he had met in England. The Political Agent resented this intervention and had the young barrister turned out of the house. Gandhi's cup of humiliation was full. He thought of filing a suit against the British officer for insulting him. Those who knew the world, the British bureaucratic world, advised him that such a procedure could only be ruinous to himself. The great lawyer of Bombay, Sir Pherozeshah Mehta was consulted. 'Such things,' he commented, 'are the common experience of many *vakils* and barristers. Gandhi is still fresh from England and hot-blooded. If he would earn something let him pocket the insult.' This was the heyday of British rule in India, before the political awakening. The professional classes were painfully conscious of their dependence upon local officials. The angry breath of a British officer had shrivelled the career of many a hot-headed young man.

With the continual tug of war among its petty princes and their favourites, the atmosphere of Kathiawar was too full of intrigue and corruption to be congenial to Gandhi. Most of his work lay in the court of the Political Agent, who was now irreconcilably prejudiced against him. So when an offer of a job came to him from South Africa, he gladly accepted it. The contract was for a year in connection with a civil suit involving £40,000. The remuneration was £105, a first-class return fare and actual expenses. The fee was modest, and it was not quite clear whether he was engaged as counsel or as a clerk, but he was in no position to pick and choose. Without seeking any elaboration of the offer, he accepted it.

A second voyage was in store for him. Ironically enough, like the first it provided an escape from immediate difficulties. In 1888 he had welcomed the trip to England because he had been unable to get on in the Bhavnager College. Five years later he welcomed a year's exile in South Africa because his *amour propre* and professional fortunes had suffered rude buffets in his homeland.

He could hardly have imagined the new vistas of maturity and public service which the South African adventure was to open to him. The conceited British officer who had bundled the young Indian barrister out of his house had unwittingly done a disservice to the British Empire.

# CHAPTER IV

# A Fateful Journey

GANDHI landed at Durban in May 1893. He was received by his employer Abdulla, one of the wealthiest Indian merchants in Natal.

After a week's stay in Durban, Gandhi left for Pretoria to take up the assignment which had brought him to South Africa.

His brief stay at Durban had given him disconcerting evidence of colour prejudice. He was taken by Abdulla to see the Durban court. The European Magistrate ordered him to take off his turban. Gandhi refused, left the court-room and wrote a letter of protest in the local press, in which he was mentioned as 'an unwelcome visitor'. It was a new experience for him. He had never before encountered blatant racial prejudice. The arrogance of British officials in India he had attributed to individual aberrations. And in England he had come into contact with many Englishmen whose courtesy and goodwill he treasured.

The experience in Durban, however, was nothing compared with what befell him in the course of his journey from Durban to Pretoria. When his train reached Maritzburg late in the evening, he was ordered to move to the van compartment. He refused, but was unceremoniously turned out of the first-class carriage. It was a bitterly cold night as he crept into the unlit waiting-room of Maritzburg station and brooded over what had happened. His client had given him no warning of the humiliating conditions under which Indians lived in South Africa. Should he not call off the contract and return to India? Should he accept these affronts as part of the bargain? He had already left India because his position in Rajkot had become untenable after he had incurred the displeasure of the Political Agent. Was he now to flee back to India because South Africa was too uncomfortable for him? He felt he had to draw the line somewhere. Determined to face whatever happened, he resumed his journey.

At Charlestown, then a rail terminus, he had to take a stage coach for Standerton. He was told he could not sit inside the coach with European passengers and was seated with the driver.

A little later he was asked to travel on the footboard. He refused and suggested that he might be given the seat due to him in the coach box. This impertinence was too much for the white official in charge of the coach, who fell upon Gandhi and belaboured him mercilessly until some of the European passengers intervened. Gandhi had borne the beating, but had not budged from his seat. It was a classic scene, a fit subject for a great artist; quiet courage and human dignity pitted against racial arrogance and brute strength.

On arrival at Standerton Gandhi met some Indian merchants. They explained to him that what had happened to him was the daily lot of Indians in the Transvaal. He reported the incident to the Agent of the Coach Company, though he made it clear that he did not wish to proceed against his assailant. At Johannesburg he drove to the Grand National Hotel, only to be told that Indians were barred; moreover, it required extensive quotations from railway regulations and special pleading with the Station Master of Johannesburg before he was able to buy a first-class ticket for Pretoria, and but for the intercession of a European fellow passenger he would again have been pushed out of the first-class compartment.

The five days' journey from Durban to Pretoria was a long-drawn-out agony. But it dramatized for Gandhi the condition of Indian immigrants in South Africa. Indian merchants had learnt to pocket these humiliations as they pocketed their daily earnings. What was new was not Gandhi's experience, but his reaction to it. So far he had not been conspicuous for assertiveness; on the contrary, he had been pathologically shy and retiring. But something happened to him in that bleak windswept waiting-room of Maritzburg railway station as he smarted under the insult inflicted on him. The iron entered his soul. In retrospect, this incident seemed to him one of the most creative experiences of his life. From that hour, he refused to accept injustice as a part of the natural or unnatural order in South Africa. He would reason; he would plead; he would appeal to the better judgment and the latent humanity of the ruling race; he would resist, but he would never be a willing victim of racial arrogance. It was not so much a question of redeeming his own self-respect as that of his community, his country, even of humanity. The helpless resignation of the mass of Indian settlers, the fact that they were illiterate, had few rights and did not know how to assert the rights they had—all this had the miraculous effect of dissipating his own diffidence. The feeling of inferiority which had dogged him as a student in England and as a budding lawyer in India vanished. In Bombay he had been unable to face a small-causes court, but one of the first things he did on arrival at Pretoria was to invite its Indian residents to a meeting 'to present to them a picture of their condition in Transvaal'. The meeting was a great success. Gandhi suggested the formation of an organization to voice the grievances of the Indian community. A token of this practical leadership was his offer to teach English to those Indian merchants who wanted to learn it. His first three pupils were a barber, a clerk and a petty shopkeeper, who received the free tuition on their own premises. He came to know every Indian in that town. He brought the disabilities of the Indian community to the notice of the British Agent in Pretoria, who was sympathetic but pleaded helplessness because the Transvaal was a Boer state outside the orbit of the British Empire. The Boer Government had already chased most of the Indian settlers out of the Orange Free State. South Africa seemed to have no room for a self-respecting Indian. Gandhi's mind became more and more exercised with the question of how this state of affairs could be put right.

Meanwhile, he had to attend to the civil suit which had brought him to South Africa. In this suit were involved the huge sum of £40,000 as well as trade rivalry and family feuds between two of the biggest Indian merchants in South Africa, Abdulla of Natal and Tyeb Sheth of the Transvaal. True to the litigation tradition of their native land, these two merchants were resolved to fight it out to the bitter end. Gandhi was assigned the modest role of examining the books of Abdulla's firm and serving as a link with its lawyers. The young barrister did not disdain the duties of an accountant-clerk. What may have appeared to another as an affront struck him as an opportunity. He dug deeply into the details of the case, acquired a knowledge of book-keeping and trade practices and improved his English by copious translations from Gujerati, in which the firm's accounts were kept. He carefully observed how the material prepared by him was sorted by the attorney and how the brief itself was prepared.

The high-water mark of the legal profession had once appeared to him to consist in feats of forensic eloquence or facile quotations from law manuals. After a year's hard labour on this suit he learnt that the function of the lawyer is to sift the facts and to find out the truth. He was conscious that he was neither eloquent nor learned, but he could depend for success upon his integrity and industry. This case taught him what a junior barrister learns in a senior barrister's chambers; it also gave him the confidence that he should not, after all, fail as a lawyer, that facts were three-fourths of law and that 'once we adhere to truth, the law comes to our aid naturally'.

On a close examination of the facts, Abdulla's case appeared to him to be strong in fact as well as in law. But he saw that the suit was ruinous to both the parties. The mounting fees of the lawyers, the inevitable dislocation in the normal work of the firms, and the bad blood engendered all round, dictated the wisdom of a settlement out of court. Not without reluctance did the two firms accept arbitration. The arbitrator's verdict went in favour of Abdulla. If it had been enforced immediately, Tyeb Sheth would have faced bankruptcy. Gandhi persuaded his client to be magnanimous in his hour of triumph and agree to payment by instalments. He could look back on his first important brief with satisfaction: 'I had learnt the true practice of law. I had learnt to find out the better side of human nature and to enter men's hearts. I realized that the true function of a lawyer was to unite parties riven asunder.'[1]

Henceforth it was his constant endeavour to reconcile opponents outside the court-room rather than let them fight it out. It was not only the litigants who gained in the process. 'I lost nothing,' he recorded many years later, 'not even money, certainly not my soul.'

---

[1] Gandhi, M. K.: *Autobiography*, Ahmedabad (1945), p. 168.

# CHAPTER V

# Plunge into Politics

THE civil suit at Pretoria having happily concluded, Gandhi's contract was over, and he returned to Durban to catch a steamer for India. At the farewell party which Abdulla, his grateful client, gave in his honour Gandhi happened to glance through the pages of the *Natal Mercury* and read a news item entitled 'Indian Franchise'. A bill was being introduced in the Natal Legislature to disfranchise Indian settlers, but Gandhi's host and other merchants attending the party were unable to throw any light on this measure. They knew enough English to be able to converse with their white customers, but few of them could read newspapers, much less follow the proceedings of the Natal Legislature. They had come to Natal for trade, and politics did not interest them. They had not yet realized that politics could affect their trade. Only recently, Indian traders had been hounded out of the Orange Free State, and now Natal was enacting a racial measure. 'This is the first nail into our coffin!' was Gandhi's comment. The Indian merchants pleaded with him to stay on in Natal to take up the fight on their behalf. They had so far relied on European barristers, and were therefore glad to have an Indian barrister in their midst. He agreed to defer his return to India for a month, and hoped that by then a decision on the disenfranchisement of Indian voters would be taken.

Gandhi lost no time in settling down to work: the farewell party converted itself into a political committee to plan Indian opposition to the bill. A sound instinct seems to have guided the twenty-five-year-old barrister in organizing his first political campaign. The insight he had acquired, while at Pretoria, into the Indian settlers' problems stood him in good stead. His strategy was threefold. In the first place, a spirit of solidarity had to be infused into the heterogeneous elements composing the Indian population. The Muslim merchants and their Hindu and Parsi clerks from Bombay, the semi-slave 'indentured' labourers from Madras, and the Natal-born Indian Christians had all to realize their common origin. On the Indian Christians it was to be impressed that because they were Christians they did not cease to be Indians. The merchants had to accept their kinship with the poor indentured labourers, whom extreme poverty had brought to a life of toil in far-off Natal. Secondly, the implications of the disfranchising measure had to be brought home to the Indian community, as well as to the saner section of European public opinion and the Natal Government. Finally, the widest publicity had to be given to the Indians' case, to quicken the conscience of the peoples and governments of India and Great Britain.

It is a measure of Gandhi's success as a publicist that the Indian National Congress in its annual session in December 1894 recorded its protest against the disfranchising bill, and in the next three years the London *Times* devoted eight leading articles to the Indian problem in South Africa. A petition drafted by Gandhi and signed by nearly 500 Indians was presented to the Legislative Assembly of Natal. The petition created a stir in the Natal Legislature and the Government, but the bill was passed nevertheless. The Indians were not dismayed by their failure; they had at least been roused from their political lethargy. As for Gandhi, this first experience of political agitation into which he had been pitchforked cured him of what once had seemed an incorrigible self-consciousness. Not that he had a sudden attack of egotism. He explained his limitations in a letter dated July 5, 1894, to Dadabhai Naoroji, the eminent leader of the Indian National Congress, and at that time a member of the British Parliament: 'A word for myself and I have done. I am inexperienced and young and, therefore, quite liable to make mistakes. The responsibility undertaken is quite out of proportion to my ability. So you will see that I have not taken the matter up, which is beyond my ability, in order to enrich myself at the expense of the Indians. I am the only available person who can handle the question. You will, therefore, oblige me very greatly if you will kindly direct and guide me, and make necessary suggestions which shall be received as from a father to his child.'[1]

The concept of inferiority is a relative one; in a community looking to him for leadership, Gandhi forgot his own limitations. As 'the only available person', he undertook a task from which elsewhere he might have shrunk.

One last chance remained. The bills passed by the Natal Legislature required the Queen's assent before they became law.

[1] Masani, R. P.: *Dadabhai Naoroji*, London, p. 468.

Gandhi decided to send a monster petition to the Colonial Secretary in London. The petition bore 10,000 signatures, cover-
ing almost the entire population of free Indians in Natal. It was
part of Gandhi's technique to use every move in this campaign
for the political education of the community. For example, no
one was allowed to sign the petition until he had understood
and accepted its contents. A thousand copies were printed and
mailed to prominent politicians and newspapers. Both in India
and Britain, the case of the Natal Indians had a good press.

Meanwhile the month for which Gandhi had postponed his
departure for India came to an end. The Indians of Natal begged
him to stay on. It was not certain that the British Government
would veto the offending measure. Moreover, had he not warned
them that this was the first nail in their coffin? Would he leave
them in the lurch and see his own work undone? Gandhi agreed
to prolong his stay, but how was he to make a living? Since he
would not hear of payment for public work, twenty merchants
offered him retaining fees to produce a minimum of £300 a year,
which he reckoned enough to pay his way in Durban.

The Bar Society of Natal opposed Gandhi's admission as an
advocate to the Supreme Court. The Chief Justice admitted
him, but in keeping with the etiquette of practising barristers,
ordered him to take off his turban. A year before, as a visitor
in a lower court in Durban, Gandhi had walked out rather than
give in to this humiliation. Now, as an advocate of the Supreme
Court, he swallowed the bitter pill with the reflection that, if
he was to fight colour prejudice, he must choose bigger issues
and other occasions.

Gandhi felt that what the Indians urgently needed was a permanent organization to look after their interests. Out of deference to Dadabhai Naoroji, who had presided over the Indian
National Congress in 1893, he called the new organization Natal
Indian Congress. He was not conversant with the constitution
and functions of the Indian National Congress. This ignorance
proved an asset, as he fashioned the Natal Congress in his own
way to suit the needs of the Natal Indians. The Indian National
Congress of this period was a debating society of the intelligentsia
which was hardly heard of between its annual pageants of
speeches and petitions and protests. The Natal Indian Congress
was, however, designated as a live body, functioning throughout
the year and dedicated not only to politics but to the moral and
social uplift of its members. Though it served a community
which had very little political experience, it was not a one-man

show. Indefatigable secretary though he was, Gandhi enlisted popular interest and enthusiasm at every step. He made the enrolment of members and the collection of subscriptions into something more than a routine. He employed a gentle but irresistible technique for exerting moral pressure on half-hearted supporters. Once in a small village, he sat through the night and refused to take his dinner until at dawn his host, an Indian merchant, agreed to raise his subscription for the Natal Indian Congress from three to six pounds.

Since his student days in London Gandhi had kept a meticulous account of his daily expenses. He exercised a similar vigilance on the finances of the Natal Indian Congress. So efficiently were its accounts maintained that thirty years later he could write: 'I dare say, the account books of the year 1894 can be found intact even today in the records of the Natal Indian Congress'. For himself he refused to accept anything from public funds. He felt that if he became a paid advocate of the Indian community, he could not remain its fearless servant; honorary public service was thus not only a duty to his people, but also a safeguard of his own independence. In these early years of his political apprenticeship, he formulated his own code of conduct for a politician. He did not accept the popular view that in politics one must fight for one's party right or wrong. The passion for facts, which he had recently cultivated in his practice of law, he brought to bear on politics; if the facts were on his side, there was no need to embroider them. He avoided exaggeration and discouraged it in his colleagues. The Natal Indian Congress was not merely an instrument for the defence of the political and economic rights of the Indian minority, but also a lever for its internal reform and unity. He did not spare his own people and roundly criticized them for their shortcomings. He asked them to improve their standards of living and integrity in business. He was not only the stoutest champion of the Natal Indians, but also their severest critic.

To appreciate the role which Gandhi and the Natal Indian Congress were to play in the Dark Continent, it would be well at this stage to look back and to see the problem in its historical perspective.

'The Asiatics,' wrote Lord Milner, 'are strangers forcing themselves upon a community reluctant to receive them.' In fact, the Indian emigration to South Africa in the eighteen sixties started at the instance of the European settlers, who were in possession of vast virgin lands ideal for tea, coffee and sugar plantations, but lacked man-power. The negro could not be compelled to work after the abolition of slavery. The Government of India was therefore approached by the Europeans of Natal for Indian labourers to be permitted to emigrate to that country. Recruiting agents of the planters toured some of the poorer and most congested districts of Madras and Bengal and painted rosy prospects of work in Natal. Free passage, board and lodging; a wage of ten shillings a month for the first year, rising by one shilling every year; and the right to a free return passage to India after five years' 'indenture' (or alternatively, the chance to settle in the land of their adoption), drew thousands of poor and illiterate Indians to distant Natal.

The first shipload of 'indentured labourers' from India arrived in Durban in November 1860. By 1890 nearly 40,000 Indians had been imported as indentured labourers. Theirs was, to use Sir W. W. Hunter's phrase, a condition of semi-slavery. Not all employers were cruel, but it was difficult to change employers on the plea of ill-treatment, and if a labourer did not renew his 'indenture' after five years, he was hemmed in by all sorts of restrictions. Nevertheless, many of these labourers, already cut off from their roots in India, preferred to settle in Natal. They bought small plots of land, grew vegetables, made a decent living and educated their children. This excited the jealousy of the European traders, who began to agitate for the repatriation of every Indian labourer who did not renew his term. In other words, the Indian was wanted in Natal as a slave or not at all. In 1885 a commission on Indian immigration found European public opinion heavily weighted against the presence of free Indians, whether in agriculture or in trade. The commission considered the ex-indentured Indian an asset and his repatriation not only unjust to him but ruinous to the economy of the colony. The argument of enlightened self-interest did not, however, appeal to those who were haunted by the fear that the Indian would under-live and under-sell the European.

The grant of responsible government to Natal in 1893 removed whatever little restraint the Colonial Office in London exercised on the policy of racial discrimination. A delegation from Natal took to India proposals for compulsory indenture or compulsory repatriation of all Indian labourers; alternatively it suggested an annual poll tax of £25 per head. The British Indian officials' ignorance of the conditions in Natal was equalled only by their eagerness to help the European planters in that country. The Government of India agreed to the levy of a £3 tax payable by every member of the family of the ex-indentured labourer, who was merely exercising his right to settle in Natal in terms of the agreement which had governed his emigration from India. It was a crippling tax for the poor wretches whose wages as indentured labourers ranged between ten and twelve shillings a month. Poor, illiterate and unorganized, they were helpless and the only quarter from which they could hope for sympathy and support was the Indian merchant.

The Indian merchant had followed the Indian labourer to South Africa and found a ready market among the Indian labourers and the negroes; the latter found that the Indian merchant was more courteous and a little less rapacious than the European merchant. The growing prosperity of the Indian merchant, however, became an irritation to his European rivals. The legislation to disfranchise Indians, which had led Gandhi to prolong his stay in Natal, was aimed at the Indian trader. The possession of immovable property worth £50 or an annual rental of £10 being the minimum qualification for a vote, only 250 Indians were on the electoral list as against 10,000 European voters. The enrolment of even a few Indians as voters appeared a danger signal to the Europeans, who would not admit the 'niggers'—black, brown or yellow—to a share in the wealth or government of Natal. The politicians of Natal made no secret of their object which, as one of them put it, was 'to degrade the Indian to the level of a Kaffir' and 'to prevent him from forming part of the future South African nation that is going to be built'. The measure was designed, declared another politician, 'to make the Indians' life more comfortable in their native land than in Natal'.

The bill disfranchising the Indians was passed by the Natal Legislature and received the assent of its Governor. The Colonial Office in London, largely influenced by the agitation organized by Gandhi, vetoed the bill on the ground that it discriminated against the inhabitants of another part of the British Empire. The Europeans of Natal were not discouraged by this veto; they sought their object without avowing a colour bar as such. An amended bill was passed according to which, 'no natives of countries (not of European origin) which had not hitherto possessed elective representative institutions founded on parliamentary franchise were to be placed on voters' lists unless they obtained an exemption from the Governor-General'. Though the amended bill was as effective a check on the Indian franchise as the one which had been vetoed by the British Government,

it was something of a gain that racial discrimination had not
been written into the statute-book.

Indian trade and immigration also came under galling restrictions. No one could henceforth trade in Natal without a
licence, which a European could have for the asking and an Indian only after much effort and expense, if at all. And since an
educational test in a European language was made a *sine qua
non* for an immigrant, the door was barred and bolted against
the majority of potential immigrants from India, except, of
course, the semi-slave indentured labourers who continued to
be imported.

In this anti-Indian campaign, the Europeans of Natal were only
following in the footsteps of their Boer neighbours in the Transvaal and Orange Free State. Kruger, the bellicose president of
the Transvaal (Boer) Republic, had told an Indian deputation:
'You are the descendants of Ishmael and, therefore, from your
very birth bound to slave for the descendants of Esau.' A representative of the British Government was stationed in Pretoria,
but he pleaded helplessness. When the Boer War broke out, the
maltreatment of Indians was part of the indictment against the
Boers. The Indians had still to learn that in South Africa they
could get no more justice from the Briton than from the
Boer.

The legal disabilities of Indians were bad enough, but the
daily humiliations they suffered were worse. Every Indian without distinction was called 'a coolie'—a contemptuous word for
a labourer. Indian schoolmasters were 'coolie schoolmasters';
Indian storekeepers were 'coolie store-keepers'. Gandhi was a
'coolie barrister'. Even the steamers owned by Indians were
called 'coolie ships'. Indians were commonly described as 'Asian
dirt to be heartily cursed, chockful of vice, that lives upon
rice, and the black vermin'. In the statute-book they were described as 'semi-barbarous Asiatics, or persons belonging to the
uncivilized races of Asia'. They were not allowed to walk on
footpaths or to be out at night, without a permit. First and
second-class tickets were not issued to them. If a white passenger
objected, they could be unceremoniously bundled out of a railway
compartment; they had sometimes to travel on the footboards of
trains. European hotels would not admit them. 'Natal,' wrote the
*Cape Times*, 'presents the curious spectacle of a country enter-
taining a supreme contempt for the very class of people she can
least do without. Imagination can only picture the commercial
paralysis which would inevitably attend the withdrawal of the

Indian population from that colony. And yet the Indian is the most despised of creatures.'

In the Transvaal, Indians could not trade or reside except in specified locations which the London *Times* described as ghettoes. In the Orange Free State, there was a law prohibiting Asiatics and other coloured persons from trading or carrying on any business whatsoever. 'Wherever the Indian goes,' wrote the *Cape Times*, 'he is the same useful well-doing man, law-abiding under whatever form of government he may find himself, frugal in his wants and industrious in his habits. But these virtues make him a formidable competitor in the labour markets to which he resorts.' As Lionel Curtis told Gandhi many years later, it was the virtues rather than the vices of the Indians which had aroused the jealousy of the European and exposed them to political persecution.

# CHAPTER VI

# Lynched

WHAT with his public activities and what with his legal work it looked as if Gandhi was now settled in Natal. In the middle of 1896 he visited India to fetch his family and, incidentally, to canvass whatever support he could for the Indian cause in South Africa.

From Calcutta, where he landed, he took a train for Bombay *en route* to Rajkot.

On arrival at Rajkot, Gandhi devoted the better part of a month to the writing of a pamphlet on the Indian problem in South Africa and had it printed and despatched to influential public men and newspapers all over the country. This pamphlet covered, though more cautiously, the same ground as his earlier pamphlets in Natal, *An Appeal to Every Briton in South Africa* and *The Indian Franchise.*

He followed up this pamphlet with a country-wide tour to educate public opinion. In Bombay he had an audience with the 'uncrowned king' of that town, Sir Pherozeshah Mehta, whom he had regarded since his student days in London with a reverence bordering upon awe. Under the distinguished patronage of Sir Pherozeshah, a meeting was called to hear Gandhi on South Africa. As he rose to read the script he had been warned to prepare, the crowded hall seemed to whirl before him, his hands trembled and his voice trailed away into nothingness. The rest of the speech was read with good effect by Wacha, a local orator.

In Poona, he met the two giants of Maharashtrian politics—Gokhale and Tilak. Gokhale, who had devoted himself wholeheartedly to public life, was always on the look-out for patriotic young men; the earnestness of the young barrister from South Africa impressed him at once. On Gandhi's side it was a case of 'love at first sight'. Immediately—and this is an interesting fact—Gokhale and Tilak, who disagreed about almost everything, agreed jointly to sponsor a public meeting in Poona to hear the grievances of the Indians in South Africa. The great Tilak, a politician to his finger-tips, could not help observing that the young lawyer from Natal was hopelessly unfamiliar with Indian politics.

The poise and leadership which had come so naturally to Gandhi in South Africa was missing on Indian soil. He became morbidly conscious of his youth and inexperience. Sir Pherozeshah Mehta reminded him of the Himalayas, Tilak of the ocean and Gokhale of the holy Ganges. The 'débâcle' at the meeting in Bombay, when he was unable to finish his speech, was painfully reminiscent of the breakdown four years earlier in a local court, which had compelled him to quit Bombay and the legal profession for that of a scribe at Rajkot. It was a fortunate circumstance that his political career began in South Africa. If he had entered politics in India at that time, the odds were heavy that he would have floundered hopelessly. Apart from the sense of immaturity which haunted him in the homeland, Indian politics at this time offered few outlets for his constructive genius, and were beginning to be riddled with personal and factional rivalries. The uniform kindness which he received from prominent politicians was due to the fact that the cause he championed, that of Indians overseas, was common ground among politicians of all shades.

The Presidency of Madras, from which the majority of indentured labourers in Natal hailed, gave Gandhi a very warm welcome. He received unstinted support from leaders of public opinion and the Press, particularly the influential *Hindu*. The pamphlet on the Indians' condition in South Africa sold like hot cakes and a reprint became necessary. In Calcutta, the response from the local leaders and the Press was not so cordial. Nevertheless, two British-owned papers, the *Statesman* and the *Englishman*, featured interviews with him.

While plans were afoot for holding a public meeting in Calcutta, Gandhi received a cable from Natal urging him to return immediately. The trip ended abruptly, but it had served the cause nearest to his heart. It had stimulated the interest of the homeland in the condition of Indians overseas. Public meetings had been held under influential auspices in the principal towns, and the Press, including its Anglo-Indian section, had pulled out the skeleton in the imperial cupboard.

Distorted versions of his activities and utterances had reached Natal and inflamed Europeans of that colony. A four-line cable from Reuter's London office was featured prominently in Natal papers. It ran: 'September 14. A Pamphlet published in India declares that the Indians in Natal are robbed and assaulted and treated like beasts and are unable to obtain redress. The *Times of India* advocates an inquiry into these allegations.'

The reference was to the pamphlet which Gandhi had published in India. The leading paper of Johannesburg, the *Star*, had once complimented Gandhi for 'writing forcibly, moderately and well', and the *Natal Mercury* had commended 'the calmness and moderation' of his writings. The pamphlet published in India was, if anything, more subdued in tone than what Gandhi had said and written in Natal. His speeches in India had been delivered from carefully prepared texts. So transparent was his sense of fairness that the editor of the *Englishman* of Calcutta had let him see the draft of an editorial on the Indian question in South Africa.

The truth about Gandhi's activities in India did not, however, percolate to Natal. Meanwhile, the cable from London made him the most hated man in the colony. He was accused of smearing the country which had harboured him and of 'dragging the Europeans of Natal in the gutter and painting them as black as his own skin'. He was alleged to have organized an agency to flood Natal with Indian immigrants. It so happened that the ss *Courland*, by which the Gandhi family travelled, and another ship the ss *Naderi* had left Bombay for Natal about the same time. Gandhi's first client and friend Abdulla was the owner of one ship and the agent of the other. The two ships had about 800 passengers on board, half of them bound for Natal. It was just a coincidence that the two ships had sailed almost at the same time at the end of November 1896, and that they arrived together in Durban harbour on December 19. To the Europeans of Natal, already excited by Reuter's report, the coincidence looked like a conspiracy. Two thousand Europeans met in the town hall of Durban and called on the Natal Government to prevent the 'free Indians' from disembarking.

After the ships had cast anchor in the port, the Europeans did their best to coax, cajole or coerce the Indians. A free return passage was dangled before those who would agree to go back; and those who declined were threatened that they would be pushed into the sea. The shipowners were warned to return their unwelcome cargo to India or incur the implacable wrath of the Government and Europeans of Natal. The ships were placed under quarantine; when the duration of quarantine was prolonged from five days to three weeks, its political use was obvious. These tactics had the support of influential Europeans, including Harry Escombe, the Attorney-General of Natal. If

the Indians, most of whom were illiterate and on their first
voyage with their families, did not succumb to these threats, it was
due to Gandhi's infectious courage and optimism. For him these
were anxious days. The lives of these passengers, most of whom
he did not know, and those of his own family were in jeopardy
on his account; it was he who was the *bête noire* of the Europeans of Natal. On Christmas Day, 1896, there was a small
party in the Captain's cabin and somebody asked Gandhi what
he would do if the Natal Europeans were as good as their word
and forcibly prevented the landing of Indians. 'I hope,' he said,
'God will give me the courage and sense to forgive them, and to
refrain from bringing them to law. I have no anger against them.
I am only sorry for their ignorance and their narrowness.'

When twenty-three days of this political quarantine and threats
failed to browbeat the Indians, the ships were permitted to
enter the harbour, on January 13, 1897. The Indians were
allowed to disembark with the exception of Gandhi, who had
received a message from Escombe to wait till the evening, when
he would be escorted by the Superintendent of the Water
Police. In the afternoon, however, Laughton, a European lawyer
and friend of Gandhi, came aboard and announced that all
danger was at an end and that in any case it was undignified
for Gandhi to slip into Durban 'like a thief in the night'. It was
therefore decided that Mrs Gandhi and the children would immediately drive to the house of Rustomji, the Gandhis' host, and
Gandhi and Laughton would join them later on foot. They had
not walked far when some European boys recognized Gandhi.
A crowd began to collect; as it swelled, it became more and
more menacing. Laughton hailed a rickshaw to save his friend,
but the Zulu boy pulling the rickshaw was scared away. Laughton
and Gandhi began to walk together, followed by the mob.
When they reached West street, Laughton was torn away. A
hailstorm of rotten eggs and brickbats raged round Gandhi. 'Are
you the man who wrote to the Press?' shouted a European, and
gave a brutal kick. Gandhi nearly fainted, held on to the railings
of a house to regain his breath, and staggered along. He had
given up hope of reaching home alive; he recalled later that even
at this critical moment his heart did not arraign his assailants.
'Then a beautiful and brave thing happened'. Mrs Alexander,
the wife of the local Superintendent of Police, came on the
scene. She recognized Gandhi, began to walk alongside him and
opened her sunshade to keep off the flying missiles. The
Europeans had run amuck, but they dared not raise their

hands against a white woman. Meanwhile, a few constables arrived and escorted Gandhi to the house of his host.

Hardly had Gandhi's wounds been dressed when a European mob surrounded the house and threatened to burn it if Gandhi did not surrender. Superintendent Alexander posted himself at the gate and began to humour the mob to gain a little time. Meanwhile, he sent word to Gandhi to agree to being smuggled out of the house if he did not want to have all the inmates, including women and children, roasted alive. Dressed as an Indian constable, with a metal saucer under his turban, and attended by a detective dressed as an Indian merchant, Gandhi slipped through the crowd and after jumping fences, squeezing between rails and passing through a store, reached the police station.

He did not have to remain in the police station for long. The Natal Europeans had been provoked by Reuter's brief and somewhat garbled report of Gandhi's activities in India. On the morning of the day on which he was assaulted, in an interview with a Press correspondent, he had explained away the various charges against him. There was a belated recognition that he had been the victim of a misunderstanding.

The Secretary of State for the Colonies in London cabled to the Natal Government to prosecute Gandhi's assailants. Gandhi's reaction was characteristic. It was, he said, a principle with him not to seek redress of a personal wrong in a court of law; and in any case it was hardly fair to haul up a few hot-headed young men for acts of violence without calling influential Europeans to account, including members of the Natal Government who had worked up the Europeans of Durban to white heat.

That day, January 13, 1897, was fateful. Gandhi had escaped from the very jaws of death. His poise and magnanimity had raised him not only in the affections of the Indians, but in the esteem of the saner Europeans in Natal. He continued to serve the Natal Indian Congress and to organize the Indian community. In 1899, when the Boer War broke out, he was faced with a major decision on the attitude which the Indian community should adopt towards the conflict which was to change, for better or for worse, the history of South Africa.

# CHAPTER VII

# Stones for Bread

THE outbreak of the Boer War in 1899 was the final phase in the struggle between the Boer and the British for hegemony in South Africa. The Indians had been badly treated by both Boers and British, though more blatantly by the former, and some of them were not sorry at the prospect of the two races bleeding each other white. Gandhi's own ideas on non-violence and pacifism had not yet matured. It was, he felt, neither possible nor desirable for each citizen to determine in such a crisis on which side the balance of justice lay. The Indians in Natal had been denied elementary rights as citizens, but Gandhi argued that those who even claimed rights could not escape corresponding obligations. The suggestion that the Boers were likely to win and that Indian neutrality would pay dividends after the war he dismissed as downright cowardice.

He succeeded in swinging the majority of the Indians in Natal to his point of view. The Government, however, was in no hurry to avail themselves of the Indians' co-operation. Jameson, a member of the Natal Legislative Council, told Gandhi: 'You Indians know nothing of war. You would only be a drag on the army; you would have to be taken care of, instead of being a help to us.' 'But,' pleaded Gandhi, 'is there nothing we can do? Can we not do ordinary servants' work in connection with the hospitals? Surely, that will not demand very great intelligence?' 'No,' replied Jameson, 'it all needs training.' It was only when General Buller's forces were suffering heavy casualties on the banks of the river Tugela and British morale touched a low ebb that the Indians' offer was accepted, and the formation of an Indian Ambulance Corps permitted. The corps consisted of nearly 1,100 Indians with Dr Booth of the Indian Anglican Mission as Medical Superintendent and Gandhi its *de facto* leaders. The corps reached the front on the eve of the action at Colenso, where it spent a strenuous week. The next summons came on the eve of the battle of Spionkop. The corps was in the field for about three weeks. It was the duty of the 'bearers', as the rank and file of the Indian Ambulance Corps were known, to receive the wounded outside the line of fire, and to tramp with them to the base about twenty miles away. Even though their terms of service did not require them to serve within the firing line, the Indians did so cheerfully on several occasions.

Vere Stent, the editor of the *Pretoria News*, has left a pen-portrait of Gandhi on the battlefield: 'After a night's work which had shattered men with much bigger frames, I came across Gandhi in the early morning sitting by the roadside—eating a regulation army biscuit. Every man in Buller's force was dull and depressed, and damnation was heartily invoked on everything. But Gandhi was stoical in his bearing, cheerful and confident in his conversation and had a kindly eye.'

The work of the Indian Ambulance Corps was mentioned in General Buller's despatches and the thirty-seven 'leaders' of the Indian Ambulance Unit received war-medals. The Indian effort, considered as a contribution to the British victory in the Boer War, may have been, as Gandhi would have been the first to admit, insignificant, but it was a fine gesture on the part of an oppressed minority. For a while the Indians were flattered on being greeted in the European Press as the 'Sons of the Empire'. And among those who personally complimented Gandhi were a number of Europeans who had been the ringleaders of the anti-Indian demonstration in Durban which had nearly ended in the lynching of Gandhi in January 1897.

When the issue of the war was no longer in doubt Gandhi felt that the change in the political climate had made it possible for him to return to India. The Natal Indians released him reluctantly and on condition that he would return, if they required him, within a year.

He landed at Bombay at the end of 1901, just in time to attend the Calcutta session of the Indian National Congress. After the Congress session he stayed on for a month with Gokhale, whose kindly interest in Gandhi had not abated since they first met during Gandhi's visit to India in 1896. It was Gokhale's ambition to launch Gandhi into Indian public life. There was a strong bond of mutual respect between the two men; Gokhale was fascinated by Gandhi's sincerity, zeal and method, and Gandhi by Gokhale's complete dedication to the service of India.

After practising for a while in the Rajkot courts, he moved down to Bombay, where Gokhale had urged him to settle and take a hand in the affairs of the Indian National Congress. He moved into a fine bungalow in Santa Cruz, and quickly built up a good practice. Gokhale was happy; an able and earnest worker had been added to the not-too-thick phalanx of Indian patriots. But all the plans, Gandhi's and Gokhale's went by the board when a cable arrived from South Africa, urging Gandhi to return to lead the Indian settlers in the crisis that faced them.

The occasion for the urgent summons was the visit to South Africa of Chamberlain, the Colonial Secretary in the British Cabinet, and the opportunity it provided for representing the grievances, new as well as old, of the Indian settlers.

At the end of the Boer War, the British Government appointed a committee to scan the Boer statute-book, and to repeal the laws which were repugnant to the spirit of the British Consitution and inconsistent with the liberty of Queen Victoria's subjects. The committee interpreted the liberty of the subject as the liberty of the white subject; the Indians thus remained outside the pale of the reformed code. In fact, all the anti-Indian laws of the Boer régime were compiled in a handy manual.

When Gandhi landed at Durban in December 1902, he found that the Indians had to free themselves not only from the old chains fastened on them in Natal, but also the new chains being forged for them in the Transvaal. He headed a deputation of Natal Indians, which waited on the Colonial Secretary at Durban. Chamberlain gave the usual 'patient hearing' to the Indian deputation, but argued that the colonies were self-governing and the Indians had better come to terms with the colonists.

The assignment for which he had been recalled from India—the interview with the Colonial Secretary—was over. For Gandhi the temptation to return to his family, and professional and public activities in India was strong; but the peril to the Indian community was so palpable and its trust in him so great that he decided to prolong his self-imposed exile. In 1893 he had come to South Africa for a year and stayed for eight years; in 1902 he had come for six months and was to stay for twelve years. He resolved that he must live in South Africa until 'the gathering clouds were dispersed or until they broke open and swept all away, all our counteracting efforts notwithstanding'.

He had himself enrolled as an attorney of the Transvaal Supreme Court and set up his office at Johannesburg, which was henceforth to be the centre of his activities.

A new phase opened in Gandhi's career. The racial and anti-

Indian policies of the European colonies in Natal and the Transvaal, far from being reversed by the victory of the British over the Boers, were receiving a new impetus. The Indians had to fight not for equality with Europeans but even for elementary civic rights, and for the preservation of interests which they had built by dint of hard work over a quarter of a century. Evidently the struggle was an unequal one and there was no knowing how long it would be protracted. Gandhi, by taking upon himself the responsibility of leading it, had burnt his boats: his own career and family were as nothing beside the cause he had taken up. His life underwent a transformation, not only in externals, in his style of living, but also in the acquisition of new values.

The story of this transformation is not only fascinating in itself, but reveals the springs of that moral and spiritual strength which enabled him to play a unique role in the public life of two continents.

# CHAPTER VIII

# The Religious Quest

WHEN at the age of nineteen Gandhi arrived in London his acquaintance with the religion of his birth was of the meagrest. It was with some embarrassment that he owned to his theosophist friends, who had invited him to read Sir Edwin Arnold's *The Song Celestial*, that he had never read the *Bhagavad Gita* in Sanskrit, or even in Gujerati, his mother tongue. This was his introduction to a book which was to become his 'spiritual reference book'. Another book of Sir Edwin's, *The Light of Asia*, also fascinated him; the story of Gautama Buddha—his life, renunciation and teaching—stirred him to his depths.

Gandhi did not join the Theosophical Society, but its literature stimulated his interest in religion. It was in England too that he was introduced to the Bible by a fellow enthusiast for vegetarianism. The New Testament, particularly the Sermon on the Mount, went straight to his heart. The verses, 'But I say unto you that ye resist not evil; but whosoever shall smite thee on thy right cheek, turn to him the other also. And if any man will sue thee at the law, and take away thy coat, let him have thy cloak also', reminded him of the lines of the Gujerati poet, Shamlal Bhatt, which he used to hum as a child:

> For a bowl of water give a goodly meal;
> For a kindly greeting bow thou down with zeal;
> For a single penny pay thou back with gold;
> If thy life be rescued, life do not withhold.
> Thus the words and actions of the wise regard;
> Every little service tenfold they reward.
> But the truly noble know all men as one,
> And return with gladness good for evil done.

The teachings of the Bible, the Buddha and Bhatt fused in his mind. The idea of returning love for hatred, and good for evil captivated him; he did not yet comprehend it fully, but it continued to ferment in his impressionable mind. Before Gandhi left England, he had already crossed 'the Sahara of atheism'[1] into which he had strayed in his adolescence.

During his first year in South Africa he came across some ardent Quakers who perceived his religious bent and decided to annex him to Christianity. They loaded him with books on Christian theology and history; they preached at him, and prayed with him and for him. Finally, they took him to a Convention of Protestant Christians in the hope that mass emotion would sweep him off his feet. Gandhi was lavish in praising the nobility of the Quakers' character, but said blandly that he felt no inner call to renounce Hinduism and to embrace Christianity.

When he had read Tolstoy's *The Kingdom of God is Within You*, he felt he had learnt more from it than from all the books which his Quaker friends had given him. Tolstoy had condemned Christian churches of all denominations for perverting the true teaching of Christ to maintain their power over the masses, and had drawn pointed attention to the contradiction between Christ's teachings and the daily life of Christians. In an earlier book, *What I believe*, Tolstoy had argued that Christ was not merely the founder of a religion of worship and personal salvation, but that Christ's teachings constituted a philosophical, moral, and social doctrine. These views of a Christian anarchist proved an effective counterblast to the indoctrination attempted by the Quakers.

Though he visited a renowned Indian Christian for 'enlightenment' as late as 1901, the possibilities of his conversion had already long receded. He began to study other religions, including his own, and came to the conclusion that all religions are right and every one of them is imperfect because they are 'interpreted with poor intellects, sometimes with poor hearts, and more often misinterpreted'. The essay on 'The hero as Prophet' in Carlyle's *Hero Worship* had first introduced him to Islam. He read a translation of the Koran and the life of the Prophet Mohammed by Washington Irving, and was struck by the poverty and humility of the Prophet, and by the courage with which he and his first followers had faced the humiliations and hardships heaped upon them.

While books on Christianity and Islam were easily available in South Africa, Gandhi had to send to India for books on Hinduism. He began to correspond on religious subjects with his friend Raychandbhai, who counselled him to be patient and to seek in Hinduism 'its unique subtlety and profundity

[1] *Autobiography*, p. 92.

of thought, its vision of the soul and its clarity'. Raychand-bhai's scholarly exposition reinforced Gandhi's sentimental bond with Hinduism and was decisive during the period when his Christian friends believed him to be on the way to baptism.

The book which was ultimately to form his strongest bond with Hinduism as well as the greatest influence in his life was the *Bhagavad Gita*. He had read it in 1890, in Sir Edwin Arnold's verse rendering *The Song Celestial*. In South Africa, he studied other translations with the original, and the book became his daily reading. He memorized one verse every morning while going through his morning toilet, until he had the entire poem by heart.

The *Gita* became Gandhi's 'spiritual dictionary' and an 'infallible' guide to conduct: 'When I see not one ray of light on the horizon, I turn to the *Bhagavad Gita* and find a verse to comfort me. I immediately begin to smile in the midst of overwhelming sorrow. My life has been full of external tragedies and if they have not left visible and indelible effects on me, I owe it to the teachings of the *Bhagavad Gita*'.[1]

The two words *aparigraha* (non-possession) and *sambhava* (equability) opened to him limitless vistas. 'Non-possession' implied that he had to jettison the material goods which cramped the life of the spirit, to shake off the bonds of money, property and sex, and to regard himself as the trustee, not the owner, of what could not be shed. 'Equability' required that he must remain unruffled by pain or pleasure, victory or defeat, and work without hope of success or fear of failure, in short, 'without hankering after the fruit of action'. Only thus could he treat alike 'insulting, insolent and corrupt officials, co-workers of yesterday raising meaningless opposition and men who had always been good' to him. Years later, Gandhi confided to a group of Christian missionaries: 'Hinduism as I know it entirely satisfies my soul, fills my whole being, and I find solace in the *Bhagavad Gita* which I miss even in the Sermon on the Mount.' The Hindu belief in the oneness of all life confirmed and sustained his own faith in *ahimsa* (non-violence). He did not accept every Hindu tenet or practice. He applied the 'acid test of reason' to every formula of every religion. When scriptural sanction was cited for inhumane or unjust practices, his reaction was one of frank disbelief. The oft-quoted text, 'for women there can be no freedom', ascribed to Manu the law-

[1] Natesan: *Speeches and Writings of Mahatma Gandhi*, Madras (Fourth Edition), p. 1061.

giver, he regarded as an interpolation, and if not then he could only say that in Manu's time women did not receive the status they deserved. Similarly, he lashed out against those who supported untouchability with verses from the Vedas. His Hinduism was ultimately reduced to a few fundamental beliefs: in the supreme reality of God, the unity of all life and the value of love (*ahimsa*) as a means of realizing God. In this bedrock religion there was no scope for exclusiveness or narrowness. It was in his view a beauty of Hinduism that: 'in it there is a room for the worship of all the prophets of the world. It is not a missionary religion in the ordinary sense of the word . . . Hinduism tells every one to worship God according to his own faith or *Dharma* and so it lives at peace with all religions'. He chided Christian missionaries for their 'irreligious gamble' for converts. It was the way a man lived, not the recital of a verse, or the form of a prayer, which made him a good Christian, a good Muslim, or a good Hindu. The missionaries' bid to save souls struck him as presumptuous. Of the aborigines and hillmen of Assam he said: 'What have I to take to (them), except to go in my nakedness to them? Rather than ask them to join my prayer, I would join their prayer.'

The study of comparative religion, the browsing on theological works, the conversations and correspondence with the learned brought him to the conclusion that true religion was more a matter of the heart than of the intellect, and that genuine beliefs were those which were literally lived. This was something beyond the grasp of those who had acquired, in the words of Swift, enough religion to hate one another, but not enough to love one another. In his lifetime Gandhi was variously labelled a *Sanatanist* (orthodox) Hindu, a renegade Hindu, a Buddhist, a Theosophist, a Christian and 'a Christian-Mohammedan'. He was all these and more; he saw an underlying unity in the clash of doctrines and forms. 'God is not encased in a safe,' he wrote to a correspondent who had urged him to save his soul by conversion to Christianitv, 'to be approached only through a little hole in it, but He is open to be approached through billions of openings by those who are humble and pure of heart.'[1]

[1] *The Diaries of Mahadev Desai*, Vol. I, entry dated September 4, 1932.

# CHAPTER IX

# *Transformation*

TOLSTOY has recorded that before his 'conversion' his philosophy of life was 'that one should live so as to have the best for one-self and one's family and not to try to be wiser than life and Nature'. Gandhi had his 'conversion', but even in the years which later seemed to him as unregenerate, he did not live only for himself and his family. In Durban, as well as in Johannesburg, he kept an open table. His clerks and junior counsel usually lodged with him and were treated as members of the family. There were, in addition, almost always guests in the house, Indians as well as Europeans. For his wife this community living was often an ordeal. There was once a scene, graphically des-cribed in the autobiography, when Kasturbai declined to clean a chamber-pot for a Christian clerk of *panchma* (untouchable) parentage. Her prejudice struck her husband as entirely irra-tional. He insisted that she should not only perform the distaste-ful task but do so cheerfully, or else leave him. His moral zeal had blinded him with anger, and he could not see how much strain it placed on his wife. Years later he recorded that he had been a 'cruelly kind husband'.

Even in those days of 'ease and comfort', as he described them later, money-making as such did not interest him. As a budding barrister he had been anxious to make good and to contribute to the family coffers, but he would not stoop to lucra-tive but immoral expedients. He was told that a certain law-yer with a practice of Rs. 3,000 a month was attracting briefs through touts by paying illegal commission. 'I do not need to emulate him,' he replied, 'I should be content with Rs. 300 a month. Father did not earn more.' The nadir of his fortunes was reached when he was turned down for the post of part-time teacher in a Bombay school with a paltry salary of Rs. 70 a month. It was only in South Africa that he found himself as a lawyer. From the £300 which had been promised to him in 1894 as the minimum retaining fee, his income steadily rose to the peak figure of £5,000 a year. His public life helped him in building up his practice, but it also made heavy inroads on his time. Nor did he accept every brief that came to him. He did not view it as his professional obligation to defend a client if he was in the wrong. If he was convinced during the progress of a case that his client had withheld material facts from him, he did not hesitate to repudiate him openly in the court. He had never forgotten how as a child his frank confession of a petty theft had moved his father to forgiveness and himself to repentance. He believed that an error must be confessed and atoned for. Parsi Rustomji, a wealthy merchant of Durban and close friend of Gandhi, once found himself in trouble for evasion of customs duties and came to him for advice. Instead of preparing a defence for him Gandhi persuaded him to make a clean breast not only of this but also of other dubious transactions, and to pay up the tax as well as the penalty. To cap it all, the repentant merchant recorded a confession of his misdeeds and had the document framed and hung in his house for the edification of his descendants.

There were doubtless abler and richer lawyers among Gandhi's contemporaries, but few of them could equal his human approach to the profession of law. When a client failed to pay his dues, Gandhi would not have recourse to law; it was, he said, his own error of judgment which was responsible for the loss. Again, to a colleague who protested that clients came even on Sundays, his answer was: 'A man in distress cannot have Sunday rest.'

One day there was much amusement in the Durban courts when Gandhi appeared with the starch dripping from his shirt-collar. This was not the handiwork of a careless launderer; it was his own first experiment in washing clothes. On another occasion his fellow-lawyers held their sides with laughter when they saw his hair cropped in a crazy fashion. He explained that the white barber had declined to attend to him, and he had become his own barber. He trained himself as a dispenser in a charitable hospital, attending the indentured labourers, the poorest of the Indians in South Africa. He read diligently on nursing and obstetrics and acted as a midwife at the birth of his youngest son, when the nurse who had been engaged did not turn up in time. Barber, launderer, dispenser, nurse, he was also a schoolmaster. Since he would not accept as a favour for his children what was denied to other children as a right, his children had to stay out of European schools, and to content themselves with the scraps of instruction they could get from their father as they walked with him the ten miles to and from his office in Johannesburg. These peripatetic lessons were often interrupted by clients or colleagues, but despite their mother's protest, Gandhi refused to put his children into European schools.

The trend towards simplicity received a tremendous fillip in 1904. One evening that year, as Gandhi was taking a train from Johannesburg to Durban, his journalist friend Polak gave him a book to read. It was Ruskin's *Unto This Last*. Gandhi sat through the night and read it from cover to cover. Ruskin had denounced classical economists for not conceiving economics in terms of human welfare, and condemned the poverty and the injustice which industrialism had brought or intensified; these and other ideas were to ferment in Gandhi's mind and to colour his outlook. But what immediately impressed him most was Ruskin's reference to the ideal of a simple life in which manual work should be the joy of existence. 'The book,' records the autobiography, 'confirmed and strengthened some of my own deepest convictions.'

When the train reached Durban next morning, Gandhi was intent on reducing Ruskin's theories to practice. With Albert West, a European friend, who was at this time looking after the *Indian Opinion* press at Durban, he discussed a plan for transferring the journal to a farm where the settlers would literally live by the sweat of their brow. A 100-acre estate situated amidst sugar plantations, served by a spring, and full of fruit trees and snakes, was purchased for £1,000. The nearest station, Phoenix, was two and a half miles from the estate and fourteen miles from Durban. The first settlers included, besides Polak and West, a few cousins and nephews of Gandhi who had accompanied him to South Africa. A hall seventy-five feet long and and fifty feet wide housed the press. Eight buildings of corrugated iron and thatched roofs were put up in the little colony.

*Indian Opinion* began to be published from Phoenix. The little colony was a busy hive on the day the paper had to be printed and made ready for despatch. Gandhi and Polak corrected the proofs, the printers ran off the corrected pages, the children folded and wrapped the journal.

Gandhi's cottage was the pivot of the corporate life of the settlement. Every Sunday all the residents met in his room for a community prayer in which recitations from the *Gita* and the Bible, Christian hymns and Gujerati *bhajans* mingled to lift the audience above their immediate surroundings, beyond the boundaries of race and religion. As for Gandhi, he had found a quiet

corner away from the heat and the dust of towns, away
from men's greed and hatred; working on the farm among
people who shared his ideals, he had time to pose questions
about his inner growth.

For Gandhi the 'fulfilment of Phoenix' was not to last long.
Both public and professional work made it imperative for him to
return to Johannesburg. A vivid account of the Johannesburg
household has been given by one of its inmates, Millie Graham
Polak, in her book *Mr Gandhi: The Man*. It was community
life in miniature. Gandhi as the benevolent patriarch had no
special privilege except perhaps that of looking after everybody
else. He was amusing and easily amused. The house resounded
with laughter as the children joined with the parents every
morning in the grinding of wheat in a hand-mill. The evening
meal was a pleasant hour, interspersed with light conversation
and serious discussion, and occasionally enlivened by Kasturbai's
ventures into the English language. After dinner Gandhi would
debate religion and philosophy and recite from the *Gita*. An
intimate pen-portrait of Gandhi as he was in his late thirties
has been left by Joseph J. Doke, Gandhi's first biographer, and a
Baptist minister of Johannesburg.[1] In December 1907 he saw
Gandhi for the first time:

'. . . to my surprise, a small, lithe, spare figure stood before me,
and a refined earnest face looked into mine. The skin was dark,
the eyes dark, but the smile which lighted up the face, and
that direct fearless glance, simply took one's heart by storm. I
judged him to be some thirty-eight years of age, which proved
correct. But the strain of his work showed its traces in the sprinkling of silver hairs on his head. He spoke English perfectly
and was evidently a man of great culture . . .

'There was a quiet assured strength about him, a greatness
of heart, a transparent honesty, that attracted me at once to the
Indian leader. We parted friends . . .

'Our Indian friend lives on a higher plane than most men do.
His actions, like the actions of Mary of Bethany, are often
counted eccentric, and not infrequently misunderstood. Those
who do not know him think there is some unworthy motive behind them, some Oriental 'slimness', to account for such profound unworldliness. But those who know him well are
ashamed of themselves in his presence.

'Money I think has no charm for him. His compatriots are
angry; they say, "He will take nothing. The money we gave him

[1] Doke, Joseph J.: *M. K. Gandhi*, Madras, pp. 6-8.

when he went as our deputy to England he brought back to us again. The presents we made him in Natal, he handed over to our public funds. He is poor because he will be poor."

'They wonder at him, grow angry at his strange unselfishness, and love him with the love of pride and trust. He is one of those outstanding characters with whom to walk is a liberal education, whom to know is to love.'

# CHAPTER X

# Discovery of Satyagraha

NATIVE policy in South Africa, Sir Alan Burns[1] has pointed out, degenerated into a defence of the 'poor white', who himself is a product of the system intended to degrade only the non-white. Behind the specious pleas of cultural differences, of conflicting ways of living, has always been economic rivalry. Lionel Curtis, a British official in the Transvaal who played a part in the formulation of the system of dyarchy in the Indian reforms of 1919, recalled a conversation he had with Gandhi in 1903:

'He (Mr Gandhi) started by trying to convince me of the points in the character of his countrymen, their industry, frugality, patience. I remember that after listening to him I said, "Mr Gandhi you are preaching to the converted. It is not the vices of the Indians that Europeans in this country fear, but their virtues." '[2]

The Europeans of Natal, who had imported thousands of indentured Indian labourers—semi-slaves—to work their sugar plantations and mines, were unwilling to suffer 'free Indians' as traders and farmers, in their midst, while after the Boer War the Europeans of the Transvaal raised the bogey of an 'Asiatic Invasion'. In 1905 a committee appointed by the British High Commissioner found that the accusation of secret smuggling of Indians into the Transvaal lacked foundation. Even though many Indian families who had left the Transvaal after the outbreak of war returned with the cessation of hostilities, the total Indian population of the Transvaal in 1903 was less than what it was in 1899.

Fear among Europeans that South Africa was being flooded with Indian immigrants were exaggerated. Gandhi considered them irrational, but he recognized the strength of European feeling on the subject. He was prepared to go so far to accom-

[1] Burns, Sir Alan: *Colour Prejudice*, London, 1948, p. 73.
[2] *Mahatma Gandhi: Essays and Reflections on His Life and Work*, edited by S. Radhakrishnan, London, 1939, p. 67.

modate European prejudices as to agree to a total embargo on the 'export' of Indian labour.

No more indentured labourers might be admitted, but a limited number of educated Indians were required to serve as clerks and accountants to the Indian merchants. Gandhi was prepared to meet the Europeans more than half-way even on other issues between the Indian community and the Europeans, backed by the local governments. The regulation of Indian trade by licences could be continued provided the local bodies issued them subject to the supervision of the Supreme Court. The Indians were similarly prepared to submit to local and municipal regulations regarding the ownership of land and the right of residence, provided the regulations applied to Europeans and Indians alike. Gandhi did not ask for the right to vote. 'What we (Indians) want,' he told the British High Commissioner in South Africa, 'is not political power; but we do wish to live side by side with other British subjects in peace and amity, and with dignity and self-respect.' This was precisely what the Boer and Briton did not want. General Smuts declared later that the Government had made up its mind to 'make this a white man's country, and however difficult the task before us in this direction, we have put our foot down and would keep it there'.

A stage was soon reached when Gandhi's policy of conciliation, of 'live and let live', was to meet with a rude rebuff. Matters came to a head on the question of the registration of Indians in the Transvaal. At first it had been considered sufficient to obtain the signature or (in the case of illiterate immigrants) the thumb impression. Later, a photograph was also required and Indians had to take out new permits. When Gandhi returned from the 'Zulu Rebellion', after doing his duty (as he then conceived it) as a citizen of the Empire, he found that a new measure had been devised to make the registration of Indians as irksome and humiliating a process as possible. He was stunned when he read the clauses of the bill in the *Transvaal Gazette* of August 22, 1906, which had been prepared for the Transvaal Legislature. It required every Indian—man, woman and child above eight years —to register and to give finger and thumb impressions on the registration form. If parents failed to give finger-prints of minor children, the latter were required to do so on attaining the age of sixteen, or to face the penalty, which might be a fine, imprisonment or deportation. In courts, revenue offices, indeed almost at any time or place, an Indian could be challenged to produce his registration certificate; police officers could enter an Indian's house to examine permits. 'Dog's collar' was indeed an apt description of this measure. The professed object of this drastic measure was to check the illicit influx of Indians into the Transvaal. Not only was there no proof of an influx on any large scale, but the existing laws were severe enough. During the years 1905-6 the Government had successfully conducted 150 prosecutions of Indians for unauthorized entry into the country. In one case a poor Indian woman had been torn away from her husband and ordered by the European magistrate to leave the country within seven hours. A boy under eleven years was arrested and sentenced to a fine of £30 or three months' imprisonment.

The object of the new registration measure was apparently to humiliate and demoralize the better educated and prosperous Indian, and to make the Transvaal too hot for him. Gandhi became convinced that if this measure became law and the Indians accepted it, it would 'spell absolute ruin to them'. It was better he felt, for Indians to die rather than submit to this law. But how were they to die? What should they dare and do, so that there would be nothing before them except a choice between victory and death? An impenetrable wall was before him; he could not see his way through it.

In the autumn of 1906, the political prospects for Indians in South Africa seemed dim. The British victory in the Boer War had brought no relief to Indians in the British colonies; in the former Boer states it had made their lot worse. The new régime in South Africa was to blossom into a partnership, but only between the Boer and the Briton. As Gandhi looked back on the twelve years he had devoted to the agitation for elementary civic rights for the Indian community in Natal and the Transvaal, he could not help feeling that 'love's labour had been lost'. His hopes of securing an amelioration of the Indians' condition by educating public opinion in South Africa, India and Britain had been frustrated. With the exception of a few Europeans, Christian missionaries or youthful idealists, he had been unable to make a perceptible impression upon the South African Europeans, who regarded the Indian question not as a matter of political ethics but one of 'bread-and-butter and of their children's bread-and-butter'. In India there was plenty of sympathy and a rare unanimity among all shades of opinion, reflected in the resolutions on South Africa passed every year by the Indian National Congress. Indian politicians were conscious of their limitations, however; the unreality of these verbal protests was brought out bluntly in Sir Pherozeshah Mehta's remark to Gandhi when they were travelling to Calcutta for the 1901 session of the Indian National Congress: 'But what rights have we in our own country? I believe that so long as we have no power in our own land, you cannot fare better in the colonies.'

In England, Gandhi was on occasions able to win influential support for his struggle for Indians' rights, particularly that of the London *Times*, but the British Colonial Office, in its anxiety to humour the South African whites, continued to dwell on the 'logic of self-government', according to which the colonies were free to do what they liked—even to grind the Indian subjects of the Empire.

It was clear that to resist the latest attack upon their self-respect, namely the measure for the registration of Asiatics, the Indians had to depend upon their own resources. They had no vote and no representation in the legislature. On September 11, 1906, they held a meeting at the Empire Theatre in Johannesburg which was 'packed from floor to ceiling'.[1] The main resolution on the agenda drafted by Gandhi was that the Indian community was determined not to submit to the proposed measure for registration of Asiatics. When one of the speakers declared in the name of God that he would never submit to that law, Gandhi was 'startled and put on his guard'. The suggestion of a solemn oath helped him to think out 'the possible consequences in a single moment', and his 'perplexity gave way to enthusiasm'. A solemn oath meant much to Gandhi. His life had been moulded by the vows he had taken; the three-fold vow he had taken on the eve of his departure for England had had a profound effect on him, and only recently he had snapped the common ties of family and property in order to give undivided allegiance to public service. The idea of a pledge of resistance to an unjust law, with God as witness, and with no fear of consequences, demolished the wall which had been obscuring his vision. He experienced the relief and exhilaration of a mathematician who suddenly discovers the solution to an intractable problem. The solution was no fluke; his whole life had been a preparation for it. Since his childhood in his personal life truth had been his guiding principle and he had tried to practise it at any cost. He had shed those smaller loyalties which make cowards of most men. The courage and the faith he evinced on this historic occasion had behind them a life-long discipline. To his fellow-Indians assembled in that Empire

[1] *Satyagraha in South Africa*, p. 161.

Theatre hall in Johannesburg he spoke out fearlessly: 'There is only one course open to those like me, to die but not to submit to the law. It is quite unlikely, but even if everyone else flinched leaving me alone to face the music, I am confident that I would not violate my pledge.'[1]

He asked them to search their hearts. He warned them that those who resisted the Government would run the risk of confiscation of property, imprisonment, starvation, flogging and even death. The meeting ended with a solemn oath by 'all present standing with raised hands, with God as witness not to submit to the (Asiatic Registration) Ordinance if it became law'. Gandhi did not explain the mode of resistance; perhaps he was not himself clear about it. Of one thing there was no doubt; it was to be free from violence. Gandhi was vaguely aware that some new principle of fighting political and social evils had come into being. The term 'passive resistance' was at first employed to describe the new principle, but the association of this term with the verbal and physical violence practised by the suffragettes in England made it unsatisfactory. *Indian Opinion*, which was to become the voice of Gandhi's movement, invited suggestions for an appropriate name. The word 'sadagraha' (which means firmness in good conduct) appealed to Gandhi; he amended it to 'Satyagraha' (firmness in truth). The principles and the technique of the new movement, however, were to evolve gradually in the ensuing months and years; its author was a man for whom theory was the handmaid of action.

It is not surprising that the movement should have borne the impress of his peculiar evolution. In 1908, Doke questioned him on the genesis of Satyagraha and recorded:

'Mr Gandhi himself attributes the birth and evolution of this principle (Passive Resistance), so far as he is concerned, to quite other influences. "I remember," he said, "how one verse of a Gujerati poem, which as a child I learned at school, clung to me. In substance it was this: If a man gives you a drink of water and you give him a drink in return, that is nothing. Real beauty consists in doing good against evil. As a child, this verse had a powerful influence over me, and I tried to carry it into practice. Then came the Sermon on the Mount".'

' "But surely," I said, "the *Bhagavad Gita* came first?"

' "No," he replied, "of course, I knew the *Bhagavad Gita* in Sanskrit tolerably well, but I had not made its teaching in that particular a study. It was the New Testament which really

[1] *Satyagraha in South Africa*, p. 168.

awakened me to the rightness and value of Passive Resistance. When I read in the Sermon on the Mount, such passages as 'Resist not him that is evil, but whosoever smiteth thee on thy right cheek turn to him the other also', and 'Love your enemies and pray for them that persecute you, that ye may be sons of your Father which is in heaven', I was simply overjoyed, and found my own opinion confirmed where I least expected it. The *Bhagavad Gita* deepened the impression, and Tolstoy's *The Kingdom of God is Within You* gave it permanent form." [1]

[1] Doke, Joseph J.: *M. K. Gandhi*, p. 88.

# CHAPTER XI

# First Satyagraha Movement

IN spite of the unanimous and vehement opposition of the Indian community, the Asiatic Registration Bill was carried by the Transvaal Legislature almost *in toto*. The royal assent was received. It was announced that the new law would take effect from July 1, 1907.

The Indians had failed to make themselves heard. The time had come for Gandhi to fulfil the pledge of resistance to this unjust law. He formed a Passive Resistance Association to conduct his campaign. Though the oath of resistance to the hated law had been taken by Indians present at that historic meeting in the Empire Theatre in September 1906, he had it readministered to give the waverers a chance to withdraw. *Indian Opinion*, which had been for many years a drain on his purse, was to prove a handy instrument for the political education of the Indian community. It played the part in South Africa which *Young India* and *Harijan* were to play later in India; it was read not only by his colleagues and co-workers but also by his opponents, as it unreservedly indicated his plans. Its popularity is shown by its circulation, which reached a peak figure of 3,500 in a country where the total number of potential Indian readers did not exceed 20,000 and where copies were also circulated from door to door.

The Government opened permit offices in the principal towns, and called upon all Indian residents in the Transvaal to register by July 31, 1907, or face the penalties prescribed by law. The Passive Resistance Association advised the Indian community to boycott the permit offices. Posters appeared with the striking caption: 'Loyalty to the King demands loyalty to the King of Kings . . . Indians be Free.' Gandhi planned the picketing of the permit offices to the minutest detail. He recruited volunteers— some of them boys in their teens—and posted them outside the permit offices to dissuade Indians from taking out the registration certificates under the new law. But volunteers were forbidden to be violent or even discourteous towards those who insisted on registering themselves. And they surrendered themselves cheerfully if the police wished to arrest them. Though pressure of every kind was ruled out in this campaign, the force of public opinion was itself strong enough for the blacklegs. There were a few instances in which permits were taken out at night in collusion with the permit offices, but by and large the boycott was effective. The Government extended the date of registration, but by November 30, 1907, only 511 Indians had taken out the registration certificates.

On December 28, 1907, Gandhi and twenty-six of his prominent colleagues attended a Johannesburg court to show cause why, through failure to register under the law, they should not be deported from the Transvaal. Gandhi received two months' simple imprisonment. If the Government had hoped to break the spirit of the rank and file by locking up their leader, they had made a serious miscalculation. There was lively competition among the Indians in courting imprisonment. The fear of imprisonment had gone; gaol came to be known as King Edward's Hotel. Johannesburg gaol began to fill, until it had 155 passive resisters where it could accommodate only fifty. They slept on the ground and the food served to them was such that only the kaffirs could relish it; their morale was high. They asked for manual labour, but since their sentences were in most cases without hard labour, those in charge of the gaol could not oblige them.

Gandhi had hardly begun to feel settled in prison when he received a visit from his friend Albert Cartright, a liberal European, whose paper *The Transvaal Leader* had often supported the Indian cause. Cartright told Gandhi that he had seen General Smuts and had brought with him the draft of a settlement, according to which the Asiatic Registration Act was to be repealed provided the Indians registered voluntarily. Two days later, Gandhi, still a prisoner, was received by General Smuts in his office at Pretoria. The General praised the perseverance of the Indians, pleaded his helplessness on the registration issue in view of the strong European feeling and repeated the assurance already conveyed by Cartright that the Asiatic Registration Act would be taken off the statute-book if Indians registered on their own. The General accepted some amendments which Gandhi suggested. 'Where am I to go?' asked Gandhi. The General laughed and replied: 'I am phoning the prison officials to release the other prisoners tomorrow morning.'

It was seven o'clock in the evening. Gandhi did not have a farthing with him. Borrowing the railway fare from General Smuts' secretary, he rushed to the railway station to catch the last train for Johannesburg. He called a meeting of the Indian community within a few hours of his arrival to discuss the informal agreement he had reached with Smuts. There was a good deal of criticism. Was he not playing into the hands of the Government? Why did the repeal of the Registration Act not precede rather than follow voluntary registration? What would happen if the Transvaal Government did not keep their word? Gandhi explained that it was part of the duty of a Satyagrahi to trust the word of even an adversary. If the Government went back on its word, it was open to the Indians to resume their resistance. A rugged Pathan hailing from the North-West frontier of India persistently heckled Gandhi and even accused him of having sold the Indian community to General Smuts for £15,000. On the morning of February 10, 1908, Gandhi left his residence to take out, as he had publicly promised, the first registration certificate in accordance with the understanding he had reached with General Smuts. In Von Brandis Street the Pathan, Mir Alam and his friends attacked Gandhi, who fainted with the words 'He Rama' (Oh God!) on his lips. Were it not for some companions who warded off some of the blows, and for the intervention of European passers-by, Gandhi would have been killed on the spot.

Bleeding profusely, he was carried into the nearest shop. As he regained consciousness, his first thought was for his assailant. 'Where is Mir Alam?' he asked his friend Doke, who had arrived on the scene. 'He has been arrested along with the rest,' replied Doke. 'He should be released,' said Gandhi. Doke replied: 'That is all very well but here you are in a stranger's office with your lip and cheek bandaged. The police are ready to take you to the hospital, but if you will go to my place, Mrs Doke and I will minister to your comforts as best we can.' Gandhi preferred to go to the Dokes's house.

Gandhi had risked his life to fulfil his part of the compact with Smuts. But the Boer General backed out with a brazenness which left not only Gandhi but Albert Cartright, the honest broker, gasping. The Transvaal Government did not repeal the Asiatic Registration Act; it brought forth a new measure to validate the voluntary registration of the Indians. This meant that Indian immigrants who entered the country in future would still be subject to the 'Black Act'. Gandhi gave vent to his feelings in *Indian Opinion* in an article entitled 'Foul Play'. His colleagues taunted him with gullibility; he wrote to Smuts and recalled conversations with Albert Cartwright and with the General. Unfortunately the General's recollections did not coincide with Gandhi's.

# CHAPTER XII

## *Second Round*

THE Indians' discomfiture looked complete. They had voluntarily put on 'the dog's collar', and the law against which they had agitated nevertheless remained on the statute-book. The Government refused to return the Indians' original applications for voluntary registration. Gandhi declared that the Indians would burn their registration certificates and 'humbly take the consequences'.

The earlier campaign in the autumn of 1907 had planned itself. Now, with better knowledge of his people and a surer grasp of the technique which he was evolving, Gandhi planned the second round in the Satyagraha struggle. A huge bonfire was held at which a large number of Transvaal Indians consigned their registration certificates to the flames. The scene was compared by the Johannesburg correspondent of the *Daily Mail* with the 'Boston Tea Party'. The Indians' struggle in the Transvaal may not have been as historic an event as the American War of Independence, but the burning of the certificates was certainly a bold act of defiance. General Smuts, who may have chuckled over Gandhi's discomfiture, did not have the last laugh. The highlight of the demonstration came when Mir Alam, now out of jail, stepped forward and shook hands with Gandhi, who assured him that he had never harboured any resentment against his assailant.

Meanwhile the Transvaal Legislature had passed another measure which effectively excluded new immigrants from India. Gandhi wrote to the Government that the Satyagraha movement would also be directed against the new measures. General Smuts accused Gandhi of raising new issues; he warned the Indians that their spokesman was a person 'who, when given an inch, asked for an ell'. In fact Gandhi had been straining hard to restrict the scope and area of his struggle, and had, with some difficult, held back Indian settlers in other colonies in South Africa from launching sympathetic movements.

The Indians were prepared to fill the prisons. In August 1908 a few prominent Indians from Natal, who had an old right of domicile in the Transvaal, crossed the frontier, not to settle in the Transvaal but to defy the Registration Act. They were arrested. In the Transvaal the easiest passport to King Edward's Hotel—as Gandhi called the gaols—was to hawk without a licence. Hawkers who had licences refused to produce them on demand and trooped into prisons. Their example was followed by well-to-do Indian merchants and barristers, who turned hawkers overnight, peddled vegetables without a licence and marched into prison. The terms of imprisonment in this second Satyagraha campaign were, unlike those in the first, usually with hard labour. The treatment of Indians in gaol became harsher. Boys in their teens were made to break stones, sweep the streets and dig tanks. One of them named Nagappa, an eighteen-year-old boy who was taken to work in the early winter mornings, died of pneumonia.

Gandhi himself had a taste of this severe treatment in a Transvaal prison when he landed there in October 1908. He spent the first night in the company of some kaffiir criminals, 'wild-looking, murderous, vicious, lewd and uncouth'. He kept his composure by repeating verses from the *Gita*. This was the hardest term he ever had in prison. At seven in the morning he was one of a gang of prisoners, led by a relentless overseer, which dug hard ground with spades. As the day wore on, with his bent back and blistered hands Gandhi was seen cheering up his companions, many of whom all but broke under the strain. In the evenings and on Sundays he pored over the *Gita* and books by Ruskin, Thoreau and others, which he could get in gaol. The rigorous prison routine harmonized with the philosophy of life which he had been working out, the renunciation of creature comforts and the sublimation of self in the service of humanity. His personality developed and took on that steely strength which was to become a powerful force in years to come. 'Each time he returned,' writes Mrs Polak, 'one felt that some almost indefinable growth had taken place in him during his absence in gaol.'[1]

Prosecutions, deportations and economic pressure did not crush the Satyagraha movement. Nevertheless, it could not continue at a high pitch all the time and gradually fell to a low ebb. A sort of war-weariness crept over the Indian community, particularly over its richer section. There was a stalemate; the Indians did not give up the fight, though they were unable to make a spectacular impression.

[1] Polak, M.: *Mr. Gandhi: The Man*, p. 94.

After a fruitless trip to England in 1909, Gandhi saw that
the Indians' struggle for their rights would be a protracted affair.
Repression by the Transvaal Government had told on the small
Indian community. Many merchants had suffered heavy losses
and had retired from politics. A small band of Satyagrahis, however, continued to court imprisonment. To the families of these
Satyagrahi prisoners the Satyagraha Association had been giving
subsistence allowances, but the funds of the Association were
running out. Since 1906 Gandhi's political preoccupations had
brought his practice at the bar to a standstill, and all his savings
had been sunk in the movement. Money was needed not only
to help the distressed families, but to run the offices of the
movement in Johannesburg and London, and to keep *Indian
Opinion* going. In this war of attrition, time was evidently on
the side of the Transvaal Government and the Indian resisters
were in danger of being starved into surrender. Gandhi felt that
if the Satyagraha struggle was to be sustained, financial commit-
ments must be drastically cut. He came to the conclusion that
the most economical arrangement was to lodge the families of
Satyagrahi prisoners at a co-operative farm. The Phoenix Settlement in Durban which he had founded in 1904 was the
obvious choice; but it was ruled out, owing to its distance from
Johannesburg, thirty hours away by train.

Kallenbach, a German architect who had thrown in his lot
with Gandhi, came to his rescue. He bought a 1,100-acre farm
twenty-one miles from Johannesburg and gave it rent free for
the use of the Satyagrahis. The estate, which was styled
'Tolstoy Farm', had about a thousand fruit trees and a small
house. With such local labour and materials as they could muster,
Gandhi and Kallenbach put up a small colony of corrugated structures. The residents of Tolstoy Farm, whose number varied
between fifty and seventy-five, hailed from almost all parts of
India, and included Hindus, Muslims, Parsis and Christians.
They were served by a common vegetarian kitchen and led a
frugal and hard life, which was in fact harder than life in jail.
All the residents, including children, had their quota of manual
labour. The colony tried to be self-sufficient; its workshop,
under the expert supervision of Kallenbach, manufactured
odds and ends. Kallenbach learnt shoe-making from the monks
of a German monastery and taught the craft to his fellow residents, including Gandhi. 'We had all become labourers', writes
Gandhi, 'and therefore put on labourers' dress, but in the European style, viz. workman's trousers and shirts, which were

imitated from prisoners' uniform.'[1] Those who went to the town on private errands had to walk the forty-two miles to and back from Johannesburg. Gandhi himself, though past forty and living only on fruits, did not think much of walking forty miles a day; he once did fifty-five miles without feeling any the worse for it.

Gandhi was in high spirits; his 'faith and courage were at their highest on Tolstoy Farm.'[2] He became a firm believer in nature-cure and it was during this period that he wrote his *Guide to Health*. 'There was not,' he writes, 'a single case of illness on the farm in which we used drugs or called in a doctor.' In Kallenbach he found an enthusiastic comrade for his experiments. They tried to work out the implications of *Ahimsa* (non-violence) and to apply the principle to snakes. They ran a school for the children of the colony where Gandhi tried his ideas on education, which he had so far tested only on his children. He laid emphasis on the culture of the heart, rather than on the sharpening of the intellect, and made manual work an integral part of the curriculum.

The children of Tolstoy Farm merrily dug pits, felled trees, lifted loads, learnt carpentry and shoe-making. Gandhi had a high conception of his duty as a teacher: 'It would be idle for me if I were a liar to teach the boys to tell the truth. A cowardly teacher would never succeed in making his boys valiant . . . I saw, therefore, that I must be an eternal object-lesson to the boys and girls living with me. They thus became my teachers, and I learnt I must be good, and live straight, if only for their sakes.'

The increasing discipline and self-restraint Gandhi cultivated at Tolstoy Farm was attributed by him to his awakened sense of responsibility as a teacher. Tolstoy Farm was another milestone in his growth; it also made a valuable contribution to the Satyagraha struggle. Not only did it offer an asylum to the families of Satyagrahi prisoners, but the spectacle of a handful of Indian patriots cheerfully leading a life of voluntary poverty and austerity, rather than surrender to the organized might of the Transvaal Government, was to prove an inspiring example to the rest of the Indian community when Gandhi led it in the last phase of his Satyagraha campaign. And the men, women and children who had known the austere discipline of Tolstoy Farm could have little fear of gaol.

The Satyagraha struggle had continued for four years. The

[1] *Satyagraha in South Africa*, p. 375.
[2] *Idem*, p. 371.

Indians went in and came out of gaol. The weaker and the richer members of the community could not sustain the tempo of the struggle, but the morale of the minority which held out under Gandhi's leadership was high. Public opinion in India was becoming restive. Gokhale piloted through the Imperial Legislative Council a resolution banning the emigration of indentured labour to South Africa. As the coronation of King George V drew near, the Imperial Government was also anxious to pour oil on troubled waters and appease Indian opinion. The result was an announcement in February 1911 by the South African Government that it would remove the racial bar; the entry of Indians into the Transvaal was to be restricted not as Asiatics, but by means of a severe education test.

On May 27, 1911, *Indian Opinion* announced that a provisional settlement with the Government had been reached, and that Indians and Chinese were free to resume their occupations. On June 1st, the Satyagrahi prisoners were released. The truce lasted till the end of 1912.

The great event of 1912 was a visit from Gokhale. For fifteen years, Gokhale had been in touch with, and lent his powerful support to, Gandhi from inside and outside the Imperial Legislative Council at Calcutta. His tour of South Africa was planned with the consent of the British Government; he came as a state guest and was given a saloon for his rail journeys. Gandhi received him at Cape Town, and acted as his secretary—and valet—throughout the one-month tour. Railway stations were illuminated and red carpets rolled out for Gokhale. The Indian community showered addresses and caskets on him, and gave him a right royal welcome. In Pretoria, the capital of the Union, he had a conference with Union ministers at the end of which he told Gandhi, 'You must return to India in a year. Everything has been settled. The Black Act will be repealed. The racial bar will be removed from the emigration law. The £3 tax will be abolished.' 'I doubt it very much,' replied Gandhi, 'you do not know the ministers as I do.'

As Gokhale turned his back on South Africa, it became clear that he had been bluffed. General Smuts told the South African Parliament that, in view of the European feeling in Natal, it was not possible to abolish the £3 tax on the ex-indentured labourers, and their families.

Another 'breach of faith' gave a new lease of life to the Satyagraha movement.

# CHAPTER XIII

# Final Phase

GANDHI decided to launch his final campaign and to throw his 'all' into it. Gokhale had written from India enquiring about the strength of 'the army of peace' which was to wage this campaign; Gandhi replied that he could count on at least sixteen and, at the most, sixty-six Satyagrahis. Gokhale, a seasoned politician, was somewhat amused at these statistics and wondered how a handful of Indians could bring the Transvaal Government to terms. But Gokhale could not foresee Gandhi's strategy, which was soon to unfold itself and suck thousands of Indians into the movement.

Gandhi's first move was to send a party of sixteen, including Mrs Gandhi, from Phoenix settlement in Natal to the Transvaal. They were arrested for entering the Transvaal without a permit on September 23rd and imprisoned. A few days later, a party of eleven women from Tolstoy Farm in the Transvaal crossed into Natal without a permit, and proceeded to Newcastle; before they were arrested, they had persuaded the Indian miners to go on strike.

The strike in the coal mines was a serious affair. Gandhi hastened to Newcastle to take charge of the situation, and to guard against any disorder or violence on the part of the strikers. The mine owners invited him to Durban. 'You have nothing to lose,' they taunted him, 'but will you compensate the misguided labourers for the damage you will cause them?' The workers, replied Gandhi, were aware of the risks they ran, and in any case there could be no greater loss than the loss of self-respect, which they had suffered for many years in the form of the £3 poll tax. On returning to Newcastle, Gandhi told the miners of the threats made by their masters, but the miners did not flinch; their faith in 'Gandhibhai' (Brother Gandhi) was complete. Their employers began to tighten the screws on them. They cut off water and electricity from the miners' quarters, so the poor Indians with their scanty belongings left their quarters. Gandhi did not know what to do with these jobless and home-

less men. The Indian traders of Newcastle were reluctant to
help the miners for fear of incurring the Government's displeasure. An Indian Christian family offered to feed them,
but how long could it afford to do so? There were great risks
involved in allowing hundreds of illiterate and unemployed
labourers to idle about. So Gandhi decided to march this
'army' to the Transvaal, hoping that en route it would be
taken out of his hands by the Government and deposited in
gaol. But if by some miracle the miners and their families
escaped imprisonment, they were to support themselves by
working on Tolstoy Farm.

The labourers covered in two days—on a ration of a pound
and a half of bread and an ounce of sugar—the 36 miles from
Newcastle to Charlestown, which was close to the Transvaal
border. A week later, on November 6, 1913 began the march
across the border. There were 2,037 men, 127 women and 57
children. 'The pilgrims whom Gandhi is guiding', wrote the
Sunday Post 'are an exceedingly picturesque crew. To the eye
they appear most meagre, indeed emaciated; their legs are mere
sticks, but the way they are marching on the starvation rations
show them to be particularly hardy.' There were a few instances of indiscipline, but on the whole the courage, the discipline and the fortitude of these poor, illiterate labourers were
amazing. They knew little of politics but they knew their leader,
whose word was law to them. One of the women was marching
with a baby; the baby fell down from her arms as she was crossing a stream and was drowned. 'We must not pine for the dead',
she said, 'it is the living for whom we must work,' and marched
on.

Gandhi was arrested at Volksrust. At Balfour station the
marchers were placed under arrest and put into three special
trains which were to deport them to Natal. There was a critical
moment when the strikers refused to board the train without
orders from Gandhibhai. They were, however, persuaded to
obey. On the way, they were starved, and on reaching Natal
were prosecuted and sent to gaol. The Government hit upon
an ingenious device for working the mines and at the same time
punishing the strikers. It declared the mine compounds as 'out-
stations' to the Dundee and Newcastle gaols, and appointed
the mine-owner's European staff as the warders. To complete
the cruel joke, working the mines was made part of the sentence. The labourers were brave men and flatly refused to be
forced underground, and for this they were brutally whipped.

The news of this ruthless repression spread and led to spontaneous strikes in the north and west of Natal, where Indian labourers came out of plantations and mines. The Government adopted a policy of 'blood and iron'. Racial feeling and vested economic interests combined in savage punishment of the poor Indian labourers, who were chased back to work in the mines by mounted military police.

In Volksrust gaol Gandhi was made to dig stones and sweep the compound. Later he was transferred to Pretoria gaol and lodged in a dark cell ten feet long and seven feet wide, which was lit at night only to check up on the prisoners. He was denied a bench, refused permission to talk in the cell and subjected to numberless pinpricks. Summoned for evidence in a case, he was marched to the court with handcuffs on his hands and manacles on his feet.

The 'blood and iron' policy of the South African Government stirred India deeply. Gokhale, who had been in touch with Gandhi by letter and cable, toured India in a campaign to mobilize moral and financial support for the Satyagrahis. Bishop Lefroy, the Metropolitan of India, backed the Indians' cause in an outspoken letter to the Press. The viceroy, Lord Hardinge, was impressed by the strong feeling in the country; he was advised that 'there had been no movement like it since the Mutiny'. He declared that the Indian resisters in South Africa had the sympathy of India, and 'also of those like myself who without being Indians themselves, have feelings of sympathy for the people of this country.'[1] The Viceroy went on to ask for an impartial enquiry into the charges of atrocities levelled against the South African Government.

General Smuts found himself in an unenviable position between his own bad conscience and the South African Europeans' intransigence which he himself had encouraged. 'He was in the same predicament as a snake which has made a mouthful of a rat but can neither gulp it down nor cast it out.'[2] He resorted to the time-honoured face-saving device of appointing a Commission of Inquiry. There was no Indian on it, and two of its three members had been noted for their anti-Indian bias. Gandhi felt that unless the commission was reconstituted the Indians could expect no justice from it. Gokhale sent Andrews and Pearson to assist in the mediation.

The major points on which the Satyagraha struggle had been

[1] Hardinge of Penshurst: *My Indian Years*, London, 1948, p. 91.
[2] Smuts, J. C.: *Jan Christian Smuts*, p. 106.

waged were conceded to the Indians. The £3 tax on the ex-indentured labourers was abolished; marriages performed according to Indian rites were legalized, and a domicile certificate bearing the holder's thumb-imprint was to be a sufficient evidence of the right to enter the Union of South Africa.

General Smuts's son has recorded that 'Gandhi's outwitting by my father was complete, and it was in this sense of failure that he set out dejectedly to brood and scheme in India'.[1] This was, however, not the opinion of his father, who wrote in 1939 that it had been his 'fate to be the antagonist of a man for whom even then I had the highest respect'. As for the Satyagraha movement, he recalled: 'Gandhi himself received—what no doubt he desired—a short period of rest and quiet in gaol. For him everything went according to plan. For me—the defender of law and order—there was the usual trying situation, the odium of carrying out a law which had not strong public support, and finally the discomfiture when the law had to be repealed. For him it was a successful coup.'[2]

In gaol Gandhi had prepared a pair of sandals for General Smuts, who recalled that there was no hatred and personal ill-feeling, and when the fight was over 'there was the atmosphere in which decent peace could be concluded'.

---

[1] *Satyagraha in South Africa*, p. 485.
[2] Radhakrishnan, S. (Ed.): *Mahatma Gandhi*, London, 1939, pp. 277-8.

# CHAPTER XIV

# A Hero on Probation

---

GANDHI'S work did not provide an enduring solution for the Indian question in South Africa; it only postponed the evil day for the Indian minority. Forces, some of which he knew and fought, and others which were to emerge in the years to come, were to forge a new racial tyranny more ruthless and shameless than the pre-1914 world could conceive. The issues on which for eight years the Satyagraha struggle was waged and won by Gandhi have indeed only an academic interest today.

What Gandhi did to South Africa was, however, less important than what South Africa did to him. He had gone to South Africa as a junior counsel of a commercial firm for £105 a year; he stayed on to command, and then voluntarily give up, a peak practice of £5,000 a year. In Bombay, as a young lawyer, he had a nervous breakdown while cross-examining witnesses in a petty civil suit; in South Africa he had founded a new political organization with the sure touch of a seasoned politician. The hostility of the European politicians and officials and the helplessness of the Indian merchants and labourers had put him on his mettle. 'I am the only available person who can handle the question,' he had written to Dadabhai Naoroji. The Natal Indians, who had no franchise and no representation in the Legislature, had to be saved from being pushed over the precipice; Gandhi could not avoid giving them a helping hand. No glittering rewards awaited him; the perils ranged from professional pinpricks to lynching. Nevertheless, it was a piece of good fortune that he began his professional and political career in South Africa. Dwarfed as he had felt by the great lawyers and leaders of India, it is unlikely that he would have developed much initiative in his homeland. When he founded the Natal Indian Congress at the age of twenty-five he was writing on a *tabula rasa*; he could try out ideals which in an established political organization would have been laughed out of court. What had truth and vows to do with politics? It was a question which often recurred in Indian politics, and if Gandhi was not confounded by it, it was because, far back in South Africa, he had observed and confirmed the connection. For a man who was no doctrinaire, and whose theory often lagged behind practice, it was a decided advantage that the scene of his early activities should have been one where he was unfettered by political precedents or professionals. Natal and the Transvaal were no bigger than some of the smaller provinces of India. The struggle for Indian independence was conducted by Gandhi on a much larger scale and on much bigger issues, but there were not a few occasions when he derived inspiration from his experience in South Africa. He had seen Hindus and Muslims co-operating in Natal and the Transvaal, and therefore never lost his faith in Hindu-Muslim unity. He had seen the vicissitudes of the Satyagraha struggle against the Asiatic Registration Act, and was never dispirited by the ebb and flow of the freedom movement in India. He had seen thousands of poor, unlettered labourers, bereft of almost all worldly goods, briskly marching, oblivious to the perils of imprisonment, flogging and shooting which awaited them; no wonder that he believed in the practicability of Satyagraha for the masses.

Not only his politics, but his personality took shape in South Africa. The most formative years of his life had been spent there. His interest in moral and religious questions dated back to his early childhood, but it was only in South Africa that he had an opportunity to study them systematically. The Quaker friends who made a dead set at him on his arrival in Pretoria failed to convert him to Christianity, but they whetted his innate appetite for religious studies. He delved deep into Christianity and other religions including his own. From the *Gita* he imbibed the ideal of 'non-possession' which set him on the road to voluntary poverty. The ideal of 'service without self' and of 'action without attachment' broadened his vision and equipped him with extraordinary stamina and faith for his public life.

Few men read so little to so much profit as Gandhi did. A book was for Gandhi not a mere diversion for the hour, it was embodied experience which had to be accepted or rejected. Books could thus exercise an amazing impact on him. Ruskin's *Unto This Last* drove him with compelling urgency from the capital of Natal to the wilderness of Zululand to practise a life of voluntary poverty, and literally to live by the sweat of his brow. It was in Tolstoy's books that we may seek one of the strongest influences on Gandhi. He was, of course, not given to indiscriminate imitation, but in Tolstoy he found a writer whose

views elaborated his own inchoate beliefs. It was not only on the
organized or covert violence of the modern state and the right of
the citizen to civil disobedience that Gandhi found support in
Tolstoy. There were innumerable subjects, ranging from modern
civilization and industrialism to sex and schools, on which he
tended to agree with Tolstoy's analysis. There was an exchange
of letters between the two which gives an impression of gratitude
and reverence on the part of the young Indian on the threshold
of his career, and of delighted surprise on that of the aged
Tolstoy, already under the shadow of domestic tragedy and
death. Many of Tolstoy's ideas were to be tested and tried by
his Indian admirer.

*Hind Swaraj* or 'Indian Home Rule', which was written in
1909 during Gandhi's return voyage from London to South
Africa, bears the impress of Tolstoy and Ruskin. Directed at the
'school of violence', the young anarchists who sought the salvation of India by using against the West its own weapon of bomb
and pistol, *Hind Swaraj* is a compendious political manifesto.

Before he left South Africa Gandhi remarked that India was a
strange country to him. Between the year 1888, when he sailed
for England, and 1914, when he finally left South Africa, he had
spent less than four years in India. He, however, was no stranger
to India. Gokhale had told his countrymen, after his tour of
South Africa in 1912, that Gandhi 'is without doubt made of the
stuff of which heroes and martyrs are made. Nay, more, he has
in him the marvellous spiritual power to turn ordinary men
around him into heroes and martyrs'.

A hero's welcome awaited him when he landed on January
9, 1915 at the Appollo Bunder in Bombay, and the Government
of India joined with the people in showering honours on him. He
received a Kaiser-i-Hind gold medal in the New Year's Honours
list of 1915. His association with Gokhale was guarantee enough
of his being a 'safe' politician. He had, of course, led an extra-
constitutional movement in South Africa, defied laws and filled
gaols, but the cause for which he had fought appeared as much
humanitarian as political, dear to all Indians and all Englishmen
whose sense of humanity had not been blunted by racial arrogance or political expediency. Lord Hardinge's open support of
the Satyagraha movement had removed any stigma of 'rebellion'
from South Africa's Indian movement.'

One of the first things Gokhale did was to extract a promise
from Gandhi on his return to India that he would not express

himself upon public questions for a year, which was to be 'a year of probation'.

Gokhale was very keen that Gandhi should join the Servants of India Society. This society, founded by Gokhale, consisted of a small band of carefully selected social workers and scholars living on a subsistence wage and pledged to devote their lives to the cause of the country. Gandhi was only too willing to fall in with the wishes of Gokhale, but several members of the Society feared there was too great a gap between the ideals and methods of the Society and those of Gandhi. His critical approach to Western civilization and modern science, and his use of religious jargon to describe everyday social and economic problems, his extra-constitutional method of political agitation (Satyagraha) jarred on the small coterie of the 'servants of India'. While the question of Gandhi's admission as 'a servant of India' was being debated, Gandhi visited his home towns of Porbandar and Rajkot and went on to Santiniketan in West Bengal, the cosmopolitan university of the poet Rabindranath Tagore.

The trip to Santiniketan ended abruptly with a telegram from Poona telling him that Gokhale was dead. Gandhi was stunned. For a moment he felt lost. 'Launching on the stormy sea of Indian public life,' he wrote later, 'I was in need of a sure pilot. I had had one in Gokhale and had felt secure in his keeping.'[1] He mourned Gokhale by going barefoot for a year, and out of respect for the memory of his friend, philosopher and guide, he made another effort to seek admission to the Servants of India Society. Finding a sharp division of opinion in the Society on this point, he wrote to Srinivasa Sastri, who had succeeded Gokhale as the head of the Society, that he wished to withdraw his application for admission and save those opposed to him from an awkward position.

During 1915—the year of probation—Gandhi eschewed politics severely. In his speeches and writings during this period he confined himself to the reform of the individual and society, and avoided the issues which dominated Indian politics. His restraint was partly due to self-imposed silence and partly to the fact that he was still studying conditions in India and making up his mind.

While his political views were yet unformed, Gandhi's immediate problem was to settle the small band of relatives and associates in the South African struggle who had cast their lot in

[1] Gandhi: *Autobiography*, p. 471.

with him. A party of eighteen boys from Phoenix in Natal, led by Maganlal, had arrived in India while Gandhi was still in England. They had enjoyed the hospitality of two great cultural and educational institutions, Gurukul Kangri and Santiniketan. At Santiniketan Tagore received them kindly and wrote to Gandhi thanking him 'for allowing your boys to be our boys as well, and thus form a living link in the *sadhana* of both our lives'. Gandhi was, however, anxious to set up an 'Ashram' where he could lodge these boys and other co-workers to enable them to resume the life of simplicity and service in which they had been nurtured in South Africa.

Gokhale had promised to finance the Ashram, but he died in February 1915. Gandhi received invitations to found the Ashram in various parts of the country, from his home town Rajkot, from holy Hardwar, and from Calcutta, but he chose Ahmedabad. Apart from the fact that some of the local industrialists promised to find the money for the setting up and running of an Ashram, he felt that he could best serve the people of the province of his birth. Ahmedabad, a great textile centre, was also best suited for experiments in hand spinning and weaving which appeared to him the only practicable supplementary occupations for the underworked and underfed masses in the villages of India.

In his *History of the Satyagraha Ashram*, which was begun in Yeravda gaol in 1932 but published after his death, Gandhi defined an Ashram as 'group life lived in a religious spirit'. The word 'religious' was used here in the widest sense. Gandhi's Ashram did not enforce any theology or ritual, but only a few simple rules of personal conduct. Some of the vows administered in the Ashram, such as those of truth, non-violence and chastity, were of universal application; others, such as those to eradicate untouchability, to do bodily labour and to practise fearlessness, were intended to meet the peculiar conditions of contemporary Indian society, which was caste-ridden, discounted the dignity of labour, and was dominated by an alien government.

The vows were to be observed in an intelligent and creative way. They were not intended to be mechanical formulae, but as practical aids to moral and spiritual growth. They may appear to be platitudes, but nevertheless they embodied ancient truths which were none the less valid for not having been realized by the common run of mankind in workaday life.

We may begin with the vow of truth. 'The Satyagraha Ashram,' wrote Gandhi, 'owes its very existence to the pursuit and the attempted practice of truth.'[1] There was no ready-made formula for truth. He conceded that what appeared as truth to one person might not do so to another. 'There is nothing wrong,' he added, 'in everyone following truth according to his lights. Indeed it is his duty to do so.'

The vow of *ahimsa* (non-violence) was not only a negative concept of non-injury to others. Nor was it carried in daily life to its logical but impossible conclusion that breathing and eating vegetables destroyed living organisms. The motive force of *ahimsa*, the love for all that lives, had to be intelligently interpreted. Orthodoxy in India received a rude shock when Gandhi permitted in Sabarmati Ashram the mercy-killing of a calf suffering from an excruciating but incurable pain. He did not regard non-violence simply as avoidance of physical injury to animate beings. He knew that guns and bombs and daggers probably take a smaller toll of human life than ill will, malice and hatred, which cramp and kill humanity inch by inch. The Gandhian non-violence aimed at liberating men and women from inner as well as outer violence.

Another vow was that of *brahmacharya* (celibacy), meant for those who wished to consecrate themselves wholly to the service of their fellow men. It may appear that Gandhi was imposing a puritanical tyranny and straining human nature to the limit, but we must remember that celibacy was part of a wider discipline he advocated, including an appropriate regimen of food, manual labour, social service, prayer and sleep.

The vow of non-stealing may appear a truism for an Ashram of this type, but it had a deeper social meaning. From the *Gita* Gandhi had imbibed the ideal of non-possession. Ideally, 'man should like the birds have no roof over his head, no clothing and no stock of food for the morrow'. This is evidently impossible of attainment in the world in which we live, but Gandhi wanted human wants to be reduced to the minimum. He had already stripped himself of money and property, and brought himself down to a level of material possession where he could feel a twinge of conscience even for 'usurping' the food and the shelter which might be more urgently needed by the hungry and homeless everywhere.

The story of a theft in Sabarmati Ashram is interesting for the light it sheds on the social philosophy of Mohandas Karamchand Gandhi. The thieves had taken away a box belonging to Kasturbai. Instead of reporting to the police, Gandhi observed

[1] Gandhi: *From Yeravda Mandir*, p. 1.

that the thieves apparently believed the Ashram had things worth stealing and that he had failed to imbue the people of the locality, including the potential thieves, with the spirit of the Ashram. As for Kasturbai's box he was, he said, surprised that she had possessed one! When she explained that it contained her grandchildren's clothes, she was told that it was for her children and grandchildren to mind their own clothes. From that day hers was the tiniest kit in the Gandhian entourage.

Two more vows administered in Sabarmati Ashram, one of fearlessness, and the other of anti-untouchability, had a limited but contemporary interest; the fear of British rule, and the ill-treatment of the untouchables had cramped the Indian people in different ways, and the members of the Ashram had to rise above those limitations.

A mere enumeration of the vows is enough to indicate that life in the Ashram was austere. It was also busy. Everyone had to put in some manual work. There was a spinning and weaving department, a cow-shed and a large farm. Every inmate of the Ashram cleaned his own plates and washed his own clothes. There were no servants. The atmosphere, however, was not so much that of a monastery as of a large family under a kindly but exacting patriarch. Gandhi was *Bapu*, the father of this household; Kasturbai was *Ba*, the mother. It was a motley group including little children and octogenarians, graduates of American and European universities and Sanskrit scholars, devout whole-hoggers, and thinly-disguised sceptics. It was a human laboratory where Gandhi tested his moral and spiritual hypotheses. It was also to him what the family is to most people; a haven from the dust and din of the world. It was a family linked not by blood or property but by allegiance to common ideals. The patriarch was a great democrat, and once appointed a committee to select verses for morning and evening prayers. When confronted with a request or a complaint he would laugh and say, 'I am a guest in the Ashram.' He ruled the Ashram but his authority there, as well as in the rest of the country, was moral. When things went wrong or a member of the Ashram was guilty of a serious lapse, he would take the blame upon himself and atone for it by undertaking a fast.

The Ashram was a laboratory in which Gandhi experimented with himself and others. It was also a military academy, if the term may be used for the training of men and women for a war without violence. Early in 1915 he had told C. F. Andrews that he did not anticipate an occasion for Satyagraha for five years.

Nevertheless, in his Ashram a band of young men and women were being trained in the moral and emotional controls essential for a Satyagrahi, so that his grip would not give way to hatred or violence, even under provocation. The Sabarmati Ashram was to do for the Satyagraha struggles of 1920 and 1930 what the Phoenix and Tolstoy farms had done in South Africa. It was also to provide men and women for constructive activities which, between spells of Satyagraha, built up the nation's morale.

# CHAPTER XV

# Indian Nationalism

WHEN Gandhi came on the Indian scene, the nationalist movement had already secured a foothold among the educated and professional classes in the country. In December 1885, nearly three years before he had left for England to qualify as a barrister, the Indian National Congress had held its first meeting at Bombay. Neither in England, nor after his return to India had he evinced any interest in politics. For twenty years, from 1894 onwards, he was wholly absorbed in the struggle for survival of the Indian community in South Africa. Nevertheless, within a few years of his return from South Africa, the reins of the nationalist movement of which he had been only a distant spectator were to fall into his hands, and were to remain with him until his death. A brief flash-back on the movement at this stage may help us to understand the state of Indian politics in 1915 and the nature of Gandhi's impact on it.

That the British conquest of India could not be a permanent feature was foreseen by far-sighted British administrators like Thomas Munro and Mountstart Elphinstone. India had been invaded before the British from the north-west and governed by foreigners for more than seven centuries, but they had gradually been assimilated within the Indian body politic. As Thomas Munro pointed out, there had been foreign conquerors who had been more violent and more cruel, but none had treated Indians with such secret scorn as the British, by stigmatizing 'the whole people as unworthy of trust'. Sir Henry Lawrence had commented caustically on the tendency among the British administrators to talk of the 'black fellows' as if they were very much in the way (of the British administrators) in their own country, except in so far as they might be turned to the comfort and aggrandizement of the rulers. The Mutiny led to a further severing of the races. It may not have been a purely military nor a primarily Muhammadan outbreak. On the contrary it was far from being a War of Independence, though in northern and central India it fed upon anti-British feeling Since its leadership was feudal it was fighting for a lost cause and foredoomed to failure.

The Mutiny was a war without pity, and there were crimes on both sides. The British continued to cherish the heroism and suffering of those who had fought and foiled the rebellion. The Indians cherished the memories of those who had fought and failed against the superior might of the foreigner. The victors had no doubt that Providence had tilted the scales in their favour. 'Those who had counted the English as few at the beginning of the war had forgotten to ask on which side God was to be counted.' A bitter legacy of suspicion and fear was left by the Mutiny. The Governor-General, Lord Canning, who was nicknamed 'Clemency Canning' for not being tough enough with the 'natives', wrote to Queen Victoria of 'a rabid and indiscriminating vindictiveness' which was abroad. The correspondent of *The Times* reached the melancholy conclusion that 'perhaps confidence will never be restored'. The British commanders and civilians seemed to be less worried about restoring confidence than about tightening their grip on the country to make sure that 'it will not happen again'.

The official report on the reorganization of the Indian Army after 1857 pointed out that next only to 'the grand counterpoise of a sufficient European army, comes the counterpoise of natives against natives'. The British proportion in the army of occupation was henceforth to be adequate, and the recruitment of sepoys (soldiers) to be confined to areas and communities whose loyalty had successfully stood the test of the Mutiny. The Indian States were treated with tenderness, and built up as breakwaters against a future rebellion. A new chasm, wider and deeper than any in the first half of the nineteenth century, divided the world of the British officials and the Indian masses; there was too much authority or arrogance on one side and excessive sensitiveness or servility on the other. Not for another sixty years was an Indian who was not a prince to meet the ordinary run of Englishmen, official or non-official, as Ram Mohun Roy had met them.

The pacification of India seemed to be complete with the disarming of the country and the strengthening of the British garrison. One can, however, do anything with bayonets except sit on them—for ever. The social, economic and political forces opposing foreign rule could not be dammed for ever. The British administrators poised peacefully in their sequestered cantonments and 'civil lines' could no more hold them back than King Canute could stop the waves of the ocean.

There were seven famines in India in the first half of the nineteenth century; there were twentdy-four in the second half. In the 1870s East Bengal and the Deccan seethed with agrarian discontent, which led the Government to enact legislation for the protection of tenants and to evolve a famine code. The agrarian trouble in the countryside was accompanied by rumblings of discontent in the towns. The educated classes, who had been nurtured on John Stuart Mill, were applying the principles of British liberalism in India and noting the gap between precept and practice.

Rabindranath Tagore has recorded his early admiration of the British. As a boy in England the poet had the opportunity of listening to John Bright in and outside parliament, and the large-hearted liberalism of those speeches, transcending national barriers, made a deep impression on him. Madan Mohan Malaviya had asked as a young man, 'What is an Englishman without representative institutions?' and answered himself- 'Why, not an Englishman at all, a mere sham, a base institution.' There was something in the scepticism of the British officials who had seen red at the introduction of Western education in India: the products of Macaulay's Western education could call upon his successors to live up to their own traditions. The British officers who governed India were not liberals or radicals, but it was with liberal politics and radical economics that the rising middle class in India associated all the best in Britain. The first demand of Western-educated Indians was for a share in the administration of their country.

The question of the recruitment of Indians to the civil service provoked the first organized agitation in India in 1877-8, when Surendranath Banerjea, the great orator of Bengal, toured the country and pleaded before crowded meetings for simultaneous examinations in India and England for recruitment to the Indian Civil Service.

The middle classes were also stirred by movements of religious and social reformation, which harked back to the golden age of Indian history. Swami Dayananda, Ramakrishna Paramahamsa, and Swami Vivekandand stirred Hinduism, and by emphasizing its spiritual and cultural heritage helped to compensate for the political demoralization inevitable under foreign rule. Foreigners, including thesophists like Olcott and scholars like Max Muller, raised the self-esteem of the intelligentsia by

drawing upon the rich reservoir of Indian philosophy and religion.

The segregation of the races since the Mutiny and the cold
aloofness of the ruling races were a source of continual humiliation to sensitive Indians. There were not a few cases where a
European got away with the murder of an Indian coolie or
servant on some flimsy plea; enlarged spleen of the native
was the usual explanation which the courts swallowed without
any qualms. The obsequiousness of the classes which flourished
on official bounty was met with a mixture of contempt and
patronage. An interesting example is the permission granted in
1868, by a formal resolution of the Government of India, to
native gentlemen wearing boots and shoes of European fashion
to appear 'thus habited' at Durbars and other ceremonial occasions, and the injunction to those who wore shoes of Indian
fashion, to take them off 'within customary limits'. The clamor-
ous agitation from European officials and businessmen against
the Ilbert Bill (by which Lord Ripon attempted to do away with
racial distinctions in the administration of justice) was an eye-
opener to the Indian middle class; its success indicated that
organized agitation alone could bring the Government to its
knees.

An important ingredient was added to the nationalist ferment
by the emergence of modern industry in India. The first cotton
mill was established in Bombay in 1854; in the next fifty years
the number of textile mills rose to nearly 200. The Government was unsympathetic to Indian industry when it competed
with industry 'at home'. When in 1882 the duties on cotton
imports were withdrawn, the Indian industrialists knew that the
real beneficiary was not the Indian consumer, but the British
manufacturer in Lancashire and Manchester.

It is a strange irony of history that the Indian National
Congress, which contributed most to the liquidation of British
rule in India, was conceived and founded by a Briton. Allan
Octavian Hume, a former Secretary to the Government of India
who had retired from the Indian Civil Service in 1882 after
more than thirty years' service, believed that though England
had given India peace, she had not solved her economic problems, that the Government was out of touch with the people,
and that it was essential to leaven the administration with a
representative Indian element. He thought of an organization
which could act as a 'safety valve for the great and growing
forces generated by our own action'. When he met the Viceroy,

Lord Dufferin, and unfolded his scheme of an All-India meeting every year to discuss social matters, the Viceroy suggested that it should also discuss problems of administration. Hume visited the principal towns in India to canvass support, paid a hurried visit to England and returned just in time for the projected All-India meeting. On December 28, 1885, seventy-two representatives from different parts of India met in Bombay under the chairmanship of a Calcutta barrister, W. C. Bonnerjee, who declared that the Indians' 'desire to be governed according to the ideas of government prevalent in Europe was in no way incompatible with their thorough loyalty to the British Government'. The first speech on the first resolution in 1885 spoke of 'the merciful dispensation of Providence' which had brought India under the dominion of the great British power.

This thick veneer of loyal phrases has led present-day critics to debunk the early phase of the Congress as that of 'political mendicancy'. Of the first twenty-five sessions of the Congress, five were presided over by Europeans. In 1892 there was even a serious proposal to hold a session in London, and in 1911 the Congress session would have been presided over by Ramsay MacDonald but for his wife's death. The resolutions of the congress repeated year after year what, today, seem to be verbal exercises. To the contemporary British administrators, however, even this rhetoric was a danger signal. The official attitude to the Indian National Congress quickly changed from a benevolent patronage to a thinly-disguised antagonism. Lord Dufferin, who had blessed the birth of the Congress in 1885, belittled it three years later as a 'microscopic minority'. In 1890 government officials were directed not to attend Congress sessions. In 1898 Lord Elgin declared in a speech in the United Services Club, Simla: 'India was conquered by the sword, and by the sword it shall be held'. Lord Elgin's successor, Lord Curzon, tried to put the educated Indian in his proper place, and assured the Secretary of State for India in 1900 that 'the Congress is tottering to its fall and one of my great ambitions while in India is to assist it to a peaceful demise'.

It was Lord Curzon's destiny to put new life into the nationalist movement and the Indian National Congress. The partition of Bengal, whatever its administrative merits, was taken by the Bengalis as an attack on the integrity of their province and evoked a vehement agitation. There was a movement for the boycott of British goods, and stray acts of terrorism against Europeans took place.

From 1905 onwards there was a struggle within the Congress
between its moderate and extremist wings. A split was avoided
in 1906 by inviting the eighty-one-year-old Dadabhai Naoroji,
who came from England, to preside over the annual session
held at Calcutta. The following year the Congress met at Surat in
a tense atmosphere. While the moderates were confident of
their majority in the Congress session, the extremists were
conscious of their popularity in the country. There was pande-
monium and the session broke up in disorder. The moderates,
with nearly 1,000 adherents out of the 1,600 delegates, met in
conference under the protection of the police and drew up a
constitution which reaffirmed their faith in the steady reform of
the existing system of government 'by constitutional means'. The
extremists had lost in the first round.

'What happened in the 1907 Congress session,' wrote Valen-
tine Chirol, a shrewd observer, 'was but a pale reflection of
what was happening outside . . . The cry of Swaraj was caught
up and re-echoed in every province of British India.' The discontent expressed itself in sporadic violence aganst British officials and loyal Indians. The Indian language papers, particularly B. G. Tilak's *Kesari* in Maharashtra and Aurobindo Ghose's
*Bande Matram* in Bengal, stirred popular feeling. Anarchist
societies grew up. 'Elaborate, persistent and ingenious' was a
comment on the revolutionary movement made by an official
committee which later investigated its ramifications. Gandhi,
then resident in South Africa and a detached observer of Indian
politics, was so alarmed by the rising tide of violence that
he attempted a re-education of Indian anarchists by a series of
articles in his paper *Indian Opinion*.

Meanwhile the Government was trying to rally moderate public opinion by doling out measured doses of constitutional reform. Unfortunately, each dose was pitifully small, belated, and
grudgingly conceded; it succeeded not so much in satisfying as in
whetting the appetite for reform. The Minto-Morley Reforms
increased the elected element in the legislatures but not to the
point where it could outvote the government bloc. The Government was very anxious, wrote Lord Morley, 'to avoid any appearance of a parliamentary franchise . . . We didn't want a Parliament at all; we wanted councils'. And worst of all, communal
electorates were introduced for Muslims, and the evolution of
democracy was thus poisoned at the source.

The general political ferment in the first decade of this century could not but suck in the Muslim middle classes. Valen-

tine Chirol had written in his *Indian Unrest* (1910) that 'never before had the Muhammadans of India as a whole identified their interests and their aspirations with the consolidation and permanence of the British rule'. The Muslim middle class was not so staid as Chirol made himself believe. The Muslim League, since its inception in 1906, had been a mouth-piece for affirming Muslims' loyalty and demanding a greater representation for Muslims in councils and in the services. The younger generation in the League, however, was chafing at the strait-jacket of loyalty in which the old guard had so firmly wrapped it. The initial discontent was not to spring from local or national grievances but from foreign sources. The Mutiny had shattered the Imperial day-dreams of the Muslim middle class, which turned for inspiration to Muslim countries. Events in the Middle East had disconcerted Indian Muslims. Persia had been carved into two spheres of influence between Russia and Britain. The Balkan Wars, from which Britain kept out, had stripped the Turkish Empire of some of its European provinces. The Balkan Wars may be viewed historically as a conflict between outmoded Turkish Imperialism and the forces of nationalism in South-eastern Europe, but to the Indian Muslims they looked like the hopeless struggle of Islam against the Christian Powers. Poets such as Iqbal and Shibli, scholars and publicists such as Abul Kalam Azad and Mahomed Ali, roused the Muslim middle class to the many dangers which beset Islam in the world. The professions of Muslim loyalty began to wear thin. In 1913 the objective of the Muslim League was declared to be not only the protection of Muslim rights, but also 'the attainment of a system of self-government suitable to India'. The same year a Muslim, Nawab Syed Mahomed, presided over the Indian National Congress, welcomed the enlarged objective of the League and expressed the hope that the two bodies would co-operate for the good of the country.

The outbreak of the world war in 1914 created a dilemma for the Muslim middle class. The dilemma arose, in the words of a Muslim leader, from the fact that 'the Government of our Caliph (Turkey) should be at war with the Government of our King-Emperor'. The political consciousness of the Muslim middle class was thus heightened by events abroad. The Hindu middle class had become politically conscious and sensitive by the acts of commission or omission of the Government at home. The two streams of discontent were to converge in 1916 into a pact signed between the National Congress and the Muslim League.

Early in 1915, however, when Gandhi landed at Bombay, Indian political life was at a low ebb. The Government had assumed vast powers under the 'Defence of India Rules'. The Congress was dominated by the moderate leaders, Pherozeshah Mehta, Banerjea and Gokhale; Tilak, the great leader of Maharashtra and of the extremist group in the Congress, recently released from prison, was lying low; Lala Lajpat Rai, the fiery orator from the Punjab, was in exile; Aurobindo Ghose had retired from politics to Pondicherry. Abul Kalam Azad and the Ali brothers, the critics of British policy towards Turkey, were within a few months to find themselves in gaol. The result was to be a lull in Indian politics—a welcome lull for a government preoccupied with the war.

# CHAPTER XVI

# *Splendid Isolation*

INDIAN politics, which seemed so stagnant early in 1915, were stirred deeply the following year by the Home Rule Movement. Its founder was Mrs Annie Besant, who had carved for herself a unique position in India's public life. A leader of the Theosophist movement, and one of the foremost educationists in the country, she had completely identified herself with India. A few months before the outbreak of World War I, she had told a London audience that the price of India's loyalty was India's freedom. In a series of articles in *New India* in the spring of 1915 she had outlined a political campaign which she intended to conduct. She canvassed support for this campaign at the annual Congress session in December 1915, and undaunted by the opposition it evoked from moderates in the Congress, she founded the Home Rule League in September 1916.

Mrs Besant had sought but failed to secure Gandhi's support in launching the Home Rule League. Gandhi was opposed to a political movement which was likely to embarrass the Government during the war; he felt that the time for constitutional reforms would come when the war was over. Mrs Besant was amused at Gandhi's conviction that India was bound to get self-government after the war. She told him that only a Britain hard-pressed by the exigencies of a a world war could be made to give freedom to India. 'Mrs Besant,' replied Gandhi, 'you are distrustful of the British; I am not, and I will not help in any agitation against them during the war.'[1]

Self-government for India within the British Empire through law-abiding and constitutional means, the declared objective of the Home Rule League, might seem tame in the light of later history, but in 1916-17 the impact of this organization on Indian politics was swift and strong. The appeal of the movement to the educated classes was due to the fact that it answered some of their own inchoate aspirations, and offered an outlet to the ferment which the war had generated.

[1] Kanji Dwarkadas: *Gandhi Through my Diary Leaves*, p. 10.

Mrs Besant's genius for propaganda and organization helped her in raising the political barometer. George Bernard Shaw, who knew her in her youth, once remarked that she was capable of bearing the burden of three men. A great organizer, an eloquent speaker and a forthright writer, she quickened the political consciousness of the educated classes.

The Government of India watched the progress of the Home Rule Movement with growing anxiety. In a minute dated January 17, 1917 the Home Member, Sir Reginald Craddock, pointed out that the minds of the people who read newspapers were being poisoned against the British Government, that Home Rule was being advocated not so much as a constitutional reform but as the only salvation from the innumerable wrongs and grievances under which India was groaning. The popular support the movement had evoked was, from the point of view of the Government, its most deplorable feature: 'The position is one of great difficulty. The moderate leaders can command no support among the vocal classes, who are being led at the heels of Tilak and Besant. The greater figures among the moderates have passed away, and so far they have no successors.'

Craddock went on to ridicule Mrs Besant as 'a vain old lady' who was influenced by 'the passionate desire to be a leader of movements', and Tilak as a man who was 'impelled by a venom and hatred against everything British'. Nevertheless he did not underrate the gravity of the problems, administrative and constitutional, which these two politicians had posed to the Government: 'Sedition in India is like the tides which erode the coast line as the sea encroaches. The last high tide was in 1907-8. The tide went out, but it is flowing in now rapidly and it will reach a point higher than ever before. We must have a dam in order lest it inundates sound land.'

The Home Rule agitation was thus to provide a powerful impulse for the famous declaration of August 1917 that the policy of His Majesty's Government was 'that of increasing association of Indians in every branch of the administration and the gradual development of self-governing institutions with a view to the progressive realization of a responsible Government in India as an integral part of the British Empire'.

The fact that Gandhi had not taken part in the Home Rule agitation, nor in the negotiations which had led to the Lucknow Pact between the Indian National Congress and the All-India Muslim League in 1916, showed that he was largely isolated from the main currents of Indian politics. It was not Gandhi but the Besant-Tilak combination which dominated the political scene and impressed the Government. In 1917 Edwin Montagu recorded in his diary that Tilak was 'at the moment probably the most powerful man in India'. Of Gandhi, Montagu's impression was of 'a social reformer with a real desire to find grievances and to cure them not for any reasons of self-advertisement, but to improve the conditions of fellow men. He dresses like a coolie, forswears all personal advancement, lives practically on the air and is a pure visionary'.

Gandhi did not figure much in contemporary politics because of his self-denying ordinance on participation in political agitation during the war. There was also another reason. His ideas and methods did not quite fit in with those of the two dominant groups in the Indian National Congress. Gokhale, the leader of the moderates, whom Gandhi avowed as his mentor in Indian politics, had paid high tribute to him; he had said at the annual session of the Indian National Congress in 1909 that in Gandhi 'Indian humanity has reached its high watermark'. But in 1915 Gokhale had found his own closest associates reluctant to admit Gandhi into the Servants of India Society. In any case Gokhale died soon after Gandhi's return to India. The fact that Gandhi had been so close to Gokhale could not add to his popularity with the extremists, who may have respected him for his South African record but did not understand, much less appreciate, his policy of non-embarrassment towards the British during the war.

In these early years in India (1915-18), even though Gandhi seemed to be ploughing a lonely furrow, his personality and politics had been firmly cast in moulds peculiarly his own. Explaining why he did not join the Home Rule League he told his friends: 'At my time of life and with views firmly formed on several matters, I could only join an organization to affect its policy and not be affected by it. This does not mean that I would not now have an open mind to receive new light. I simply wish to emphasize the fact that the new light will have to be specially dazzling in order to entrance me'.[1]

No light could be more dazzling than that of Satyagraha, the technique of non-violent action with which, for a decade, he had sought to guide his life in personal as well as public spheres. Gandhi believed he had discovered an effective instrument for rectifying injustices, righting wrongs and ironing out conflicts.

[1] G. A. Natesan in an article entitled 'Reminiscences' in *Gandhiji*, p. 215, on Gandhi's 75th birthday in 1944.

Having discovered it and wielded it with a measure of success in South Africa, he felt he could not deny it to those of his country-men who came to him for help. The fact that he was committed to abstention from political agitation during the war did not pre-vent him from championing just grievances which could not brook delay.

One of the first calls for help came to Gandhi from a quarter he had not thought of. Champaran in Bihar had been seething with agrarian discontent for some time. The racial factor gave additional acerbity to relations between the European indigo fac-tory owners and Indian cultivators. Gandhi was present at the Calcutta session of the Indian National Congress in December 1916 when the Champaran troubles came up for discussion. He was invited to take part in it, but declined, for the simple reason that he knew nothing about the matter: Champaran was for him no more than a dot on the map of India. After the Con-gress session Rajkumar Shukla, a peasant from Cham-paran, requested Gandhi to visit the district and see things for himself. Shukla's tenacity was remarkable; he followed Gandhi from one end of the country to the other, until he escorted him to Champaran and confronted him with a problem which had strained relations between the planters and the peasants for nearly a century.

Rajkumar Shukla had given Gandhi some details of the planter-tenant conflict in Champaran. After arriving in Bihar, Gandhi learnt enough to become anxious to investigate the facts for himself. From Patna he went to Muzaffarpur and from Muzaffar-pur to Motihari, the headquarters of the district of Champaran. He was served with a notice to quit the district 'by the next available train' as his presence was considered a danger to public peace. He refused to comply. He told the magistrate who tried him on April 18, 1917: 'As a law-abiding citizen, my first instinct would be, as it was, to obey the order served on me. I could not do so without doing violence to my sense of duty to those for whom I came . . . I am fully conscious of the fact that a person holding in the public life a position such as I do, has to be most careful in setting examples . . . I have dis-regarded the order served upon me, not for want of respect for lawful authority, but in obedience to the higher law of our being —the voice of conscience.'

The Commissioner of Tirhut Division had ordered Gandhi's arrest without consulting his superiors, but these orders were cancelled by the Government of India. Gandhi was now at liberty to continue his investigations into the peasants' grievances; he carefully sifted the evidence, cross-examined each witness searchingly and discouraged exaggeration. A portrait of Gandhi at work, which is as intimate as it is honest, is sketched in a letter (April 29, 1917) written by a young British officer, W. A. Lewis, I.C.S., Sub-divisional officer, Bettiah, to W. H. Heycock, District Magistrate, Champaran:

'Mr Gandhi arrived last Sunday and called on me on the morning of Monday. He explained to me the object of his investigation which is to secure redress for certan definite wrongs to which he claims the *raiyats* (peasants) are now subjected. I gathered that he is already in possession of a large mass of information on local problems. Mr Gandhi impressed on me that he wishes his investigation to be impartial.

'On Wednesday afternoon, I rode out to . . . one of the villages where he was then collecting information. I sat with him for a time while his enquiries were being conducted. Each witness is subjected to severe cross-questioning as Mr Gandhi is determined to get his facts on an incontrovertible basis. Mr Gandhi is accompanied by Babu Brijkishore who is working on similar lines. . . . He also records depositions in writing.

'In a sense he (Mr Gandhi) has superseded the local authority . . . Mr Gandhi claims that the local administration has been very largely dominated by planters' influence. . . .

'By the planters Mr Gandhi is very naturally regarded as their natural enemy. The affairs of the great majority of factories, even those which we consider well managed, will not under present circumstances stand the severe critical analysis on all points of economic detail to which they are now being subjected, and Mr Gandhi will have in his hands material based on indisputable facts to form the basis of a very formidable indictment . . .

'It is with the effect of Mr Gandhi's presence on the *raiyats* that I wish especially to deal with . . . We may look on Mr Gandhi as an idealist, a fanatic, or a revolutionary according to our particular opinions. But to the *raiyats* he is their liberator, and they credit him with extraordinary powers. He moves about in the villages asking them to lay their grievances before him, and he is transfiguring the imaginations of masses of ignorant men with visions of an early millennium. I put the danger of this before Mr Gandhi, and he assured me that his utterances are so carefully guarded that they could not be construed as an incitement to revolt. I am willing to believe Mr Gandhi, whose sincerity is, I think, above suspicion: but he cannot control the tongues of all his followers . . .

'On matters which require redress Mr Gandhi is prepared to go to any length to secure it and would willingly immolate himself in that cause: nor will he disengage himself from the district until very great changes are effected: but he is, I am sure, amenable to reason in his treatment of these difficult problems.'

The Government of India felt perturbed at Gandhi's presence in Champaran and the possibilities of a Satyagraha struggle developing in the indigo districts of Bihar. At the suggestion of Craddock, the Home Member, the Viceroy wrote to Sir Edward Gait, the Governor of Bihar suggesting the appointment of a Commission of Inquiry on which a seat could be offered to Gandhi as well. Sir Edward at first resisted the suggestion. 'It would be a device,' he wrote to Lord Chelmsford, 'for heading off Mr Gandhi; and it is by no means certain that it would be effective.' The Champaran Agrarian Committee was thus appointed at the instance of the Government of India and not because, as Gandhi suggested in his autobiography, the Governor was 'good'.

With the evidence of 8,000 tenants in his hands, there was no aspect of the agrarian problem with which Gandhi was not thoroughly acquainted. Knowledgeable, persuasive and firm he was able to make out an irresistible case for the tenants. The Commission unanimously recommended the abolition of the oppressive 'tinkathia system', and of the illegal exactions under which the tenants groaned.

While Gandhi was engaged in Bihar, trouble was brewing in the textile industry of Ahmedabad. Since August 1917 a 'plague bonus', equivalent in some cases to eighty per cent of the wages, was being paid to dissuade the workers from fleeing the plague-ravaged town. When the epidemic was over, the employers wanted to discontinue the 'bonus'. The workers resisted the move, arguing that the cost of living had more than doubled during the war and the bonus only partially set off the loss in purchasing power.

Apprehending a showdown between the millowners and their employees, the British Collector of Ahmedabad wrote to Gandhi to exert his influence with the mill owners for a compromise. One of the leading mill owners, Ambalal Sarabhai, was a friend of the Gandhi family; it was his anonymous charity that had saved the Sabarmati Ashram in its early days, when the admission of an untouchable family had brought a storm over Gandhi's head. Gandhi had long discussions with the representatives of the mill owners and the workers, as a result of which both parties agreed to arbitration by a tribunal consisting of three representatives of the employers and three representatives of labour with the Collector as chairman. Before this tribunal could commence its work, the mill owners took advantage of a stray strike, declared the agreement void, backed out of arbitration and announced that the workers who declined to accept a twenty per cent bonus would be dismissed.

When the mill owners threatened 'united action' against their employees, Gandhi's comment was that they were organizing 'a union of elephants against a union of ants'. He took up the workers' cause as another experiment in Satyagraha. The crucial question was whether the just demand of textile labour at Ahmedabad could be won by a peaceful, non-violent strike. This demand has been brought down to the thirty-five per cent bonus which he adjudged to be an irreducible minimum. The strike, organized on the principles of Satyagraha, was to be different from the familiar pattern. The morale of the workers was not to be boosted by working up their passions. There was to be no violence, neither against the employers nor against blacklegs. There was no room for bitterness, for fabrication of grievances, exaggeration of claims, or competition in invective. The strikers' enforced idleness was to be utilized in constructive activities: alternative trades were to be learnt, houses were to be repaired, and roads in workers' colonies were to be swept.

Not the least interesting feature of this dispute was that Gandhi's chief lieutenant in organizing the strike was Ambalal Sarabhai's sister Anasuyabehn. As the strike progressed, Gandhi watched it with some anxiety. The workers' morale after the first few days began to sag. It was impossible for most of them to exist without work and wages. It was at this moment that Gandhi announced that he would undertake a fast. Had he not declared at the beginning of the strike that if it led to starvation he would be the first to starve? The object of the fast was to rally the workers. Nevertheless, it could not but affect the mill owners, some of whom respected and even loved Gandhi. The result was an unintended but definite pressure on the mill owners.[1] It was this feeling, that the fast was exercising an element of coercion, which led Gandhi after three days' fast to accept a compromise. The fundamental issue on which the breach had

[1] Desai, M. D.: *Ek Dharam Yudh* (A Righteous Struggle), p. 45.

occurred had been the refusal of the employers to accept the
principle of arbitration; on this issue they now yielded. The
arbitrator's award went in the workers' favour and the thirty-
five per cent bonus was ultimately won.

The labour dispute at Ahmedabad had scarcely been settled
when Gandhi was drawn into a conflict between the peasants of
Kheda district in Bombay Presidency and the local administration on the remission of land revenue. A drought had blighted
the crops in this district. The 'revenue code' provided for a total
remission of the land revenue when the crops were less than
twenty-five per cent of the normal yield. But opinion was
sharply divided on the exact damage to the crops. On-the-spot
inquiries by three members of the Servants of India Society and
estimates by V. J. Patel, then a member of the Bombay Legislative Assembly, and Gandhi, put the damage at more than three-
fourths of a good year's yield. The officials belittled these estimates as emanating from 'outsiders'.

*Gujerat Sabha,* of which Gandhi was president at this time,
took a leading part in this agitation. When petitions, interviews
and press statements failed to bring relief to the peasantry, the
agitation passed into Gandhi's hands. This was the first real
agrarian Satyagraha which Gandhi organized in India. The basic
problem was to rid the peasantry of fear: the fear of officials,
the fear of forfeiture of land and property. Gandhi and Vallabhbhai Patel toured the villages of Kheda to train the people in
the hard school of Satyagraha. The Government tightened up the
tax collection. Those who refused to pay were sternly dealt
with; cattle and household goods were seized and even standing
crops were attached. The peasantry showed much courage and
fortitude, but the repression told severely on a district already suffering from the after-effects of drought, plague and high
prices. Gandhi felt that the peasantry had reached the verge of
exhaustion and it was prudent to prevent it from being driven
to utter ruin. When the Government issued instructions that
land revenue should be recovered only from those who had the
capacity to pay and that no pressure should be exercised on
genuinely poor peasants, he felt justified in calling off the no-tax
campaign.

To put these early experiments in Satyagraha in proper perspective we must remember that during these years World War
I was in progress, and that Gandhi had no intention of distract-
ing the Government. He avoided any collision as far as possible. In Champaran and Kheda he could not altogether avoid

one, but he endeavoured to localize these conflicts and sought solutions which secured a modicum of justice to the peasantry without creating a national crisis.

His attitude to the war had indeed marked him off from other prominent leaders; he cherished the hope—which few knowledge-able politicians shared—that India would receive self-govern-ment at the end of the war if she whole-heartedly supported the British war effort.

When World War I broke out Gandhi was on the high seas; he was homeward bound, though he hoped to spend a few weeks in England. On August 6, 1914 he landed on English soil and lost no time in calling a meeting of his Indian friends to raise an ambulance unit.

Were it not for a severe attack of pleurisy he might have con-tinued to serve in the ambulance unit he had raised, and his return to India may have been indefinitely delayed.

When he arrived in India he found that nationalist opinion was opposed to unconditional support for the war effort. Only those who were politically backward or flourished on official patronage were for loyalty at all costs. Gandhi did not favour a bargain with the Government by offering co-operation at a price and he told the Gujerat Political Conference in November 1917: 'That we have been loyal at a time of stress is no test of fitness for Swaraj. Loyalty is not merit. It is a necessity of citizenship all the world over.'[1]

Early in 1918 the war was going badly for the Allies; a Ger-man thrust was expected on the western front and the Viceroy summoned prominent leaders of Indian opinion to a War Con-ference in Delhi. A number of nationalist leaders including Tilak, Jinnah and Khaparde, were not invited, as they had raised the question of the terms on which co-operation should be accorded to the Government. Indian political opinion had swung heavily against vague promises unbacked by any con-cession in the constitutional sphere. Gandhi's first impulse was to boycott the conference, but he was persuaded to attend. He sup-ported the resolution on recruitment with a single sentence in Hindi: 'With a full sense of my responsibility, I beg to sup-port the resolution.'

He threw himself heart and soul into a recruiting campaign. There was something comic in this votary of non-violence tour-ing the villages of Gujerat to secure recruits for the British Indian army to fight on the battlefronts of Europe and the

[1] Natesan: *Speeches and Writings of Mahatma Gandhi*, p. 409.

Middle East. He went to Kheda district, where a few months earlier he had organized a no-tax campaign. He found that it had been easier to persuade the villagers to queue up for prison than for the army. Gandhi and Vallabhbhai Patel, who accompanied him, discovered that they were no longer the heroes they had been in this part of the country only recently. In a village which had been conspicuous for resistance to the Government no one came out even to meet them; for three days they stayed on the outskirts of the village and cooked their own food.

Not infrequently, unable to get carts for their journeys, Gandhi and his colleagues had to march on foot twenty miles a day. The strain was too much for him and at last a severe attack of dysentery laid him low. Averse to taking medicines he fasted, but in vain. He did not agree to injections owing to what he described later as his 'ridiculous ignorance' about them. His friend Ambalal Sarabhai took him to his palatial house in Ahmedabad, but he would not submit to medical treatment and devoted nursing alone could not restore him to health. One day while still suffering from high fever, he insisted on being moved to Sabarmati Ashram. Dr Rajendra Prasad, who saw him next day, found him emaciated in body and in spirit resigned to the approaching end. His whole life had been, Gandhi reminisced sadly, one in which he had taken up things and left them half-done, and now he was to pass away; but if that was the will of God, it could not be helped.

Gandhi believed that he was at death's door. He recited verses from the *Gita* and summoned the inmates of the Sabarmati Ashram. They trooped in silently. 'My last message to India,' he said, 'is that she will find her salvation through non-violence, and through non-violence alone India will contribute to the salvation of the world.'

While he lay in agony watching his body slowly wear away, an 'ice-doctor' came on the scene. Gandhi let him experiment with ice-therapy, which infused into him fresh energy and hope. The will to live returned; one symptom was that he was persuaded by Kasturbai to take goat's milk on the plea that the vow he had taken many years before not to take milk applied only to cow's milk. This was, of course, a mere quibble and the bluntest comment on it is in his autobiography: 'The will to live proved stronger than the devotion to truth.'

The greatest incentive for living was to be furnished to Gandhi by the Government of India. The publication of the Rowlatt Committee Report and the Rowlatt Bills stirred him to his depths. 'If I had been well,' he said, 'I would have toured the whole of India to rouse her.' Friends came to him for consultation. How was the country to fight the new legislation which attacked civil liberties? As Gandhi brooded over it all he recalled how he had pleaded for support to Britain in her hour of need in the hope of a worthy gesture at the end of the war. Once again he had received stone for bread. He had done his best to keep out of political agitation during the war. Now he felt an irresistible call to fight a wrong perpetrated in peace.

# CHAPTER XVII

# Shadow of Amritsar

THE Rowlatt Bills which had pulled Gandhi out of his sick-bed were based on the recommendations of the Rowlatt Committee, which had reported on measures to combat political violence.

Nobody had been a more vehement critic of political violence than Gandhi. Ten years before the Rowlatt Bills were conceived he had, in his *Hind Swaraj*, condemned revolutionary activities on moral as well as practical grounds. He put forward Satyagraha—'soul force'—as a superior and more effective substitute for bomb and pistol. Opposed as he was to violence, he argued that it was not right to frame drastic legislation for the whole of India because political crimes occurred in a few places. Nor did he favour investing an executive, which was not yet responsible to the people, with wide powers.

There was a rare unanimity among Indian leaders on opposition to the Rowlatt Bills. Jinnah observed that a government which enacted such a law in peace forfeited its claim to be called a civilized government. Sapru described the laws as 'wrong in principle, unsound in operation and too sweeping'. 'We think,' said V. J. Patel, 'that all our constitutional agitation for any reforms whatsoever would die if these bills are passed.'

The reaction of the Government of India to this agitation was characteristic. It discounted its strength and attributed it to mass hysteria among Indian politicians. The Government of India rushed the bill through the Imperial Legislative Council in March 1919 with almost indecent haste. All the elected Indian leaders voted against the bill; nevertheless it became law. The passage of the first Rowlatt Bill was an eye-opener to Gandhi. He had heard the debate in the Imperial Legislative Council and seen how the eloquent logic of Indian Councillors had been wasted on the official benches. 'You can wake a man,' he wrote later, 'only if he is really asleep; no effort that you may make will produce any effect upon him if he is merely pretending sleep.' The conviction grew upon him that the 'Great Civil Service Corporation' and the British commercial community had made the Government of India impervious to popular feeling. A government which really cared for public opinion would not have enacted a measure which had been opposed by every shade of Indian opinion. And a government which was hoping to introduce a substantial measure of constitutional reform could hardly have provided a worse prelude to an instalment of self-government.

The constitutional opposition to the Rowlatt Bills having proved fruitless Gandhi felt that recourse must be had to Satyagraha to secure the repeal of the Rowlatt Act. Already in February 1919, he had drafted and circulated a pledge of resistance to the Rowlatt Bills: 'In the event of these bills becoming law and until they are withdrawn we shall refuse civilly to obey these laws and such other laws as a committee to be hereafter appointed may think fit, and further affirm that in this struggle we shall faithfully follow truth and refrain from violence to life, person and property.'

Now that the Government had put the first Rowlatt Bill on the statute-book, Gandhi—though he had not yet fully recovered from his recent illness—picked up the gauntlet. He toured the country to educate the people in the implications of the Satyagraha pledge and founded a new organization, the Satyagraha Sabha. While in Madras he woke up one morning and told his host, Rajagopalachari, that 'in the twilight condition between sleep and consciousness' it had occurred to him that the country should be called upon to observe a day of 'hartal', when all business should be suspended and people should fast and pray as a protest against the hated legislation. The date fixed for the 'hartal' was March 30th, but it was later changed to April 6th. The idea of a 'hartal' as a measure of mourning or protest was not a novel one in India, but as a one-day national strike it was a masterly stroke. In Bombay, in addition to the cessation of business a beginning was made with civil resistance by selling certain books, including Gandhi's *Hind Swaraj* and *Sarvodaya,* which had been banned as seditious by the Government. And on April 7th appeared *Satyagraha, a news-sheet,* edited by Gandhi and published in defiance of the Press Act.

The hartal in Delhi, owing to a misunderstanding, was observed on March 30th instead of April 6th, and it was also marred by some rioting. Gandhi promptly condemned the excesses of the mob as well as those of the local officials who, he said, had used a hammer to crush a fly. Tension mounted in the Punjab, where the local leaders felt that Gandhi's presence would assist in maintaining peace; but the Government did not let Gandhi reach the Punjab. While he was on his way to Delhi he was taken out of his compartment at a small station and put in another train bound for Bombay, where he was released. He would have again left for Delhi, had he not discovered that in his absence disturbances had broken out in the city of Bombay, Ahmedabad, Nadiad and other places in his own province, which was the least expected to forget his doctrine of non-violence. He came to the conclusion that he had underrated the latent forces of violence. He decided to retrace his steps, to give up the idea of seeking re-arrest, restrict and finally suspend Satyagraha. He observed a three-day fast to atone for his 'Himalayan miscalculation' in launching a mass movement without making sure that the people were ready for it.

Meanwhile, events in the Punjab had moved to a tragic climax. The Punjab had been suffering from several undercurrents of discontent. Though Gandhi had never visited the Punjab, his name was already something to conjure with in that province. His arrest near Delhi had agitated the people. On April 10th, at Amritsar, following the arrest of two local leaders, a mob ran amuck, burnt down the town hall and the post office, cut telegraph wires and injured a few Europeans, including two women. Order was restored by drafting troops into the city under Brigadier-General Dyer. The city was quiet for the next two days, but on April 13th, the day of the *Baisakhi* festival, a meeting was held in Jallianwala Bagh, which became the scene of a holocaust. Dyer decided to break up the meeting. The entrance was too narrow to admit armoured cars, but he marched into the garden with his troops, who fired 1,650 rounds in ten minutes. The holiday crowd of unarmed men, women and children, unable to escape from the walled compound, were caught 'like rats in a trap'. The Punjab Government estimated the number of killed at 379. Sir Chimanlal Setalvad, a member of the Hunter Committee, estimated that 400 persons had been killed and 1,200 injured.[1]

Later, Dyer explained that his object was to create a 'moral effect' by resolute action. He could not have dealt a bigger blow to the Empire which he was professing to save. Amritsar became a turning point in Indo-British relations almost as im-

[1] Setalvad: *Recollections and Reflections*, p. 307.

portant as the Mutiny.[1] The tragedy of Amritsar should not be viewed as an isolated act, but as a symptom of the 'mutiny complex' to which the British in India periodically succumbed. The Punjab Government, with Sir Michael O'Dwyer at its head, had persuaded itself of the existence of a widespread conspiracy to overthrow the Government.

The 'mutiny complex' from which the official and particularly the European community seemed to suffer at this time is the key to the tragic events in the Punjab in the spring and early summer of 1919, when a number of military and civil officers heaped nameless indignities and harsh penalties on Indians, particularly the educated and politically-conscious classes. It is unnecessary to recount the details of this draconian régime. The most notorious order of General Dyer was the one which required Indians to crawl on their bellies in the street where a European woman had been assaulted. Indians were made to alight from vehicles if a European passed on the road and salute him. A number of villages were machine-gunned by armoured cars and aeroplanes. Motor-cars owned by Indians were requisitioned. Colonel Johnson ordered nearly a thousand students of Lahore colleges to march four times daily for three weeks—sixteen miles a day—in the scorching heat of May to answer a roll-call. When a notice pasted on the outer wall of the college building was found torn every male in the precincts of the college, including the professors, was arrested. These military officers doubtless believed that they were holding the bastions of the British Empire at a critical moment in its history. Many of them, having recently returned from European or Middle Eastern battle-fields, were impatient of half-hearted methods. Rabindranath Tagore, who renounced his knighthood as a protest against the events in the Punjab, diagnosed the root of the trouble: 'What happened at Jallianwala Bagh was itself a monstrous progeny of a monstrous war.'

The Government drew a discreet veil over the Punjab tragedy. Gandhi had called off civil disobedience on April 18th and was anxious to go to the Punjab. Since he wished to avoid a clash with the Government, he sought the Viceroy's formal permission to enter the province. This permission he could not get for nearly six months. C. F. Andrews sent him disconcerting accounts of the conditions in that province. The Government appointed a Committee of Inquiry headed by Lord Hunter to

[1] Thompson and Garratt: *Rise and Fulfilment of British Rule in India*, p. 609.

enquire into the genesis of the Punjab disturbances. The Indian
National Congress decided to boycott the Hunter Committee
and appointed a non-official committee consisting of eminent
lawyers, including Motilal Nehru, C. R. Das, Abbas Tyabji,
M. R. Jayaker and Gandhi. It was as a member of this non-
official committee that Gandhi learnt the truth about the martial-
law régime in the Punjab. He discovered shocking instances of
high-handedness based on incontrovertible evidence which he
himself scrupulously sifted. The fanciful image of the British
Empire as a merciful dispensation of Providence that he had
cherished seemed to crumble to the ground. Nevertheless, he tried
to make himself believe that the Punjab had been wronged by a
few erratic officers and that the Government would, when it
knew the truth, make amends.

On December 24, 1919 King George V issued a proclamation
granting his assent to the Indian Reforms Act and an amnesty
to political prisoners. The King called upon officials and the
people to co-operate. 'This is a document,' wrote Gandhi, 'of
which the British people have every reason to be proud and
with which every Indian ought to be satisfied. The proclamation
has replaced distrust with trust, but it remains to be seen whether
it will filter down to the civil service.'

What Gandhi believed to be the spirit of the Royal Proclamation of December 1919 did not filter down to the British
administration in India. In vain did he appeal to the Central and
the Provincial Governments for 'a change of heart'. When in
March 1920 the appeals of twenty martial-law prisoners from
the Punjab against sentence of death were turned down, he
wrote: 'Judgments even of the highest tribunals were not unaffected by subtle political considerations.' He noted with surprise that the officers responsible for misrule in the Punjab had
not been recalled; they were being lionized by the European
community. The report of the Hunter Committee, when it came
out, struck him as little better than 'thinly disguised whitewash'.
Was there, he asked, some secret code of conduct governing
the official class in India 'before which the flower of the great
British nation fell prostrate?'

Reluctantly and almost painfully, Gandhi was driven to the
conviction that the system of government which he had been
trying to mend needed to be ended. In December 1919 he had
advised the Indian National Congress to make a success of the
new instalment of reforms granted by the British Government
and thus prepare for a fuller measure of responsibility. In Sep-

tember 1920 he declared that reformed councils and governorships for Indians were 'subtle methods of emasculation'.

Besides the 'Punjab Wrong', the 'Khilafat Betrayal' had contributed to this conversion.

# CHAPTER XVIII

# Road to Rebellion

EVENTS in the Punjab had placed a great strain on Gandhi's loyalty in 1919, but his links with the British Empire would not have snapped so dramatically during the following year were it not for another strand in Indian politics, represented by the Khilafat movement.

During his brief sojourn in England in 1914, Gandhi had formed some idea of the conflict that tore the politically-conscious Muslims. During the years 1915-18, when he was deliberately avoiding controversial politics, his advice was often sought by Muslim leaders on the future of the Caliphate or, as it came to be known, the Khilafat. He had opportunities of addressing the Muslim League and the Muslim University of Aligarh. Always his advice to his Muslim compatriots was to exercise patience, and in spite of their deep frustration to give up thoughts of violence. He remained in touch by correspondence with Mahomed Ali, one of the leaders of the Khilafat movement who had been imprisoned. During his visit to Delhi for the War Conference in 1918, Gandhi had pleaded for Mahomed Ali's release and for an assurance by the Government that Muslim sentiments about the future of Turkey would be respected.

The end of the war in November 1918 again brought the Khilafat question to the fore. A Muslim deputation waited on the Viceroy in January 1920, but all that Lord Chelmsford could promise was that if a deputation of Indian Muslims wished to proceed to England he would arrange for the necessary facilities.

Some Muslim leaders, including Abul Kalam Azad, the editor of *Al Hilal*, had already ceased to set much store by petitions to the Viceroy and deputations in England. A meeting of the Khilafat leaders debated for six hours without reaching a decision; Gandhi, who was present by special invitation, suggested that a sub-committee should go further into the question. The sub-committee consisted of Abul Kalam Azad, Hakim Ajmal Khan and Gandhi. 'It was here,' wrote Azad, 'that non-co-operation was conceived.'[1] Next day, when Gandhi placed a programme of 'non-co-operation with the British Government' before the Muslim leaders, a majority of them could not conceal their consternation and wanted time to think.

In February 1920, Abul Kalam Azad presided at the Khilafat Conference in Calcutta and advocated acceptance of Gandhi's programme. Meanwhile, the publication of the treaty with Turkey had aggravated Muslim discontent. Turkey had been denied the leniency for which Indian Muslims had been hoping and agitating. The Viceroy's advice 'to bear with patience and resignation the misfortunes of their Turkish co-religionists' was cold comfort to Indian Muslims, whose frustration was complete. The Khilafat leaders were anxious to do something immediately to express their resentment. On June 9th, when the Khilafat Committee met at Allahabad it unanimously approved the programme of non-co-operation which Gandhi had outlined. Gandhi was in fact authorized to launch the non-co-operation programme after giving a month's notice to the Viceroy. A fortnight later Gandhi informed Lord Chelmsford that if the peace terms offered to Turkey were not revised in accordance with the British pledges to Muslims, he would call upon Muslims to cease co-operation with the Government and invite the Hindus to join the movement.

Gandhi, with his deeply religious outlook, unlike Europeans and educated Hindus, could understand and sympathize even though he may not have entirely agreed with the Muslim sentiment underlying the Khilafat. Unfortunately, what he knew of the movement was largely derived from Muslim divines and pan-Islamic enthusiasts. He failed to see that the Khilafat was a moribund institution, that the Turks themselves were sick of it, that the Ottoman Empire could no more remain intact after the war than the Hapsburg Empire, and that the smaller nations, Arab and non-Arab, were struggling to be free from the stranglehold of Turkey.

When the Indian National Congress in its special session in September, 1920 accepted the non-co-operation programme Gandhi became the leader of both the nationalist and the Khilafat struggles. He toured the country with the Ali brothers and Hindu-Muslim cordiality reached a high tide. Gandhi was heard with reverence by Hindus as well as Muslims. He was invited to address meetings of Muslim women where no male except Gandhi, who was considered pure enough to be an exception,

[1] Mahadev Desai: *Maulana Azad*, Agra, 1940, p. 27.

could be present without his eyes being bandaged. His hope of a 'heart-felt unity' between Hindus and Muslims seemed to have been realized.

He was now heading a mass struggle, the avowed purpose of which was to end alien rule. It was an open rebellion, even though a 'non-violent' one.

He had travelled far, though reluctantly, on the road to sedition against the Empire whose anthem he had sung and whose wars, his non-violence notwithstanding, had seemed to him his own.

'Lord Reading must understand,' wrote Gandhi in *Young India* of December 15, 1921 'that non-co-operators are at war with the government. They have declared rebellion against it.'

It was the same Gandhi who had said at the Madras Law Dinner in April 1915: 'It gives me the greatest pleasure this evening at this great and important gathering to redeclare my loyalty to the British Empire . . . I discovered that the British Empire had certain ideals with which I have fallen in love and one of those ideals is that every subject of the British Empire has the freest scope for his energies and honour and whatever he thinks is due to his conscience.'[1]

That there was no equality between the rulers and the ruled, white and coloured, should have been obvious to Gandhi with his twenty years' struggle in South Africa behind him. While the predominantly European colonies had been fast moving towards a position of equality with the mother country, the so-called dependencies of Britain were standing still or moving at a snail's pace towards self-government. Gandhi was not ignorant of the origins and the basis of British rule in India. In *Hind Swaraj* he had given a merciless analysis of Indian History. The East India Company's victories he had attributed to the divisions of the Indian princes. He had criticized *Pax Brittanica*; the peace was in name only, as it had emasculated the Indian nation and made it cowardly. The railways, the law courts and the educational system had all served to tighten the stranglehold of the occupying power. This was a scathing indictment of British rule, but the moral he drew from it was novel: India was ground down not by British rule but by Western civilization, which had perpetuated that rule. The English themselves were the victims of this civilization; they deserved to be pitied rather than hated. He talked of conquering the conquerors

[1] *Speeches and Writings of Mahatma Gandhi*, p. 310.

spiritually. 'I tender my loyalty to the British Government,' he declared, 'quite selfishly. I would like to use the British race for transmitting this mighty message of *ahimsa*.' During 1915-16 his emphasis on the materialism of the West and the ancient culture of the East, widow-remarriage, the abolition of untouchability, the promotion of handloom industry and the revival of Indian languages, seemed to mark him out as a visionary, strangely unpolitical and other-worldly.

Those who hoped that his energies would be diverted into the innocuous channels of social reform were, however, mistaken. In his scheme of life there was no sharp demarcation between the political and the non-political. When he exhorted the people to cultivate religion, he exhorted them to fear only God and to shed all fear of temporal authority. When he preached the gospel of *swadeshi*, 'in the religious spirit which restricts us to the use and service of our immediate surroundings,' he drew the important corollary that India could not live for Lancashire before she was able to live for herself. He protested against the use of a foreign language as *lingua franca* and threw a bomb-shell into the War Conference of 1918 by speaking in Hindustani. The Government discovered before long that this visionary was human dynamite, completely unpredictable and uncontrollable.

Speaking on the occasion of the opening of the Benaras Hindu University in 1916, he began to think audibly. He rebuked the Indian princes for their jewellery and liveries: 'Whenever I hear of a great palace rising in any great city of India, be it in British India or be it in India which is ruled by our great chiefs, I become jealous at once and I say: "Oh, it is the money that has come from the agriculturists."' 'If we trust and fear God,' he went on, 'we shall have to fear no one, not Maharajas, not Viceroys, not the detectives, not even King George.' Annie Besant, who was present at the august function, could not bear this 'audible thinking' any more and shouted to him: 'Please stop it.' A senior British Officer murmured: 'We must stop this man from talking such rot.'

But no one could stop Gandhi from saying or doing what he believed to be right. 'I have disregarded the order served upon me,' he told the magistrate in Champaran, 'not for want of re-spect for lawful authority, but in obedience to the higher law of our being, the voice of conscience.' Now this was a more revolutionary doctrine than the most radical politics of the day.

The experiences of these early years filled a gap in Gandhi's education which had been caused by his long self-imposed exile in South Africa. Something of the seamy side of the idolized British Empire he already knew. The vendetta of a British Political Agent had driven him at the age of twenty-four to seek a job in South Africa. The brief experience in the courts of Raj-kot and Bombay in 1902 had given him a glimpse of the 'inconsiderateness and ignorance of the English official'.[1] On his return voyage to India he noticed a distance between the English and Indian passengers on the boat—the social gulf between the rulers and the ruled. He had attributed all these experiences to the aberrations of individual Englishmen, and continued to cherish the belief that the system as a whole was just and beneficial to India; but closer knowledge of conditions in his homeland was to disillusion him.

Of the poverty of India he had some idea; he had referred to it in *Hind Swaraj*, but the truth proved to be worse than his wildest imagination. In December 1917 he wrote to *Indian Opinion*, the organ of the South African Indians, that they should not expect from him contributions for relief work in flood-ravaged areas in South Africa: 'The deep poverty I experience in this country deters me even from thinking of financial assistance to be sent for those who have been rendered helpless. Even one pie in this country counts. I am at present living in the midst of thousands who have nothing but roasted pulses or grain flour mixed with water and salt.'

And in his presidential address to the Gujerat Political Conference in November 1917, he spoke of 'deepening poverty'. The Government, he said, honestly believed that the nation's prosperity was increasing; 'its faith in the blue books was immovable.'

The initial deference which high British dignitaries showed to him was due to their conviction that his loyalty to the British connection was beyond question. The moment he criticized particular policies or officials, he ceased to be a *persona grata*. The officers in the districts, more than their superiors in the provincial and central secretariats, were impatient of any agitation and quickly saw red. Gandhi's first collision with authority came in Bihar with the Commissioner of the Tirhut Division, and his second in Bombay Presidency with the Commissioner of Ahmedabad, about whom he wrote: 'The Commissioner's attitude constitutes a greater peril than the German peril, and I am serving the Empire in trying to deliver it from the peril within.' By 1917, Gandhi was being shadowed by the secret police. Civil

[1] *Autobiography*, p. 300.

Service rule, he declared, was one of fear; 'it was a fetish' with the British officers that it should never be said of them that they had yielded to anything like popular agitation. His irrevocable break with the Government came when he saw how rigid was the official machine, how sensitive to prestige, how slow to recognize mistakes and how reluctant to make amends. 'It is contrary to my nature,' he wrote, 'to believe in the depravity of human beings, but there is evidence of the depravity of the bureaucratic mind that it will stop at nothing to gain its ends.'[1] And it was despair with the bureaucracy which convinced him that the system needed ending and not mending.

The Viceroy seems to have realized at an early stage that, if Gandhi could be a valuable ally, he could also be a dangerous opponent. During the years 1917-18 Lord Chelmsford made some efforts—for example during the Champaran crisis and the Delhi War Conference—to retain Gandhi's goodwill, but during the next two years he gravitated towards the view held by members of the civil service, that Gandhi was ever seeking occasions for trouble with the authorities and was irreconcilable. The British attitude to Gandhi in these early years had a curious ambivalence. Personal esteem for him was overlaid by strong, if vague, suspicions of his motives and policies. The official world saw in Satyagraha only a challenge to British rule; it did not see, what was most important to Gandhi, that the challenge had a moral and non-violent basis. The British saw no particular virtue in being evicted from India non-violently, though there is little evidence to suggest that they believed in the feasibility of a mass movement remaining non-violent. They found it difficult to appreciate Gandhi's advice that on the Rowlatt Bills or the Turkish Question the prestige of the Government could grow by stooping to conquer; to them his professions of loyalty and friendship did not carry conviction.

It is thus obvious that to seek the explanation of Gandhi's transition from a loyalist to a rebel only in the events of the summer and autumn of 1920 is a superficial undertaking. Those events only completed a process which had begun much earlier. The depth of his disillusionment in 1920 was a measure of the illusion he had been hugging, of a new heaven and earth being established after the war by a grateful Empire for the help rendered to it in its hour of need by a subject people. Given the Government's intolerance of all agitators, and Gandhi's assertion of the inherent right of non-violent opposition to political or economic

[1] *Young India*, October 20, 1921.

injustice, a conflict between the two was inevitable. What is surprising is not that it came but that it was delayed so long.

Gandhi was deeply human and almost sentimental, even in politics. In the closing months of 1919 and early in 1920 he was scanning the horizon for a gesture which would restore his faith in the sovereignty of British justice. He was clutching at every straw. The Royal Proclamation of December 1919, which he had hailed as a harbinger of a new era, turned out to be no more than the felicitous phraseology usual on such occasions. In any case its spirit was not caught by His Majesty's Government in India. On both the Khilafat and the Punjab issues, Gandhi found the authorities said one thing and did another. Trusting by nature, he could make many allowances for the Government so long as his faith in its sincerity remained. But when that faith was shaken, he saw British rule in an entirely new light. He had once attributed the faults of this rule to the aberrations of individuals; now its virtues appeared to him accidental or incidental. 'I said to myself,' he wrote in *Young India* (December 31, 1921), 'there is no state run by Nero or Mussolini which has not good points about it, but we have to reject the whole once we decide to non-co-operate with the system . . . the beneficent institutions of the British Government are like the fabled snake with a brilliant jewel on its head, but which has fangs full of poison . . .'

# CHAPTER XIX

# Swaraj within a Year

THE programme of non-violent non-co-operation with the Government which Gandhi presented to the Khilafat Committee and the Indian National Congress, however revolutionary it seemed to the Government and the people, represented features which had for long been a part of Gandhi's personality and philosophy. 'The English have not taken India,' he had written in 1909; 'we have given it to them. They are not in India because of their strength but because we keep them.'[1] A year later he had suggested in a message to the Indian National Congress, that 'for the many ills we suffer in India, passive resistance is an infallible panacea'. Hence when he came to the conclusion that the Government did not possess in itself any capacity for self-improvement, that it was 'past mending', he enunciated the right recognized 'from time immemorial of the subject to refuse to assist a ruler who misrules'.[2] His scheme of boycotting conventional schools and establishing national schools filled his eminent contemporaries—such as Rabindranath Tagore, Madan Mohan Malaviya, Srinivas Sastri, and C. R. Das—with misgivings, but Gandhi had experimented on his children. He had criticized the use of English in schools as calculated to make Indian children foreigners in their own country. He always practised what he preached. Had he not surprised the élite of Bombay in 1915 by replying to their welcome in Gujerati, and scandalized the Viceroy and his colleagues by speaking in Hindi at the War Conference of 1918?

As for the British courts in India, he had recorded his verdict on them in *Hind Swaraj* in 1908. 'The lawyers have enslaved India, have accentuated Hindu-Muhammaden dissensions and have confirmed English authority.' The law's delays and expense in India were too well known to need any elaboration. Motilal Nehru, one of the most successful lawyers in the land quoted a proverb to illustrate the ruinous effects of litigation. '*Adalat*

[1] Gandhi: *Hind Swaraj*, p. 27.
[2] Letter to Lord Chelmsford dated June 22, 1920.

*mein jo jita so hara, jo hara, so mara'* (Success in the court is defeat; defeat is death).

'Swadeshi', or the use of home-made goods, was another plank in the non-co-operation movement Gandhi had been preaching since his return from South Africa. He had told a conference of Christian missionaries in February 1916 that India could not live for Lancashire before she was able to live for herself.[1] His advocacy of the boycott of foreign cloth and the use of hand-spun and hand-woven cloth (khadi) during the non-co-operation movement was taken by the Government—and by most nationalists—as a blow aimed at Britain in her tenderest spot, her commerce with India. To Gandhi, however, the boycott of foreign cloth was not at all a pressure tactic but a means of reviving the oldest cottage industry of India. With increasing pressure on land, agriculture had long ceased to give adequate employment to the peasant; hand spinning could therefore help him to eke out a living in the normal year and act as 'a ready-made insurance policy' in periods of famine and flood.

As for the boycott of councils, which had been and was to prove the greatest bone of contention in the Congress, Gandhi did not subscribe to the claim that legislatures were a necessary training ground for self-government. Nor was he attracted by the strategy of 'capturing' legislatures for the purpose of 'wrecking from within'. As recently as December 1919, when he still had some faith in the sincerity of the British, he had pleaded for working the Montagu-Chelmsford Reforms for what they were worth. When that faith had gone the councils appeared to him only a red herring in the path of Indian nationalists.

This was in a nutshell the programme that Gandhi placed before India, the boycott of British courts, schools, councils, and cloth. With some *naiveté*, he claimed that his movement was not unconstitutional:[2] evidently in his dictionary constitutional and moral were synonymous terms. The British saw that the success of this programme of non-co-operation would paralyse their administration. Lord Chelmsford at first tried to kill with ridicule 'the most foolish of all foolish schemes', which would bring ruin to those who had any stake in the Government. He was also apparently rousing the fears of the propertied classes. A number of 'moderate' leaders joined official critics in underlining the risks inherent in mass non-co-operation. M. A. Jinnah had cried halt at the Nagpur Congress in December 1920.

[1] Natesan: *Speeches and Writings of Mahatma Gandhi*, p. 341.
[2] *Ibid.* p. 523.

Srinivas Sastri—Gokhale's political heir—warned his countrymen against the perils of the course towards which they were drifting by adopting 'an impracticable programme in unreasoning opposition to the Government'.

The chief argument against non-co-operation, whether from the British Government or the 'moderate' Indian leaders, was that it was likely to open the sluice gates of anarchy. Those who denounced the movement as negative and dangerous did not appreciate the precautions which its author had taken. 'Non-co-operation' was an incomplete and, in certain ways, a misleading description of a movement which was intended not only to dismantle some institutions but also to replace them with others. The students and teachers who walked out of schools run and aided by the Government were invited to join 'national' schools and colleges; the lawyers and litigants who boycotted the courts were to take their briefs to the arbitration boards; those who resigned from the army and the police were to become Congress or Khilafat volunteers. The boycott of imported cloth was to be accompanied by the promotion of hand spinning and hand-woven cloth to clothe the people in villages and towns. There was thus to be no vacuum as a result of these boycotts. The movement was moreover to be carefully phased. Between the surrender of titles and honorary offices to the Government and mass civil disobedience and non-payment of taxes, there were several stages to suit the level of discipline and organization achieved by each particular district and province. From his central control, Gandhi was to permit as much electrical current of non-co-operation to be transmitted as the people could take, and he made it clear that if there was a violent spark he would switch off the mains to prevent a conflagration. The greatest safeguard for peace was the stress he laid on non-violence. Non-co-operation with the symbols and institutions of British rule ruled out even hatred of Englishmen. Again and again Gandhi declared that he would not do to an Englishman what he would not do to a blood-brother. He had, he publicly recalled, non-co-operated even with his brother on matters of principle.

Repeatedly he drew the attention of the non-co-operators to the 'purifying' part of the movement, to its introspective and moral aspects. Violence, disunity and corruptibility among a people strengthened foreign rule and so all had to make themselves proof against these weaknesses. The change of heart for which he was working he expected first among Indians and then

among Englishmen. The Indian people had thus to shed fear of
the Government and also rid themselves of the curse of communalism, untouchability, use of intoxicants, forced labour and
other social evils.

Gandhi had told the special session of the Indian National
Congress at Calcutta in September 1920 that with an adequate
response to his programme of non-co-operation, Swaraj could
be attained in one year. 'The promise of Swaraj within a year,'
wrote Subhas Chandra Bose 'was not only unwise but childish.'[1]
It looked on the face of it too optimistic a proposition that
Britain's Empire in India, established for more than a century,
could be overthrown by non-violent agitation in a year. The
time limit set by Gandhi was not, however, a prediction, nor
the promise of a political tactician. A year was in Gandhi's
opinion long enough to awaken a people, to make it shed its fear
and stiffen its backbone. A moral transformation of the Indian
people could be expected to lead to a a transformation of the
British Government and people. 'Freedom,' Gandhi wrote, 'is like
a birth. Till we are fully free we are slave. All birth takes place
in a moment! He had, he declared, laid a practical programme
before the country. A nation that could throw away an age-long
curse (of untouchability), shed the drink habit, and utilize its
spare hours to manufacture sixty crores worth of cloth during
a single year would be a transformed nation. Such a nation
would have acquired enough discipline, courage and self-sacrifice to convince Britain that India could not be treated on any
basis other than that of equal partnership. Swaraj was not to
come as a gift from Britain. 'The Act of Parliament,' wrote
Gandhi, 'would be merely a courteous ratification of the declared wish of the people of India even as it was in the case of
the Union of South Africa.'

That a political programme had no chance of success without
an adequate organization to implement it Gandhi had realized
at the age of twenty-five, when he had founded the Natal Indian
Congress to fight for the rights of the Indians in Natal. The
Indian National Congress had therefore to be refashioned if it
was to prove an efficient instrument of 'non-violent non-co-
operation'. Gandhi saw that what the country needed was not
a forum for an annual pageant and feast of oratory, but a militant organization in touch with the masses. The revised constitution of the Indian National Congress, largely Gandhi's own

[1] Bose, S. C.: *Indian Struggle*, Calcutta, 1948, p. 104.

handiwork, was approved at the Nagpur session of the Congress in December 1920; it defined the creed of the Congress as 'the attainment of *Swarajya* by all legitimate and peaceful means'. Satyagraha was thus brought within the four corners of the constitution of the Congress. The Congress was reorganized not only on a more representative basis but in such a way that it could function efficiently between its annual sessions. It ceased to be the preserve of the upper and middle classes; its doors were opened to the masses in the smaller towns and villages whose political consciousness Gandhi was quickening.

The annual Congress sessions at Nagpur in December 1920 confirmed the decisions taken by the Special Session at Calcutta three months earlier. Opposition to the non-co-operation programme died hard. The president of the Congress session, Vijayaraghavchariar, was critical and so in varying degrees were Kelkar, Jinnah and Annie Besant. The enthusiasm of the rank and file of the delegates infected their leaders; non-co-operation became the official programme and Gandhi undisputed leader of the Congress. From now until his death Gandhi was to exercise a unique influence over the Indian National Congress and Indian politics.

Gandhi was now the Mahatma, the great soul; with his voluntary poverty, simplicity, humility and saintliness he seemed a *Rishi* (sage) of old who had stepped from the pages of an ancient epic to bring about the liberation of his country. Nay, to millions he was the incarnation of God. In the course of a tour of Bihar, when a tyre of his car burst, he saw an old woman standing by the roadside. She was stated to be 104 years old and had waited in rain and without food and water for the whole day. 'For whom are you waiting?' somebody asked her. 'My son, which is Mahatma Gandhi?' she answered. 'Why do you want to see him,' asked Gandhi who now stood next to her. 'He is an *Avatara*' (incarnation of God), replied the woman. For the next quarter of a century, it was not only for his message that people came to him, but for the merit of seeing him. The sacred sight of the Mahatma, his *darshan*, was almost equivalent to a pilgrimage to holy Banaras. The unthinking adoration of the multitude sometimes made him feel sick. 'The woes of Mahatmas,' he wrote, 'are known only to Mahatmas.' But this adoration was the mainspring from which was drawn the immense influence he exercised over Indian public life. He inspired old and young alike. In his autobiography, Jawaharlal Nehru has graphically narrated the story of the boy in his teens who was arrested during the non-co-operation movement, stripped and tied to a whipping post and flogged; as each stripe fell on him and cut into his flesh he shouted, 'Victory to Mahatma Gandhi' until he fainted.

Gandhi had struck some of the inner chords of Indian humanity; his appeal for courage and sacrifice evoked a ready response because he was himself the epitome of these qualities. It was because he was, to use Churchill's epithet, a 'naked fakir', because his life was one of austerity and self-sacrifice that a great emotional bond grew between him and the Indian people. The number of such 'fakirs' was to multiply fast. Among those who gave up their lucrative careers and queued up for prison under Gandhi's leadership were Motilal Nehru, Rajendra Prasad, C. R. Das, Vallabhbhai Patel, C. Rajagopalachari. Life acquired a new meaning for them. Abbas Tyabji, a former Chief Justice of Baroda, wrote from a village that he was feeling twenty years younger. 'God!' he exclaimed, 'What an experience! I have so much love and affection for the common folk to whom it is now an honour to belong. It is the fakir's dress that has broken down all barriers.' Motilal Nehru, who had given up his magnificent practice at the Allahabad Bar, wrote to Gandhi from a small health resort where he was convalescing: 'The brass cooker has taken the place of the two kitchens, a solitary servant not over-intelligent that of the old retinue—the three small bags containing rice, dal and masalo that of the mule-load of provisions . . . The *shikar* has given place to long walks, and rifles and guns to books, magazines and newspapers . . . What a fall my countrymen! But really I have never enjoyed life better.'

And it is in writing about this period that Jawaharlal Nehru has recorded how the movement absorbed and engrossed him so wholly that he 'gave up all other associations and contacts, old friends, books, even newspapers except in so far as they dealt with the work in hand . . . I almost forgot my family, my wife, my daughter.'[1]

---

[1] Nehru, J. L.: *Towards Freedom* (Autobiography), London 1945, p. 77.

# CHAPTER XX

# Climax

1921 was a year of awakening for India. The non-co-operation movement gathered momentum on the crest of rising enthusiasm. The prospect of 'Swaraj within a year' shattered bonds of centuries; the hypnosis of fear had been broken. Gandhi's call for courage and sacrifice lifted politics from the doldrums in which they had drifted for decades. The Government was anxious, but momentarily perplexed, wondering whether the old methods of fighting violent outbreaks would suppress Satyagraha or strengthen it.

For Gandhi this was a period of incessant activity which taxed him almost to the limits of his endurance. He travelled all over the country, keeping in touch with local leaders, directing, advising and admonishing. His daily mail was enormous and received his personal attention. His secretaries were often hard put to it to locate remote villages even with the help of railway time-tables and post and telegraph guide books. Sometimes, unable to decipher the name of a correspondent, they cut out the signature from the letter and pasted it on the envelope to serve as an address. In the midst of this unremitting activity, Gandhi found time to write for *Young India*, into the pages of which he poured his very soul. Many an article which inspired the country with faith and courage was scribbled in the third-class compartment of a moving train. The four or five hours' sleep which his public engagements left him was often disturbed by the uncontrollable enthusiasm of crowds, which gathered at railway stations at all hours of the day and night to see him. In Krishandas's *Seven Months with Mahatma Gandhi* there is an interesting story of the residents of an Assam village who had threatened that if the train carrying the Mahatma did not halt at their station, they would hold it up by lying across the track. They were as good as their word and broke into his compartment at the dead of night, with naked torches and shrill cries of 'Mahatma Gandhi Ki Jai'.

This hero-worship pained Gandhi deeply, but the awakening

of the people, to which his movement was contributing, pleased him. In the course of his tours he noted that 'the spirit of kindness of which the poet Tulsidas sings so eloquently is gaining ground'. His message was simple: it was not British guns but Indians' own imperfections which kept India in bondage. India could acquire a new strength by purging her corporate life of untouchability, communal strife, drink and drugs and dependence upon foreign cloth and institutions run or aided by the British Government. Swaraj was not to come as a gift from the British Parliament. 'I have had the hardihood to say,' he declared, 'that Swaraj could not be granted even by God. We would have to earn it ourselves.'

The first reaction of the Central and Provincial Governments to Gandhi's defiance of laws in April 1919 were sharp and swift. Gandhi was arrested in 1919 on his way to Delhi and put in a train for Bombay, where he was released. The disturbances which broke out in his home province in his absence, and the tragedy which occurred in the Punjab a few days later, led him to suspend civil disobedience temporarily.

The initial 'firmness' which the Governors and the Viceroy showed was not to be repeated for nearly three years. Perhaps in the first flush of excitement they had accepted the inevitability of Gandhi's arrest and prosecution too lightly. When they had had time for second thoughts, they felt less sure of the requirements of the situation and the precise scale and timing of the force required to cope with Satyagraha. The tragic events in the spring of 1919 at least revealed the tremendous hold which Gandhi exercised over the people, and the risks inherent in his arrest. At the same time, his restraint in the summer of 1919 led them to hope that he might not, after all, take the extreme step of open and large-scale defiance of the Government, or he might not be able to carry with him other leaders and groups in the Congress.

'I think,' wrote Sir William Vincent, the Home Member, on April 26, 1919, 'that a good many people will soon be tired of Mr Gandhi and his vagaries.' The same opinion was expressed by Sir George Lloyd, the Governor of Bombay, in a letter to the Viceroy on June 11, 1919:

'I am rather anxious about things here, for Gandhi is beginning to get very restless . . . He has some game on with the Punjab, but exactly what it is we have not yet succeeded in finding out. His meetings are not well attended and his followers are very disgruntled . . . The mere deportation of Gandhi will raise a considerable storm, whilst his prosecution is a course that I cannot contemplate with any degree of satisfaction. For the rest the Home Rule party is completely split up now in this Presidency. It has suffered blows in the resignations of several important leaders . . . If it were not for Gandhi, all could be extremely well here . . . but he is a real danger point. Unless he forces our hands he is less dangerous loose than bound, for he loses influence daily, but his knowledge of that fact impels him to desperate courses to recover his influence.'

It was in view of these considerations that, even after the adoption of the non-co-operation programme by the Indian National Congress in September 1920, the Government of India prescribed 'non-interference' as the 'wisest policy' in a circular dated September 4, 1920: 'The non-co-operation scheme is so intrinsically foolish that Government have every confidence that the common sense of India will reject it . . . For the time being the policy of non-interference is the wisest policy. They (the Government of India; think that it would be a mistake at the present juncture either to adopt repressive measures of an executive nature under special or emergency laws against the leaders of the movement or even to institute immediate proceedings against them under the ordinary criminal law, because any such action would only result in making martyrs of them, and gaining for them a large number of adherents who would otherwise hold aloof.'

On April 2, 1921, Lord Reading succeeded Lord Chelmsford as the Viceroy of India. At the end of the month the new Viceroy wrote: 'When in England, I was not unduly depressed . . . by the report of serious conditions in India . . . I am reluctantly compelled since my investigations here to take a more serious view.' He adopted, records his son-biographer, 'Fabian tactics' to bide his time for a massive assault on the movement. In the latter half of May he met Gandhi. The meeting had been arranged through the efforts of Madan Mohan Malaviya, primarily to clear some misunderstanding about alleged incitement to violence by the leaders of the Khilafat movement, which was of course inextricably tied up with the non-co-operation movement. The whole trouble had arisen from some references to Afghanistan made by Maulana Mahomed Ali at a time when rumours were rife about an imminent invasion of India by the Amir of Afghanistan. There were in all six meetings between Gandhi and Reading; their discussions ranged over a wide field: the Punjab disturbances of 1919, the Khilafat movement, the meaning of

*Swaraj.* In a private letter to his son, the Viceroy confessed to a feeling of excitement, almost a thrill, in meeting his unusual visitor, and described his religious and moral views as admirable though he found it difficult to understand his practice of them in politics. Gandhi agreed to ask Mahomed Ali publicly to withdraw the passages in his speeches, which were susceptible of an interpretation of incitement to violence; in doing this he wanted to leave no doubt in the minds of his own followers as well as in that of the Viceroy that non-violence was the basic principle of his movement. The Viceroy viewed the episode from another angle: 'He (Mahomed Ali) is the real factor in the situation; he is the ostensible link between the Mohammedan and Hindu. If trouble comes between him and Gandhi it means the collapse of the bridge over the gulf between Hindu and Mohammedan. If Mahomed Ali does what Gandhi desires—and that no doubt will be to make the declaration—Mahomed Ali will be lowered in the public esteem . . .'[1]

The Secretary of State telegraphed his congratulations to the Viceroy on his skilful treatment of Gandhi!

The breach between the Mahatma and the Ali brothers to which the Government was looking forward did not come. When in September 1921, the Ali brothers were arrested, and the Government of Bombay explained in a communiqué that the charge against them was that of tampering with the loyalty of the Indian soldier, a manifesto was signed by nearly fifty leaders, including Gandhi, calling upon every Indian soldier and civilian to find some other means of livelihood.

The visit of the Prince of Wales had been planned before Lord Reading became Viceroy, and in spite of the disturbed political conditions Lord Reading did not advise postponement. 'Postponement,' he wrote to the Secretary of State, 'would have the disadvantage of attributing power to this movement, and above all of creating both in England and in the Dominions, and throughout the world, the impression that India was so disloyal that it was not safe for the Prince to visit it.' On November 17, 1921, when the Prince landed in Bombay, the non-co-operators abstained from the official ceremonies. Gandhi was in Bombay on this day and was present at a big meeting held in the morning to make a huge bonfire of foreign cloth; in the afternoon rioting broke out in the town, in which assaults were made on Europeans, Parsis and others who had participated in the

[1] Reading, Marquess of: *Rufus Isaacs, First Marquess of Reading,* Vol. II, p. 199.

reception to Prince Edward. Personal appeals and a fast by
Gandhi, and frantic efforts by his colleagues, saved Bombay from
the maze of violence and counter-violence into which it
slipped. Fortunately in other towns there were no riots, but the
people left no doubt of their sullen attitude to the British *Raj*.
Wherever the Prince went, parades, receptions and banquets
were arranged in his honour by the authorities, but, as the
memoirs of the Duke of Windsor record, he did not fail to
notice 'empty streets, shuttered windows, brooding silence'.

The Prince of Wales was to visit Calcutta in the last week of
December 1921. The Viceroy, anxious to avoid a *hartal* and hostile demonstration at Calcutta, encouraged Madan Mohan Malaviya's efforts for mediation between the Government and the
Congress. Malaviya wired to Gandhi on December 16, 1921 that
he proposed to lead a deputation to the Viceroy to urge the
calling of a Round Table Conference. If the Viceroy accepted
the proposal and released the leaders, would Gandhi call off the
boycott of the visit of the Prince of Wales and suspend the civil
disobedience movement until the Conference was over? The
same proposal had been simultaneously broached by Malaviya
with C. R. Das, who was then serving a term in the Presidency
Jail at Calcutta. C. R. Das thought, and Abdul Kalam Azad
agreed with him, that the 'offer' brought by Malaviya was worth
considering; in a telegram to Gandhi they urged him to accept
Malaviya's proposal. Gandhi made his acceptance conditional
on two assurances: that the date and composition of the Conference were settled in advance, and that the Ali brothers should
be among the political prisoners to be released. Malaviya could
not give these assurances and the negotiations, to the chagrin
of C. R. Das, fell through.

In December 1921 and January 1922 nearly 30,000 people were
imprisoned. Volunteer organizations were made illegal, meetings
and processions were forcibly dispersed, midnight searches of
Congress and Khilafat offices became the order of the day, and
the treatment of political prisoners became harsher. The Indian
National Congress met at Ahmedabad in December 1921 and
appointed Gandhi as its sole executive authority. Within the
Congress there was a growing pressure on him to intensify the
struggle and launch mass civil disobedience. A mass struggle
was, in Gandhi's armoury of Satyagraha, the most effective as
well as the most dangerous weapon. He compared it to an
earthquake, 'a sort of general upheaval on the political plane
—the Government ceases to function . . . the police stations, the

courts, offices, etc., all cease to be Government property and shall be taken charge of by the people'.

Gandhi's plan was to launch civil disobedience in one district; if it succeeded in one district he proposed to extend it to the adjacent district, and so on until the whole of India was liberated. He gave a clear warning that if violence broke out in any form in any part of the country, the movement would lose its character as a movement of peace, 'even as a lute would begin to emit notes of discord the moment a single string snaps'.

The riots which had disfigured Bombay during the visit of the Prince of Wales in November 1921 had led Gandhi to postpone civil disobedience. Evidently the atmosphere did not appear too propitious for a drastic step. The wholesale arrests and prosecutions of Congress workers and volunteers in the next two months, however, made him review the position. The Government was preventing meetings and muzzling the Press. The choice, as Gandhi described it, was between 'mass civil disobedience with all its undoubted dangers and the lawless repression of the lawful activities of the people'. He decided to take the risk and to make a beginning with mass civil disobedience under his own supervision in Bardoli *taluk* in Gujerat. While selecting Bardoli as a spearhead of the mass civil disobedience, Gandhi warned its people that for refusing payment of land revenue their crops were liable to be auctioned, lands confiscated, cattle driven away, and that Bardoli *taluk* may even disappear from the map.

Gandhi communicated the step he contemplated to the Viceroy. The Government of India promptly issued a reply to the Mahatma's ultimatum and asserted that the issue before the country was 'no longer between this or that programme of political advance but between lawlessness with all its consequences on the one hand and the maintenance of those principles which lie at the root of all civilized governments'.

The Congress and the Government were now poised for a head-on collision.

# CHAPTER XXI

# *Anticlimax ?*

THE 'open letter' to the Viceroy, which struck him as an ulti-matum but was from Gandhi's view-point a sacred duty binding to a Satyagrahi, was dated February 1, 1922. Three days later a clash occurred between a procession and the police at Chauri Chaura, a small village in Gorakhpur district in the United Provinces. The facts were clear enough. The main body of the procession had passed in front of the police station when some constables jeered at the stragglers, who hit back. The con-stables opened fire, and when their ammunition was exhausted locked themselves inside the police station. The main procession then returned and in a mad fury set fire to the police station, hacking to pieces the hapless policemen as they rushed out of the burning building. Among the twenty-two victims of the tragedy was the young son of the sub-inspector of police.

The news of this outrage was a bolt from the blue to Gandhi. He inferred from it that the atmosphere in the country was too explosive for a mass movement, and decided to revoke the plans for civil disobedience in Bardoli which he had announced only a week earlier. He consulted such members of the Congress execu-tive as were not imprisoned. The All-Indian Congress Committee met at Delhi on February 24th, and at his instance passed resolutions deploring the Chauri Chaura incident, suspending mass civil disobedience, and permitting only such activities of the Congress as were not designed to invite imprisonment. With the 'aggressive' part of the movement in abeyance, the emphasis was shifted to the constructive programme.

The sudden suspension of mass civil disobedience shocked and bewildered Gandhi's closest colleagues. Subhas Chandra Bose re-called many years later: 'I was with *Deshbandhu* (C. R. Das) at the time and I could see that he was beside himself with anger and sorrow at the way Mahatma Gandhi was repeatedly bungling.'[1] Motilal Nehru and Lajpat Rai wrote from gaol urging Gandhi not to halt the movement because of a stray incident.

[1] Bose, Subhas Chandra: *The Indian Struggle*, Calcutta, 1948, p. 108.

Gandhi had a feeling that many of those who had endorsed his proposals in the Congress Working Committee and the All-India Congress Committee had done so not out of real conviction, but out of deference to him. Some of his ardent followers were troubled by doubts and torn between loyalty to their leader and their own convictions. They were at a loss to see any logic in calling off the civil disobedience movement at Bardoli after an outbreak at Chauri Chaura. Was it not open to the government to thwart the non-violent rebellion by staging such 'incidents' through *agents provocateurs* and thus turn the Satyagraha struggle into a pious futility? Was the Congress a political institution or a testing ground for the inner conflicts of a Mahatma? Were the sacrifices of the nation to go in vain, and were the non-co-operators to continue to rot indefinitely in gaol? And was not the reversal of the 'aggressive' programme an invitation to the Government to pounce upon the non-co-operators and to turn their retreat into a rout?

Such were the angry questions shot at Gandhi by a bewildered and indignant following. Few of the critics could see that Chauri Chaura was not the cause, but only the occasion for the reverse gear which he had applied. From the moment he had come out against the Rowlatt Bills and presented Satyagraha to the country as a lever for the redress of political and social injustice he had stressed the paramount importance of non-violence; this was the one theme which had recurred in his speeches and articles. And yet, as the ugly violence in Ahmedabad, Viramgan and Amritsar had shown in 1919, it was not easy to prevent outbursts of mob frenzy altogether, particularly when the local authorities were not slow to feed it with provocative acts. 'I am sorry,' he had declared on April 18, 1919 at Bombay, 'that when I embarked upon a mass movement, I underrated the forces of evil.' He was fully aware of the undercurrent of violence in the country, and one reason why he had allowed himself to be placed at the head of the Khilafat movement in 1920 was that he hoped to divert this undercurrent into non-violent channels. Conscious of the risks, he had taken extraordinary precautions to graduate his movement and condition it to the political climate. The non-co-operation programme began with the surrender of titles and honorary offices by individuals, and was to end with the suspension of taxes and mass defiance of laws. Between these two extremes there were a number of activities, which not only asserted the nationalist feeling but also disciplined the people and prepared them for a

mass movement. The improvement in the condition of untouchables, the establishment of national schools, the settlement of
disputes by arbitration boards outside the courts, the formation
of volunteer corps, the picketing of liquor shops, the boycott of
foreign cloth, and the promotion of *Khadi*, were practical
methods of organizing the masses. Gandhi's programme was
one of 'progressive non-co-operation' in which defiance of authority was to be extended according to the ability of the people
to resist repression without retaliation.

While organizing the forces of nationalism against foreign
rule, Gandhi had taken care not to rip open the latent fissures
in Indian society. He advised tenants to pay rents to landlords
even when payment of tax to the Government was suspended.
He advised workers to obtain leave from their employers for
joining 'hartals'. 'It is a most dangerous thing,' he wrote, 'to
make political use of labour until the labourers understand the
political condition of the country.' He gave much time and
thought to the organization of Congress volunteers, and wrote at
length in *Young India* on the technique of controlling crowds
and conducting public meetings. Violence on the part of the
Government he did not fear, as it could strengthen the hearts
and swell the ranks of non-co-operators. Violence on the part of
the people he dreaded, as it could dissolve the movement into
chaos, besides provoking the superior violence of the Government.

No violent outbreak in any part of the country could escape
Gandhi's notice. The Malegaon riots, in which policemen were
victims of mob violence, and the Malabar outbreak in which
Hindus suffered at the hands of the Moplahs, elicited his instantaneous and unqualified condemnation. He was in Bombay
when the Prince of Wales arrived in November 1921, and a riot
broke out in which fifty-eight persons were killed and 381
injured. In a message to the people of Bombay he said that
the non-violence of the non-co-operators had been worse than
the violence of the co-operators, 'for with non-violence on our
lips we have terrorized those who have differed from us . . .
The Swaraj that I have witnessed during the last two days has
stunk in my nostrils.'

C. F. Andrews, who saw Gandhi on return from South Africa
soon after the Bombay riots, found him 'haggard and emaciated,
as one who had just passed through the valley of the shadow of
death'. Andrews had noticed a spirit of violence enter the movement from the side of the people as the violence on the part of

the Government increased. The great masses of India had awakened to the sense of their own power, but they had not yet been trained to keep this power under control. Andrews criticized the 'subtle racial appeal' in public bonfires of foreign cloth. He had seen Satyagraha in action in South Africa during the years 1913-14; when he saw the movement in 1921 in India he felt 'it was something entirely new and less spiritual'.

So when the tragedy of Chari Chaura occurred it was more than a stray incident in an unknown village in a remote corner of the Indian sub-continent. It was, as Gandhi wrote to Jawaharlal Nehru on February 19, 1922, 'the last straw'. He recalled the complaints he had received that the rank and file had been getting out of hand in many places, and that indiscipline had been increasing. 'I assure you,' he wrote to Jawaharlal, 'that if the thing had not been suspended we would have been leading not a non-violent struggle but essentially a violent struggle,'[1] Jawaharlal, who had received the news of the suspension of civil disobedience in gaol 'with amazement and consternation', after discussing the pros and cons of the suspension of civil disobedience, records in his autobiography that the 'decision was right; he (Gandhi) had to stop the rot and build anew'.

Gandhi noted that many of his colleagues, and the mass of non-co-operators, were burning with indignation and were anxious to deliver 'telling blows', albeit non-violent ones, against the Government. Now this was rather an imperfect appreciation of the technique of Satyagraha, which sought to prick the conscience, to melt the heart and to open the eyes of the opponent. The technique of non-violent warfare is essentially different from that of the other variety, which is almost uninhibited as to the means for achieving its objective. The common view of war and politics is that everything is fair, and that the protagonists should muster overwhelming pressure at as many points as possible to defeat the opponent; such a strategy was inapplicable to Satyagraha, in which there was no room even for excitement. Gandhi defined civil disobedience as preparation for mute suffering, 'with effects which may be marvellous, but unperceived and gentle'.

'It is dangerous to assemble' wrote Romain Rolland, 'all the forces of a nation and to hold the nation panting before a prescribed movement, to lift one's arm to give the final command, and then at the last moment, let one's arm drop and

[1] Quoted in Tendulkar's *Mahatma*, Vol. II, p. 118.

thrice call a halt just as the formidable machinery has been set in motion. One risks ruining the brakes, and paralysing the impetus.'[1] If we may continue Rolland's metaphor, Gandhi was bringing the machinery not to a standstill but into third gear from a premature top gear. The suspension of the 'aggressive programme' did not affect the constructive programme, the positive aspect of the non-co-operation movement. Critics did not share Gandhi's faith that the non-co-operation movement, even without the last desperate step of mass civil disobedience, could prove effective.

It was not only Congressmen and Khilafatists who failed to understand Gandhi's action after Chauri Chaura. The Viceroy, Lord Reading, gleefully confided to his son that Gandhi 'had pretty well run himself to the last ditch as a politician by extraordinary manifestations in the last month or six weeks before his arrest'.[2]

On the evening of March 10th, Gandhi was arrested. He bade farewell to the inmates of his Ashram, heard his favourite song of the true *Vaishnava*, took his seat in the waiting car and was driven to gaol. The trial was held on March 18th, before C. N. Broomfield, the District and Sessions Judge of Ahmedabad. The prosecution relied upon three articles published in *Young India*, namely 'Tampering with Loyalty', 'The Puzzle and its Solution' and 'Shaking the Manes'. The other accused was Shankarlal Banker, the publisher of *Young India*. Sir J. T. Strangman, the Advocate-General, conducted the prosecution. The accused did not defend themselves. The judge behaved with exceeding courtesy, nodding respectfully to the accused in the dock before taking his seat. Gandhi made his task easy by pleading guilty. In a statement which would have been difficult to excel in dignified emotion or eloquence, he explained his transition from a staunch loyalist to a rebel:

'My public life began in 1893 in South Africa in troubled weather. My first contact with British authority in that country was not of a happy character. I discovered that as a man and as an Indian I had no rights. On the contrary I discovered that I had no rights as a man because I was an Indian. But I was not baffled. I thought this treatment of Indians was an excrescence upon a system that was intrinsically and mainly good. I gave the Government my voluntary and hearty co-operation, criticiz-

[1] Rolland, Romain: *Mahatma Gandhi*, London, 1942, p. 132.
[2] Reading, Marquess of: *Rufus Isaacs, First Marquess of Reading*, Vol. II, p. 249.

ing it fully where I felt it was faulty, but never wishing its destruction . . .'

He accepted responsibility for the violent outbreaks which had occurred, and asked for the highest penalty that could be inflicted upon him:

'The only course open to you Mr Judge is . . . either to resign your post or inflict on me the severest penalty if you believe that the system and law you are assisting to administer are good for the people.'

Gandhi was sentenced to six years' imprisonment. An observer noted that he was not only serene but 'festively joyful' during the 100-minute trial. 'So far as the sentence is concerned,' he told the judge, 'I certainly consider that it is as light as any judge could inflict on me; and so far as the whole proceedings are concerned, I must say that I could not have expected greater courtesy.'

Gaol-going was part of non-co-operation; in his articles and speeches Gandhi had often commented on its significance for the movement. 'Freedom is to be wooed only inside prison walls and sometimes on gallows,' he had once written. Thousands of non-co-operators had been arrested during the preceding eighteen months. The ideal non-co-operator, according to Gandhi, was to seek imprisonment not to embarrass but to convert the Government by suffering for a just cause. Arrests were to be courted 'not rudely, roughly, blushingly, certainly never violently, but peacefully, quietly, courteously, humbly, prayerfully, and courageously'. The non-co-operator was to observe gaol discipline; he was neither to seek nor to accept special privileges. The hardships of gaol life were to be borne cheerfully as 'such meek behaviour springing from strength and knowledge ultimately dissolves the tyranny of the tyrant—voluntary suffering is the quickest and best remedy for the removal of abuses and injustices'.

On entering the Yeravda prison he was told that he could not use his spinning-wheel nor sleep in the open. However, these restrictions were later removed. It was with considerable difficulty that the 'higher authorities' were persuaded to allow him to keep a few books on religion, an old dictionary and an Urdu manual. He was denied a pillow, but improvised one with his books and spare clothes. He could not be trusted with a pocket knife to slice his bread; when it was allowed, he had to deposit it with a gaol official after use. Banker, his fellow-prisoner, was taken to another cell and other prisoners were not permitted to meet the Mahatma. An African prisoner was attached to him as an attendant; unable to talk to each other, they communicated by signs. Gandhi, however, knew the language of the human heart. One day, when the African was bitten by a scorpion, Gandhi washed his wound, wiped it, sucked off the poison, and treated him until he was cured. Won over by this kindness, the African became an apt pupil at hand-spinning.

Gandhi liked the enforced solitude in gaol; it gave him the quiet and the rest which he had missed during seven years of incessant activity in India. He kept up his daily routine of morning and evening prayers and spinning. His literary and religious studies, which had been neglected in the midst of other activities, were now resumed; he read no less than 150 books, including Henry James's *The Varieties of Religious Experience,* Buckle's *History of Civilization,* Wells's *Outline of History,* Bernard Shaw's *Man and Superman,* Goethe's *Faust* and Kipling's *Barrack Room Ballads.* There is no doubt that, in spite of occasional pinpricks, prison life proved for him, as Tagore once put it, 'arrest cure'.

# CHAPTER XXII

# Councils and Communities

THE revocation of the 'aggressive' programme in the non-co-operation campaign, whatever its justification from Gandhi's point of view, confused the Congress rank and file; it also divided its leadership. Some of the Congress leaders, including C. R. Das, Motilal Nehru and V. J. Patel, had never really favoured the boycott of the new legislatures brought into being by the Indian Reforms Act of 1919. Born lawyers and orators, they were in their element in legislatures. In 1920 they had allowed themselves to be persuaded by the Mahatma to agree to the boycott. Now that mass civil disobedience was no longer in the offing they felt that the only way of keeping up resistance to the Government was to enter the Central and Provincial Legislatures, not to work the new constitution, but to expose its limited and irresponsible character.

The Government of India 'under the reformed constitution' was not answerable to the Central Legislature. The upper chamber, the Council of State, had a majority of official and nominated members. In the lower chamber, the Central Legislative assembly, nearly one-third of the members were British officials or their Indian nominees. Hardly more than one-seventh of the budget was votable by the Central Legislative assembly. The Governor-General had powers to 'certify' as law measures rejected by the legislature.

The provinces were governed under a hybrid system known as 'dyarchy', which entrusted some departments to the control of ministers responsible to the legislature, and left others, including finance and law and order, in the charge of officials directly responsible to the Governor, who possessed the power of veto. The Swarajists (as the Congress leaders who were in favour of entering the Councils came to be known) acknowledged the limited utility of the legislatures. These legislatures were, according to them, masks put on by the British bureaucracy to deceive the world, and it was for Congressmen to tear off these masks. The legislatures could not bring real power to the people, but they could be made useful instruments in political warfare; if Congressmen could muster sufficient strength in the legislatures to reject official bills and to refuse the supplies, the Government would either have to use its special powers or give in to the verdict of the legislature. Such a situation was in any case bound to expose to the world that the constitution under which the country was governed left the ultimate authority in the hands of an irremovable executive. Some of the Swarajists were influenced by the tactics which Parnell and his party had adopted with success in the House of Commons in the agitation for Irish Home Rule.[1] 'Continuous, consistent and persistent obstruction,' was intended to turn the councils from a tool in the hands of the Government into a thorn in its side.

Soon after Gandhi's imprisonment in March 1922, signs of a serious rift appeared among his followers.

C. R. Das, who had been making plans for a council-entry campaign in Alipore gaol, threw himself into this campaign after his release. In his presidential address to the Gaya session of the Indian National Congress in December 1922 he proposed that the councils should either be amended in a manner suitable to the attainment of Indian freedom or ended completely. He did not consider entry into councils as inconsistent with the non-co-operation movememt. Boycott was in fact being carried to the precincts of the council chambers, to the very heart of the official citadel. The argument did not convince Gandhi's faithful followers, to whom council-entry was not a change of tactics but a violation of the principles of non-violent non-co-operation. As one of them observed: 'Ours is a purity mvement, and as such is above diplomacy. To enter the councils with the object of making them a failure is not only diplomacy but it is also diplomatic duplicity which every non-co-operator should disdain'.[2]

V. J. Patel had declared that entry into legislatures was like smuggling oneself into the enemy's fort with a view to conquering it. His brother Vallabhbhai Patel retorted that the fortress of the enemy was not located in the legislatures, and that so long as it lay elsewhere the Government could continue to function for a hundred years without a legislature.

Vallabhbhai Patel, Rajagopalachari and others who were opposed to changes in the non-co-operation programme came to be known as 'No-Changers'. Most of them were actuated by a sentiment of loyalty to their leader who was in gaol. In spite of the

[1] Patel, G. I.: *Vithalbhai Patel*, Vol. II, p. 540.
[2] *Ibid.*, p. 537.

support he received from Motilal Nehru, Srinivas Iyengar and
V. J. Patel, C. R. Das could not secure a majority in the Gaya
Congress. The policy of boycotting legislatures remained un-
altered. Immediately after the session, Das resigned the president-
ship of the Congress and founded the Swaraj Party, with himself
as its leader and Motilal Nehru as secretary. The breach between the two groups of Congressmen was now open.

Efforts at a compromise between the Swarajists and No-
Changers were made. A special session of the Indian National
Congress was convened at Delhi in September 1923 to take a
final decision on the Congress attitude to the elections, which
were scheduled to be held in November 1923. Maulana Mahomed
Ali, the Khilafat leader, who had meanwhile been released from
gaol, threw his weight in favour of the Swarajists; he created a
stir in the Congress session by quoting a message he professed
to have received from the Mahatma ('through some spiritual
trick, maybe through telepathy') that the Congress was free to
amend non-co-operation to suit the changed conditions in the
country. The No-Changers decided to remain neutral on council
entry, with the result that the Swarajists received the approval
of the Congress to participate in the elections. The Swarajists
had barely two months to fight the elections, but they succeeded
in capturing a solid bloc of seats in the Central Legislative
Assembly, a substantial representation in provincial legislatures
and even a majority in the Central Provinces Legislative Council.
Motilal Nehru led the Swaraj Party in the Central Legislative
Assembly, while Das took up the leadership of the party in
Bengal Legislative Council.

Meanwhile, on January 11, 1924 Gandhi had been transferred
to Sassoon Hospital, Poona for an operation following an acute
attack of appendicitis. His premature release on medical
grounds did not please him; the illness of a prisoner, he argued,
did not afford a valid reason for his release. The hundreds of
telegrams of congratulation betrayed, he said, 'hopes of results
from me which stagger me'. The wish which he had once
cherished of release from gaol by the order of a 'Swaraj Parliament' had in any case been frustrated.

Lord Reading's judgment that Gandhi's energies after his release would be distracted by dissensions in the Congress was
not far wrong. The Swarajists had fought the elections and secured a firm foothold in the legislatures. They were nevertheless keen to receive Gandhi's blessing. C. R. Das and Motilal
Nehru paid a visit to Juhu, a seaside resort near Bombay,

where Gandhi was convalescing. They had long discussions, but were unable to convince Gandhi. The 'obstruction from within' which Swarajists advocated seemed to him a contradiction in terms; one could either co-operate or non-co-operate with the government; it was no use trying to sail under false colours. The councils, warned Gandhi, gave condiments not bread. Though unconvinced himself of the wisdom of council-entry, Gandhi decided not to stand in the way of the Swarajists and advised the 'No-Changers' to maintain an attitude of 'neutrality' towards legislative work.

Nehru and Das had gone to Gandhi to convince him and to get his powerful support for the Swaraj Party. In this they did not succeed. The events of the next few months, however, were to pave the way for domination of the political stage by the Swaraj Party. Gandhi realized that during his absence the political climate had changed. The non-co-operators were non-co-operating 'not so much with the government, but against each other'. Hindu-Muslim unity had gone to pieces. The constructive programme did not seem to appeal to the intelligentsia. He was anxious to prevent a split in the Congress; he knew the damage which had been done by the Surat split of 1907. He made a gesture to the Swarajists, which to many of his followers savoured of a surrender. After a visit to Bengal, where the Provincial Government had launched an offensive against the Swaraj Party by clapping its members into prison on charges of violence, he issued, jointly with Motilal Nehru and C. R. Das, a statement recommending that the non-co-operation programme should be suspended, with the exception of the boycott of foreign cloth, and that the Swaraj Party should become an integral part of the Congress organization with powers to raise and administer its own funds. The constructive programme and the spinning franchise were to continue. The new policy was, however, a definite triumph for the Swarajists.

The Gandhi-Nehru-Das pact was ratified at the Belgaum Congress in December 1924. On the eve of the session over which he presided, Gandhi held informal talks with the leaders of the two groups to prevent an open rift in the Congress session. He made another gesture to the Swarajists by omitting from his Working Committee 'No changers' such as Rajagopalachari and Vallabhbhai Patel. He was now not only for tolerating the Swarajists, but for strengthening them. To some observers, including his faithful 'No-Changers,' it seemed that he had yielded too much ground to the Swarajists. The Viceroy wrote home:

'Gandhi is now attached to the tail of Das and Nehru, although they try their utmost to make him and his supporters
think that he is one of the heads, if not the head.'[1]

If the rift in the Congress talks on council-entry was one disappointment to Gandhi after his release from gaol, the division
between Hindus and Muslims was another and greater.

The Hindu-Muslim unity of the heyday of the non-co-operation movement was now a mere memory. Trust had given way to
distrust. Apart from the riots which periodically disfigured several
towns, there was a new bitterness in politics and in the Press.
A number of Hindu leaders, such as Lajpat Rai, Madan Mohan
Malaviya and Shraddhanand, felt that the Muslim masses had
received a dangerous awakening through the coalescence of the
Khilafat and the non-co-operation movements, and that it was
necessary for Hindus to adopt measures of self-defence
against Muslim communalism, which was the more dangerous
because it appeared to them to have the backing of the British
Government. Many Muslim politicians who had been in the forefront of the Khilafat movement had also had second thoughts and
felt that they had too readily joined hands with the Congress
in fighting for a new order, in which the position of the Muslim
community was not likely to be too secure.

In an atmosphere of mutual suspicion and fear every incident
was twisted and every move of one community was suspect to
the other. The Moplah outbreak in 1921, in which the Muslims
of Malabar had wreaked their fanaticism on their Hindu neighbours was a painful memory to the Hindus. The *Shuddhi* movement for the conversion of non-Muslims to Hinduism and the
*sangathan* movement for the unity of Hindus evoked counter-
blasts from Muslims in the form of *tabligh* and *tanzim* movements. The new proselytizing twist to Hinduism was resented
by the Muslim intelligentsia who, paradoxically enough, saw
nothing wrong in the conversion of non-Muslim to Islam. But
there was no room for logic in an atmosphere clouded by hazy
memories and vague misgivings. The very Muslims who, as a
gesture to their Hindu neighbours, had voluntarily given up
cow-slaughter during the favourable climate of 1920-22, now
insisted on ostentatiously exercising it as a religious obligation. The Hindus asserted the equally provocative right to
play music before mosques while conducting their religious pro-

[1] Reading, Marquess of: *Rufus Isaacs, First Marquess of Reading*,
    Vol. II, p. 304.

cessions. Then there were the endless wrangles about discrimination in favour of one community or the other in the distribution of official patronage.

There were not a few who put down the new tension to the non-co-operation movement and its alliance with the Khilafat cause, and blamed Gandhi for having played with the masses and roused them prematurely. 'The awakening of the masses,' wrote Gandhi, 'was a necessary part of the training. I would do nothing to put the people to sleep again.' However, he wanted this awakening to be diverted into constructive channels. The two communities had to be educated out of the mental morass into which they had slipped. Through the pages of his weekly journals he gave his own diagnosis of the communal disease; a whole issue of *Young India* was devoted to the subject. He argued that Hindu-Muslim tension could never have taken the form it did if the country had understood his method; the doctrine of non-violence held the key not only to the political freedom of the country but also to peace between the communities. A civilized society which had given up violence as a means of settling individual disputes could also eschew violence for reconciling differences between groups. Disagreements could be resolved by mutual tolerance and compromise, private arbitration, and in the last resort by appeal to the courts. Hearts could never be united by breaking heads. To Gandhi, the points of friction between the two communities seemed a travesty of true religion. Was it religion that drove a group of Hindu worshippers to lead a procession noisily before a mosque just as the 'faithful' knelt for prayer? Was it a religious obligation laid on the Muslim to lead cows to slaughter to wound the feelings of his Hindu neighbours? And what was the use of proselytizing when the conversion was not a moral or spiritual uplift, but 'crossing from one compartment to another', with one thing on the lips and another in the heart? As for the competition for jobs, there were after all a limited number to go round. Gandhi was prepared to concede special educational facilities to communities which were relatively backward to qualify for higher appointments, but to make religion instead of merit the criterion of employment was to cut at the root of the administration.

By probing into the causes of antagonism, and by appealing to the good sense of the communities, Gandhi had hoped to restore sanity. But communal tension showed no signs of abatement. There were outbreaks at Sambhar, Amethi and Gulbarga. A riot in Kohat in September 1924 was particularly serious: 155 Hindus were killed and practically the whole Hindu population was driven out of the town. This carnage hurt him deeply, the more so as he felt that the awakening which the non-co-operation movement brought about had run into destructive channels.

Out of his personal anguish, Gandhi sought a way in a fast: the country's reaction was instantaneous. A 'Unity Conference' was convened at Delhi and met within a week of the commencement of the fast. The 300 delegates included the Metropolitan of India, Dr Westcott, Annie Besant, the Ali brothers, Swami Shraddhanand and Madan Mohan Malviya. The conference affirmed freedom of conscience and religion, but condemned the use of compulsion and violence. It passed a number of resolutions designed to generate goodwill and to dissipate mutual suspicion. On the morning of October 8, 1924, twenty-one days after he had begun it, the Mahatma broke his fast in the presence of leaders of all the communities. As the chanting of verses from the *Koran* and the *Upanishads* mingled with Christian hymns C. F. Andrews noted that 'hearts were drawn together'.

But this harmony was not to last long. Within a few months Gandhi had to confess that bitter experience had taught him that those who took the name of unity meant disunion, that the leaders of the two communities were fighting not for loaves and fishes, but 'fighting like the proverbial dog, not for the bone but for the shadow'. In January 1927, he told a meeting at Comilla in Bengal that the Hindu-Muslim problem had passed out of human hands into God's hands.

Though in the pages of *Young India* from 1925 onwards Gandhi continued to devote occasional attention to the Hindu-Muslim problem, he had almost despaired of a solution. He saw the urban intelligentsia split into antagonistic groups but felt he could not react on it: 'Their method is not my method, I am trying to work from the bottom upward.'

# CHAPTER XXIII

# From the Bottom Up

DURING the next three years Gandhi retired from the political scene; to be precise, he retired only from the political controversies of the day to devote his time to the less spectacular but more important task of nation-building 'from the bottom up'.

He toured the country extensively from one end to the other, using every mode of transport from railway trains to bullock-carts. He walked through bush, brier, mud and water to penetrate into the interior of the Indian countryside. Everywhere he met with a welcome, which is the prerogative in India of saints and prophets. To the thousands who flocked to his meetings in villages, most of whom knew little of modern civilization or Indian politics, he was an *Avatara*, an incarnation of God. He hated this deification and endeavoured to transmute it into something positive and constructive. He exhorted the people to shake off age-old social evils such as child-marriage and untouchability, and to ply the spinning-wheel.

In the later twenties it was usual for British observers to describe Gandhi as a spent force and for Indian politicians to speak of the retirement of the saint of Sabarmati. It was obvious enough that the politics of the day, the debates in the Central and Provincial Legislatures and the communal controversies in the Press did not excite Gandhi's interest. Political freedom was, in his opinion, dependent upon the social and economic regeneration of the country; this regeneration had to come through the efforts of the people themselves. 'The fact is,' he had written, 'that political emancipation means a rise of mass-consciousness. It cannot come without affecting all the branches of national activity.'

In his speeches and writings of these years two themes are recurrent: the spinning-wheel and untouchability. The spinning-wheel, or rather its product, *khadi*, had figured in the non-co-operation programme, but during these years of political lull Gandhi turned it into a cult. He spoke of the 'thread of destiny';

he suggested a 'khadi franchise' for the Congress organization, and even envisaged a 'yarn currency'. Western-educated Indians, even ardent Congressmen, wondered whether the khadi cult was not being overdone. To the Government, once the threat of civil disobedience was over, his emphasis on Khadi seemed only a bee in his bonnet. It was not until khadi again became part of an active political campaign in 1930 that the Government took it seriously, and then too as an economic weapon in a political struggle.

That Gandhi's almost emotional attachment to the spinning-wheel should have baffled both the British and the Western-educated town-bred Indians, is not surprising. They were both unable, the former from lack of will, the latter from lack of knowledge, to grasp the incredible poverty of the Indian village. Deeply religious as Gandhi was, he wrote: 'For the starving men and women, liberty and God are merely letters put together without the slightest meaning; the deliverer of these unfortunate people would be one who brought them a crust of bread.' Not only were the landless labourers steeped in poverty, but there were millions of peasants who spent nearly six months in enforced under-employment. Their pitifully low income, argued Gandhi, could be usefully supplemented by cottage industries. And there was no cottage industry so simple and natural to the Indian village as hand-spinning; people could spin and weave cloth in their own homes just as they cooked their food. True, the spinning-wheel could make only a meagre addition to the slender resources of the peasant, but, as Gandhi explained to the Rotary Club of Calcutta in August 1925, one-tenth of the population of India, which lived on one meal a day and could not earn on the average more than three rupees a month, was bound to consider even an income of five or six rupees from the spinning-wheel as a fortune. When Tagore expressed the fear that the emphasis on the spinning-wheel would bring about a 'death-like sameness in the country', Gandhi replied:

'I did not want the poet to forsake his music, the farmer his plough, the lawyer his brief, and the doctor his lancet. They are to spin only thirty minutes every day as a sacrifice. I have indeed asked the famishing man or woman, who is idle for work whatsoever to spin for a living and the half-starved farmer to spin during his leisure to supplement his resources.'

Thus while the spinning-wheel had an economic significance for the farmer, the labourer, or the helpless widow in the village, to the townsman its appeal was based on moral or, as Gandhi would have put it, on spiritual grounds. India's towns had flourished at the expense of the villages, but now they had a chance to make amends for their past sins by buying cloth spun and woven in village homes, and thus to forge a link, economic as well as sentimental, between town and village.

The spinning-wheel gradually became the centre of rural up-lift in the Gandhian scheme of Indian economics; round it were to be built up anti-malaria campaigns, improvements in sanitation, settlements of village disputes, conservation and breeding of cattle, and hundreds of other beneficent activities required for the resuscitation of the village. The economics of the spinning-wheel were thus the economics of a new village economy. Primarily advocated as a solution of chronic under-employment in the villages, the spinning-wheel became something more than a simple tool of a cottage industry. In his efforts to 'sell' the spinning-wheel to the people, Gandhi romanticized it. He put it forward, not only as a panacea for economic ills but also for national unity and freedom. It became a symbol of defiance of foreign rule, the 'livery of freedom', as Jawaharlal Nehru picturesquely described it.

There is no doubt that the spinning-wheel symbolized Gandhi's protest against industrialism and materialism. But it would not have meant so much to him if it had not become a means of his deep identification with the humblest and the poorest in the land. 'The more I penetrate the villages,' he wrote, 'the greater is the shock delivered as I perceive the blank stare in the eyes of the villagers I meet. Having nothing else to do but to work as labourers side by side with their bullocks, they have become almost like them.' These skeletons behind the bullocks haunted him day and night. When somebody suggested that the country could patiently wait for prohibition, he said, 'Ask the wife of a drunkard to be patient; see what she will think of you. I happen to be the wife of thousands of drunkards and I cannot be patient.' He was not only the wife of thousands of drunkards, but of millions of semi-starved villagers of India; with his imaginative sympathy he could enter into the thoughts and feelings of others. The consciousness of the poverty and misery of the villages of India had gone like iron into his soul. 'The moment someone asks me (about the spinning-wheel)', he said, 'a whole volcano surges up within me.' Often his words betrayed his anguish. He told a meeting at Jalpaiguri: 'India is dying . . . if you want to save India, do it by doing the little I ask for. I want you to take up the wheel betimes or perish.' And he told the fastidious students of Chittagong that 'the pauperism of India is coarser than the coarsest Chittagong *khaddar*'.

He used his tours to liberate the people from an age-long inertia, fear and supersititon. He frowned on gold and silver caskets in which addresses were presented to him and asked for something 'cheaper, local and artistic'. He auctioned the caskets presented to him and credited the proceeds to his *khadi* fund. He chided the people of a village for wasting money on garlands for him: 'For every rupee saved on these garlands you should give sixteen women one meal.' While in Southern India he condemned in no uncertain terms the evil of 'devadasis'. To a municipal committe in Mysore, which boasted of a project of three lakes for water supply and prospects of electrifying the town in six months, he offered his congratulations but with the question, 'Can you assure children of the town cheap and clean milk? So long as you do not take the broom and bucket in your hands,' he added, 'you cannot make towns and cities clean.'

# CHAPTER XXIV

# The Rising Tempo

WHEN Jawaharlal Nehru returned to India in December 1927, after a twenty-month absence in Europe, he sensed a change in the political atmosphere. 'Early in 1926,' he writes, 'India was still quiescent, passive, perhaps not fully recovered from the effort of 1919-22; in 1928 she seemed fresh, active and full of suppressed energy.'[1] Signs of discontent were visible in several sectors of society, particularly among industrial workers, peasants, and middle class youth. Trade unions were gaining strength and labour was restive. The All-India Trade Union Congress had become a militant and class-conscious body, and among those who took an interest in its affairs were Jawaharlal Nehru and Subhas Chandra Bose. A number of strikes took place in the late twenties, the most notable being those which affected the textile industry in Bombay, the jute bills in Bengal, and iron and steel works in Jamshedpur. The labour movement was not directly connected with the political movement but it was at least against the existing order of things.

Apart from sporadic acts of political violence which gave the Government an anxious time, Youth Leagues sprang up all over the country. A number of youth conferences were held in which radical solutions for political, social and economic ills were put forth.

Agrarian discontent was brewing in several provinces, but it was in Bardoli *taluk*, under the leadership of Vallabhbhai Patel, in Gujerat in Bombay Presidency, that it came to a head. The Government tried to break the peasants' resistance. It offered concessions to those who would pay up; it tried to win over the richer or the weaker peasants; it sold crops for a song, and forfeited, in lieu of the tax, land, household goods, and cattle. Since no one from the villages would either carry or buy the confiscated property, Pathans were imported to do the dirty work. The peasants' weapon against weaker brethren or high-handed officials was boycott, and this weapon they used with

[1] Nehru: *Autobiography*, p. 170.

deadly effect. Gandhi was deeply interested in this large-scale experiment in Satyagraha to which he gave his support in public and private. A successful struggle after years of inertia was an uplifting experience for lovers of Indian freedom; the campaign was an index to the latent energy which was waiting to be harnessed to the national cause.

Meanwhile, Indian politics had been emerging out of the doldrums of the mid-twenties. The Swaraj Party had held the political stage since 1923. It had set out to create an atmosphere of resistance to the bureaucracy and to wreck the constitution. Founded by Pandit Motilal Nehru and C. R. Das, it had counted amongst its members such outstanding men as Lajpat Rai and Madan Mohan Malaviya. It had started well. In 1923 and 1924, in two provinces, it had made the system of dyarchical provincial government unworkable. In the Central Legislative Assembly it had delivered calculated blows at the prestige of the Government in spite of the communal franchise and the solid bloc of official and nominated members; it had thrown out budgets and demanded a round table conference for a new constitution. The early official impression of the Swaraj Party may be gleaned from a letter which the Viceroy wrote to the Secretary of State in London: 'For the present, the Swarajist has it all his own way; there is none to compare with him; there is none to attack him . . . The Moderate presents a very dull and dreary appearance as compared with the Swarajists.'[1]

The high discipline of the Swaraj Party did not last long. The lack of an absolute majority in the legislatures made co-operation with other parties necessary, and this co-operation had sometimes to be purchased at a high price in terms of principles. The Government could lure the weaker members of the party by throwing crumbs of official patronage in their way—a provincial ministership or a visit to Geneva. Some of those who had been elected on the communal franchise could not escape the virus of communalism which was rampant in the country. The Muslim members gradually fell off, and the Swarajists from Maharashtra picked up the slogan of 'responsive co-operation'. The crowning blow came with the defection of Lajpat Rai, the Deputy-Leader of the party. The general elections in 1926 reduced the strength of the Swarajists both at the centre and in the provinces. Except in Madras they lost seats everywhere. In the United Provinces Motilal Nehru was the only Swarajist

[1] Reading, Marquess of: *Rufus Isaacs, First Marquess of Reading*, Vol. II, p. 283.

elected to the Central Legislative Assembly. 'It was a fight,' observed Nehru, 'between the forces of nationalism and a low order of communalism and the latter won.'

The Government now found it less difficult to have its way in the legislatures. In February 1926, before the general elections, Motilal Nehru had declared, 'We have no further use for these sham institutions.' His son records how he became more and more disillusioned and was driven to the painful conclusion that constitutional methods were ineffective and futile in India in the conditions which were then prevailing. The Swarajists' disillusionment with parliamentary methods was to prove an important factor in their return to the Gandhian fold.

In spite of the many undercurrents of discontent, Indian politics nevertheless seemed placid on the surface in 1927. Lord Reading had prophesied that his successor would have an easy interlude of eighteen months, which would be only a lull before the storm. The prophesy turned out to be true, but the storm was brought on by the British Government itself. On November 2, 1927, a number of Indian leaders including Gandhi, Motilal Nehru, Ansari and Jinnah, were summoned to the Viceroy's House at Delhi and handed a document which announced the appointment of a Royal Commission. This was the only business transacted at this meeting: Gandhi, who had travelled a thousand miles, wondered why a postcard had not been used to convey the information. The document handed to the Indian leaders was not even news, as its contents had been correctly forecast by the Press. 'Never had Indian leadership felt itself to be so affronted,' writes the Viceroy's biographer.[1] The Indian Reforms Act of 1919, under which India was being governed, contained a clause for a review of the constitutional position after ten years. This provision had been regarded as a safeguard by the British Conservatives and as a lever for further advance by Indian nationalists. The appointment of a Royal Commission in 1927, two years ahead of the schedule, raised a spate of speculation. It was suggested that the Conservative Government in England were anxious to handle the Indian question itself rather than leave it to a Labour Government which might come into power after the general elections. Support for this view is lent by the observation in Birkenhead's *The Last Phase* that 'we could not afford to run the slightest risk that the nomination of the 1928 Commission should be in the hands of our successors'.

[1] Johnson, Alan Campbell: *Viscount Halifax*, p. 190.

Whatever may have been the motive behind Lord Birken-head's move, it completely misfired. The members of the commission, with the exception of its chairman, Sir John Simon, were all 'second flight men'; the junior member of the commission (as Viscount Simon describes him in his *Retrospect*) was Clement Attlee, the future Premier of Britain, then a back-bencher in the House of Commons. What hurt Indian feelings most was that no Indian had been included in this 'all-white commission'. The argument that a Royal Commission answerable to the British Parliament could not draw its personnel from outside may have been sound constitutional practice, but it was a political blunder of the first magnitude. The commission came to be looked upon in India as an inquisition by foreigners into India's fitness for self-government; the Indian National Congress decided to boycott the commission 'at every stage and in every form'. Even moderate and Muslim politicians, whose co-operation Birkenhead had almost taken for granted, were unanimous in denouncing the commission. Black-flag demonstrations and shuttered shop-windows greeeted the 'Simon Seven' in most of the towns they visited.

The boycott of the Simon Commission had raised the political barometer and brought together a number of parties which had otherwise little in common. A challenge from Birkenhead stung Indian leaders to seek an agreed solution of the constitutional problem. 'I have twice in three years,' declared Birkenhead, 'during which I have been Secretary of State, invited our critics in India to put forward their own suggestions for a constitution to indicate to us the form in which in their judgment any reforms of constitution may take place'. 'That offer,' he added, 'is still open.' As an answer to this challenge, a series of All-Parties Conferences took place and a constitutional scheme was drafted. The *Nehru Report*, as it came to be known, envisaged a parliamentary system of government, joint electorates and some complicated formulae for the protection of minorities. When it came up for approval before the last meeting of the All-Parties Conference in August 1928, the controversy on 'dominion status' *v.* 'complete independence' flared up. The *Nehru Report* had adopted dominion status as the basis of its recommendations to secure the lowest common measure of agreement among the Congress, the moderates and other political groups. The younger wing of the Congress did not like Indian freedom to be hedged in by any limitations. But Motilal Nehru was keen on carrying through the report, which bore his name, *in toto*.

Jawaharlal Nehru and Subhas Chandra Bose threatened to resign from the Congress; their resignations were not accepted, but they founded an Independence League to promote among Congressmen the ideology of complete independence. The annual session of the Congress was due in December 1928, in Calcutta, and it looked as if a head-on collision between the old guard and the younger group in the Congress was inevitable.

Gandhi had played little part in the All-Parties Conference or in the drafting of the *Nehru Report*. Nevertheless, he had commended the report for satisfying 'all reasonable aspirations'. He had taken little active interest in the Congress session at Gauhati in 1926 or at Madras in 1927. It is doubtful if he would have taken any more interest in the Calcutta session in December 1928 were it not for an urgent summons from Pandit Motilal Nehru. The Pandit, anticipating a crisis at Calcutta, had urged the Mahatma to attend the Congress session: 'You have made me sit in the Presidential chair and put upon my head a crown of thorns; but at least do not look at my difficulties from a distance.'

A rift at the Calcutta Congress was avoided by a compromise formula framed by Gandhi. The Congress passed a resolution accepting the *Nehru Report* on the condition that, if by December 31, 1929, it was not accepted by the Government, the Congress would demand complete independence and fight for it, if necessary, by resorting to non-violent non-co-operation. Gandhi would have preferred to give the Government two years to make up its mind and for the Congress to set its house in order. To those who talked glibly of independence, he said, 'you must take the name of independence on your lips as the Muslims utter the name of *Allah* or the pious Hindu utters the name of Krishna or Rama'. The British Government, he warned the Congress, was going to concede neither dominion status nor independence until the nation was ready to assert its rights, until 'the necessary sanctions had been forged.' If the Congress were to give a non-violent battle to the Government, it had first to close its ranks. The Congress roll was, he said, a 'bogus show'; what the Congress needed was a living register of members; if Congressmen were serious about the resolution they had passed, hard work lay ahead of them.

The Calcutta Congress opened the way for Gandhi's return to politics. If the British Government did not concede the demands of the Congress—and there was little prospect of their doing so—the Congress was committed to a non-co-operation

movement and it was obvious to all that Gandhi alone could
conduct such a movement. In March 1922 he had been sentenced
to six years imprisonment and premature release in 1924 for
reasons of health had not pleased him. Not until March 1928 had
he felt 'morally' freed from his term of imprisonment. Political as
well as personal reasons were thus dictating an end of his retirement from active politics.

# CHAPTER XXV

# Year of Grace

THE Calcutta session of the Congress (December 1928) had given the British Government, to use the words of Jawaharlal Nehru, 'an offer of a year's grace and a polite ultimatum'. If dominion status was not conceded by the end of 1929, the Congress was to launch a struggle with the Government. Gandhi had been toying with the idea of visiting Europe in 1929, but having piloted the main resolution of the Congress session, he felt it would be 'an act of desertion' to leave India. By giving a year's ultimatum, the Congress had thrown the ball into their opponent's court, and the next move lay with the Government. He knew that freedom was not likely to descend as a gift from the British.

It was not part of the strategy of Satyagraha to plan moves months and years ahead. Meanwhile, the country had to be educated and disciplined. Gandhi toured everywhere, calling upon the people to spin and weave in their homes, and to boycott foreign cloth. He evolved a scheme whereby Congress organizations were to enrol volunteers to sell *khadi*, and to collect foreign cloth from door to door. Foreign cloth was to be publicly burnt and the foreign cloth shops picketed. Early in March 1929 he was at Calcutta when a large pyramid of foreign finery was ceremoniously consigned to the flames. The Bengal Provincial Congress Committee received a notice that it was an offence to burn foreign cloth in or near a public place. Gandhi had as yet no intention of breaking the law. 'I am capable,' he observed, 'of breaking all the regulations that hurt my moral sense, but that time is not for me yet.' He had been advised, however, that Shraddhanand Park at Calcutta, where the meeting was held, was not a public thoroughfare. As the bonfire was lighted he was placed under arrest. He refused to sign the bond requiring him to appear before the Chief Presidency Magistrate on March 5th. However, the case was postponed to enable him to fulfil his engagements in Burma, which he was visiting after fourteen years.

On his return from Burma three weeks later, he presented himself for trial and was fined one rupee. Someone paid the fine without his knowledge. The inevitable result of this prosecution was to give a fillip to the boycott of foreign cloth. The day of Gandhi's trial was celebrated by bonfires of foreign cloth all over the country.

The Government saw the growing signs of unrest. Apart from the ultimatum which the Congress had given, and the possibility of a clash early in 1930, there were other disquieting symptoms. Industrial labour was seething with discontent. There had been strikes in Bombay and Jamshedpur. In April 1929, when Speaker Patel rose in the Central Legislative Assembly to give his ruling on the Public Safety Bill, which sought more powers for the executive to curb the 'extremists', bombs were thrown from the visitors' gallery. Two young men, Bhagat Singh and B. K. Datt, were arrested; their intention, they deposed later, was not to kill anybody but 'to make the deaf hear'. Terrorist outrages occurred in several parts of the country, and groups of young men were rounded up and prosecuted for political violence in what came to be known as a series of 'conspiracy cases'. These anarchists became popular heroes; even those who deplored their method applauded their motive. Public feeling reached a peak when a number of them went on hunger strike as a protest against the treatment of political prisoners; one of them, Jatin Dass, died in gaol and was honoured as a martyr.

Official reaction to this heightened tension was to arm the executive with still greater authority. The Public Safety Bill, which Speaker Patel had ruled out of order, was nevertheless made law under the Viceroy's special powers. In March 1929 a number of trade union leaders, 'some of them communists, some near-communists and some trade unionists', were brought up for trial in what came to be known as the 'Meerut Conspiracy Case'. 'It seems to me,' wrote Gandhi, 'that the motive behind these prosecutions is not to kill communism but to strike terror.' He added that 'The Government were giving the usual periodical exhibition of its red claws which usually remain under cover'.

However, the Viceroy, Lord Irwin, had no intention of trying strong-arm methods only. In the summer of 1929 he visited England and conferred with British statesmen. Lord Irwin's mission was facilitated by a change of government in England. Wedgwood Benn, Secretary of State in the Labour Govern-

ment, shared Irwin's anxiety to reverse the process of estrangement of Indian opinion which had gone on since the appointment
of the Simon Commission. Benn approved of Irwin's proposal
for a Round Table Conference in London between the representatives of India and Britain to discuss the constitutional
problem. He also approved of Irwin's idea of heralding the
announcement of the conference by a declaration reaffirming
that the goal of British policy in India continued to be dominion
status. Neither Lloyd George nor Lord Reading—the two
stalwarts of the Liberal Party—gave much encouragement to
Lord Irwin. The Labour Government depended for its majority
upon the support of the Liberals, but the Secretary of State was
prepared to take the risk.

Lord Irwin returned to India on October 25, 1929. On October
31, came the issue of a 'Gazette Extraordinary' of the Government of India containing an announcement of a round table
conference. The Viceroy's announcement was an ingeniously
worded document which could mean much or little, but it had
a favourable reception in India. The moderate leaders, to
quote Lord Irwin's biographer, saw the conference as 'their
supreme opportunity for the full exercise of their intellectual
power and were henceforth Irwin's faithful allies'. The Congress
leaders, scanning the horizon for a gesture which might lead to
progress in self-government and prevent a clash with the Government, saw signs of 'a change of heart'. A 'joint manifesto'
issued under the signatures of Gandhi, Motilal Nehru, Patel,
Tej Bahadur Sapru, Annie Besant, Jawaharlal Nehru and others
expressed their appreciation of the sincerity underlying the declaration.

Lord Irwin's announcement was thus well received in India,
but a storm broke over him and the Labour Government in
England. The British Press and Parliament subjected the announcement to a protracted post mortem. The Labour Government, which did not have a clear majority in the House of Commons, was on the defensive. Wedgwood Benn explained the
declaration as a 're-statement' and an interpretation of Montagu's declaration of August 1917, and thus made out that no
radical departure had been made in British policy towards
India.

The debate in the British Parliament disillusioned Indian
leaders. Circumstances had compelled the Secretary of State to
belittle in Britain what the Viceroy had tried to boost in India.
The temporary bridge which the Viceroy's declaration had

thrown between the Government and the nationalists had been knocked down.

A last-minute effort, in which V. J. Patel and Tej Bahadur Sapru were the prime movers, was made for a reconciliation between the Congress and the Government. An interview between the Congress leaders and the Viceroy was arranged. The interview took place on December 23rd. That morning Lord Irwin had returned from a tour of South India, and as he approached the capital a bomb had exploded under the Viceregal train. Gandhi congratulated the Viceroy on his miraculous escape. There was not much progress, however, on the political plane. The Viceroy chastened by the recent debate in the British Parliament, was unable to give an assurance that the Round Table Conference would definitely discuss a scheme of reform on the basis of dominion status.

Soon after the abortive interview at Delhi, the Indian National Congress was to meet for its annual session at Lahore. The year of grace which the Calcutta Congress had offered to the British Government in December 1928 was drawing to a close; the Congress was pledged to a declaration for complete independence if dominion status was not conceded by Britain. The Congress leaders sought from the Viceroy something more than a vague indication of the direction of British policy to convince their party that India was assured of a sizable advance towards self-government. It was all very well for Lord Irwin to say 'that the assertion of a goal is of necessity a different thing from the goal's attainment', but such an approach could hardly help Gandhi and Motilal Nehru in carrying the rank and file with them at the ensuing Congress session. And the argument that it was impossible to prejudice the issue or encroach upon the constitutional responsibility of the British Parliament did not carry conviction to them. Had not the British Cabinet on several occasions committed itself to particular policies in anticipation of the Parliamentary verdict? The bland fact remained that the Labour Government had neither the courage, nor perhaps the conviction, to dismantle the imperial structure in India and to instal a self-governing dominion instead.

'All roads lead to Lahore,' Motilal Nehru had aptly summed up the political situation at the end of 1929 in a letter to V. J. Patel. The Lahore session was going to be a momentous one, as it was likely to declare a struggle which only Gandhi could lead. The choice of the Mahatma as President of the Congress seemed almost inevitable, but he declined the honour on the plea that he could not devote the necessary time to the day-to-day work of the presidency, and that in any case he could continue to serve the Congress without holding office. At his instance the All-India Congress Committee elected Jawaharlal Nehru, who thus entered this high office, to use his own words, 'not by a main entrance or even a side entrance but by a trap-door'.

Politically, the election of Jawaharlal Nehru was a masterstroke of the Mahatma. Only a year before there had been a clash between crabbed age and youth at the Calcutta Congress. Youth had looked askance at the outmoded shibboleths of the old guard. A compromise ingeniously devised by Gandhi had prevented a split. The Congress, instinct with new hope and energy, needed a young man at the helm. The forty-year-old Jawaharlal, whom Gandhi described as 'pure as crystal . . . truthful beyond suspicion . . . a knight *sans peur et sans reproche*', was to be in the fullness of time the Mahatma's politican heir. There was a bond of deep affection between the two men in spite of the twenty years and widely differing intellectual backgrounds which separated them. Gandhi had been unhappy with some of the activities of Jawaharlal since the latter's return from Europe at the end of 1927. 'You are going too fast,' he wrote to him early in 1928. 'You should have taken time to think and become acclimatized.' A few days later he confessed: 'The differences between you and me appear to be so vast and so radical that there seems to be no meeting ground between us.' This intellectual gulf widened or narrowed from time to time; it was rarely bridged, but it did not affect their emotional affinity or their mutual loyalty.

In December 1929 events were on the march, there was a promise of a struggle, and Jawaharlal was in his element.

# CHAPTER XXVI

# Civil Disobedience

THE Indian National Congress was meeting in the Punjab after exactly ten years. The Amritsar Congress was held in December 1919; the non-co-operation movement had followed in 1920. Was history going to repeat itself? There was little doubt that the Lahore Congress was going to be a momentous one. 'The year of grace' which the Calcutta Congress had granted was over. Dominion status had not been conceded; the offer of the 'minimum national demand' embodied in the *Nehru Report* would lapse; henceforth Swaraj would mean complete independence. At midnight on December 31, 1929, as the new year dawned, the Indian National Congress unfurled the flag of independence on the bank of the Ravi. The Congress called upon its members in the central and provincial legislatures to resign their seats and authorized the All-Indian Congress Committee to launch civil disobedience.

The significance of the Congress session was not lost upon the Government. According to Alan Campbell Johnson, Lord Irwin's biographer, the Viceroy seriously considered the banning of this session. Early in January, the Punjab Government advised the Government of India that, in the opinion of its legal advisers, Jawaharlal Nehru and S. D. Kitchlew should be prosecuted for speeches delivered by them as President-designate and Chairman of the Reception Committee of the Lahore Congress. The advice was not accepted, as events had already moved fast.

In an appraisement of the Congress position immediately after the Lahore Congress, the Viceroy reported to the Secretary of State 'the striking effect on the political situation made by the recent meeting at Lahore'. It had seemed clear, wrote the Viceroy, that the Lahore Congress would be the scene of a struggle between the two wings of the Congress which had clashed but compromised at Calcutta a year earlier; a split was avoided at Lahore by the 'capitulation' of Gandhi and Motilal Nehru to the left-wing Congressmen, consisting of 'revolutionaries' and 'irreconcilables' who were expected henceforth to provide the driving force of the Congress. Though the decision to boycott legislatures could still cause a split, the Congress as a whole, by passing the independence resolution, had, in the Viceroy's opinion, declared itself as a body which intended to pursue 'an illegitimate aim by illegal and unconstitutional means'.

There was little doubt that in executing the decisions of the Lahore session, the Congress would be guided by Gandhi. His writings and speeches acquired the forthright frankness which had marked them ten years earlier. The people had the right, he wrote, to alter or abolish an unjust government. If the atmosphere remained non-violent, he promised to lead a civil disobedience campaign. He was conscious of the risks inherent in a mass movement. The lesson of Chauri Chaura, however, had not been lost on Congressmen. At the same time, Gandhi made it known that there was to be no easy reversal of the movement once it was launched; while every possible effort was to be made to restrain the forces of violence, civil disobedience would continue 'so long as there is a single resister left free or alive'. In 1920-2 Gandhi had proceeded cautiously, spent months in preparing the country, graduated the programme of non-co-operation and shown an obvious reluctance in embarking upon mass civil disobedience. In 1930 he proceeded with swifter and surer steps; it was as if his labours in the previous decade had not been wasted and he was picking up the thread where he had left it in 1922. 'The call of 1920,' he wrote, 'was a call for preparation. The call in 1930 is for engaging in final conflict.'

A struggle between the Congress and the Government was now inevitable. In January 1930, Gandhi told Tagore that he was furiously thinking 'night and day'. The first step he took was to call for the celebration of 'Independence Day' on January 26. On that day, in the towns and villages of India, hundreds of thousands of people took a pledge that 'it was a crime against man and God to submit to British rule,' and undertook to join a campaign of civil disobedience and non-payment of taxes if the Congress launched it. Independence Day revealed the latent enthusiasm in the country; Gandhi felt the country was ripe for a mass movement. He suggested inaugurating the movement with a breach of the Salt Laws. The Salt Tax, though relatively light in incidence, hit the poorest in the land; but salt did not quite seem to fit into the plan of a national struggle for liberation. Salt manufacture was confined to the sea-coast or salt mines, and even if a strike could be organized among the politically backward labourers engaged in the industry, the pros-

pect of launching a successful Satyagraha struggle did not appear
to be bright. These and other doubts assailed Gandhi's closest
adherents even as they followed his lead.

Gandhi announced that he would himself perform the first
act of civil disobedience by leading a group of Satyagrahis to the
sea-shore for a breach of the Salt Laws. He communicated his
plans to the Viceroy in a letter, which was an indictment of
British rule as well as an appeal for restoring to India what
was her due:

'Dear Friend—before embarking on civil disobedience and
taking the risk I have dreaded to take all these years, I would
fain approach you and find a way out. My personal faith is absolutely clear. I cannot intentionally hurt anything that lives,
much less fellow-human beings even though they may do the
greatest wrong to me and mine. Whilst, therefore, I hold British
rule to be a curse, I do not intend to harm a single Englishman
or any legitimate interest he may have in India . . .

'I must not be misunderstood. Though I hold the British rule
in India to be a curse, I do not, therefore, consider Englishmen
in general to be worse than any other people on earth. I have the
privilege of claiming many Englishmen as dearest friends. Indeed much that I have learnt of the evil of British rule is due
to the writings of frank and courageous Englishmen who have
not hesitated to tell the unpalatable truth about that rule. . . .

'In common with many of my countrymen, I had hugged the
fond hope that the proposed Round Table Conference might
furnish a solution . . . But when you said plainly that you could
not give any assurance that you or the British Cabinet would
pledge yourselves to support a scheme of full dominion status,
the Round Table Conference could not possibly furnish the
solution for which vocal India is consciously, and dumb millions
unconsciously, thirsting.

'. . . if India is to survive as a nation, if the slow death by
starvation of her people is to stop, some remedy must be found
for immediate relief. The proposed conference is certainly not
the remedy. It is not a matter of carrying conviction by argument. The matter resolves itself into one of matching forces.
Conviction or no conviction, Great Britain would defend her
Indian commerce and interests by all the forces at her command. India must consequently evolve (non-violent) force enough
to free herself from that embrace of death . . .

'I know that in embarking on non-violence, I shall be running
what might be fairly termed a mad risk, but the victories of truth

have never been won without risks, often of the gravest character. Conversion of a nation that has consciously or unconsciously preyed upon another far more numerous, far more ancient and no less cultured than itself, is worth any amount of risk.

'I have deliberately used the word conversion. For my ambition is no less than to convert the British people through non-violence and thus make them see the wrong they have done to India. I do not seek to harm your people. I want to serve them even as I want to serve my own. I believe that I have always served them. I served them up to 1919 blindly. But when my eyes were opened, and I conceived non-co-operation, the object still was to serve them. I employed the same weapon that I have in all humility successfully used against the dearest members of my family. If I have equal love for your people with mine, it will not long remain hidden. It will be acknowledged by them even as members of my family acknowledged it after they had tried me for several years. If people join me, as I expect they will, the sufferings they will undergo, unless the British nation sooner retraces its steps, will be enough to melt the stoniest hearts.'

The Viceroy's reply was brief: it expressed his regret 'at Mr Gandhi's contemplating a course of action which was clearly bound to involve the violation of the law and danger to public peace'.

Gandhi decided to lead the first band of Satyagrahis from Ahmedabad to Dandi on the sea-shore. The Satyagrahis were selected from Sabarmati Ashram, which had, according to the testimony of one of its inmates, reached 'its zenith in physical energy and moral strength'.[1] Sabarmati was now assuming the role which Phoenix and Tolstoy Ashrams had done in South Africa; it became the recruiting ground for the vanguard of freedom and a hub of political activities. Richard Gregg has recorded how a correspondent of a British-owned paper, who had been sent to Ahmedabad to report what was going on in 'the enemy's camp', instead of being turned away was accommodated, at Gandhi's instance, in the Sabarmati Ashram, treated as a guest, and allowed to see things for himself.

The prayer meeting on the evening of March 11th had a record attendance. 'Our cause is strong,' said Gandhi, 'our means the purest, and God is with us. There is no defeat for Satyagrahis till they give up truth. I pray for the battle which begins to-

[1] Mirabehn: *Bapu's letters to Mira*, p. 101.

morrow.' That night perhaps the only person in the Ashram who slept was the Mahatma himself. Next morning, at 6.30, he began the 241-mile march to Dandi on the sea-shore. The seventy-nine Satyagrahis included scholars, newspaper editors, untouchables, weavers. The oldest was the sixty-one-year-old leader, the youngest a boy of sixteen. The people of Ahmedabad turned out in their thousands to cheer them. The roads were strewn with green leaves. Gandhi, although the oldest member of his volunteer band, walked so fast that younger men found it difficult to keep pace with him. He felt all the better for the exercise; he rose as usual at 4 a.m., conducted the morning prayers, addressed meetings in villages through which he passed, did his daily quota of spinning, wrote articles for his journals and letters to his correspondents. He announced that he would not return to Sabarmati Ashram until the Salt Tax was repealed.

Meanwhile, the authorities had been watching the movement with mingled anxiety and bewilderment. The British had no intention of liquidating their Indian Empire. Earl Russell, the Under-Secretary of State for India, had commented on the Congress demand for complete independence: 'None knows better than the Indians themselves how foolish it is to talk of complete independence. Dominion status is not possible at the moment and would not be for a long time.'

The first impulse of the Government, as of the Congress intellectuals, was to ridicule 'the kindergarten stage of political revolution', and to laugh away the idea that the King-Emperor could be unseated by boiling sea-water in a kettle. The experts of the Government of India did not take the breach of the Salt Tax seriously. Tottenham, a member of the Central Board of Revenue (the department which dealt with Salt Tax), described the breach of the Salt Laws 'as Mr Gandhi's somewhat fantastic project'. A committee of two senior officers reported early in February that salt did not appear to be a promising field for initiating a no-tax campaign; that the most that could happen was that small quantities of inferior salt would be sporadically produced in certain areas and consumed locally; that neither government revenues nor the price of salt were likely to be affected.

In the last week of March, the Government of India issued instructions 'based on past experience in handling such movements' to the local Provincial Governments, advising them to avoid situations in which they would have to make wholesale arrests or enter into a test of endurance with the Congress; it

was preferable to arrest only the leaders, whose imprisonment
was likely to discourage or disorganize the movement. If it became necessary to arrest large numbers of Satyagrahis, it was
advisable to use the minimum possible force: the use of force
against those who were not violent tended to alienate public sympathy. The local governments were exhorted to exercise special
care in avoiding congestion in gaols and in treating young boys
and women. This was sound advice, but unfortunately, as the
tempo of the movement grew, the temper of the authorities
also rose. Vallabhbhai Patel had already been arrested on March
7th under the orders of the local officials, who had acted without
consulting even the Provincial Government. Early in April Jawaharlal Nehru was arrested in Allahabad. From Dandi, where he
had made the first symbolic breach of the Salt Laws, Gandhi
sent a message that 'at present Indian self-respect is symbolized,
as it were, in a handful of salt in the Satyagrahi's hand. Let
the fist be broken, but let there be no surrender of salt'. No
less than 60,000 Indians were gaoled. Among those convicted for
breach of the Salt Laws were Rajagopalachari, Madan Mohan
Malaviya, J. M. Sen Gupta, B. G. Kher, K. M. Munshi, Devadas
Gandhi, Mahadev Desai, Bithalbhai Patel. Women from aristo-
cratic and middle-class homes picketed liquor and foreign cloth
shops.

There were stray cases of violence, such as in Chittagong,
where some terrorists raided the arsenal to seize arms. But on
the whole India remained non-violent. Those who had scoffed
at Salt Satyagraha and failed to see any connection between salt
and Swaraj had underrated Gandhi's knack for organizing the
Indian masses for corporate action. The Government also at last
did what it had been planning for so long and at the same time
dreading. It decided to arrest Gandhi.

The arrest took place on May 5, 1930 at Kradi, a village near
Dandi, under Bombay Regulation XXV of 1827, which was re-
surrected from the dusty covers of the state archives to detain
him without trial. Just before his arrest Gandhi had planned a
more aggressive phase of his 'non-violent rebellion' by 'raiding'
and taking possession of the salt depots at Dharsana. The raid,
which was led by the aged Imam Sahib, an inmate of the
Sabarmati Ashram, took place on May 21st. The leaders were
arrested and the rank and file beaten up; an account of this
raid was given in the *New Freeman* by an American correspondent Webb Miller: 'In eighteen years of reporting in twenty-
two countries I have never witnessed such harrowing scenes

as at Dharsana. Sometimes the scenes were so painful that I
had to turn away momentarily. One surprising feature was the
discipline of volunteers. It seemed they were thoroughly imbued
with Gandhi's non-violent creed.'

Meanwhile, the All-India Congress Committee had extended
the scope of civil disobedience to include the breach (besides the
Salt Tax) of forest laws, the non-payment of taxes in ryotwari
areas, and the boycott of foreign cloth, banks, shipping and insurance companies. A series of 'ordinances' issued by the Viceroy conferred extraordinary powers on the executive to enable
it to crush the Congress, or to use the official jargon, 'to cope
with the emergency'.

Gandhi's arrest stimulated rather than slackened resistance
to the Government. Though at the time official propaganda belittled it, the Government were aware of the hold Congress had
acquired over the people. In his *Rebel India*, Brailsford has
borne testimony to the influence of the Congress in several parts
of India, and particularly in Bombay. A similar testimony is available in official records; for example, in a report given by the
Director of the Intelligence Bureau to the Home Member,
after a visit to Bombay in August 1930. The Congress, he wrote,
was able to command whatever support it wanted in that town;
its volunteers and picketers were fed free by the people; its
'stranglehold' on business of every sort was complete; many
businessmen were prepared to continue in the movement,
even though ruin stared them in the face; in short, the Congress
was 'completely in command', with the initiative entirely in its
hands.

# CHAPTER XXVII

# *Truce*

SINCE his arrest in early May Gandhi had been making up arrears of rest in the Yeravda gaol in Poona, which he picturesquely described as 'Yeravda Mandir' (Yeravda Temple). In prison he maintained his routine of prayer, spinning and studies, and ceased to worry about the political situation in the country and the fate of the movement he had launched. He knew he had done his duty; he hoped the people would do theirs.

A week after his arrest, Lord Irwin published his correspondence with the British Premier and indicated that the civil disobedience movement had not deflected His Majesty's Government from its policy of constitutional reforms and the decision to hold a Round Table Conference in London. The Viceroy was at this time directing the sternest repression which nationalism had known in India, but he did not really relish the role. 'You know,' he had written to V. J. Patel as late as in April 1930, 'that no one wishes more fervently than I, that the affairs of India may speedily be again guided into smoother waters.' He did not discourage the efforts at conciliation made by George Slocombe, the correspondent of the *Daily Herald*, and the two moderate leaders Sapru and Jayakar.

George Slocombe, who had been distressed by the turn which events had taken in India, had gathered from an interview with Motilal Nehru that under certain conditions the Congress was prepared to call off civil disobedience. A little later, Motilal Nehru was arrested and lodged in Naini prison, where his son Jawaharlal had preceded him. The Nehrus were interviewed by Sapru and Jayakar on the possibility of a truce; since they would not commit themselves without consulting Gandhi, they were carried in a special train to Poona. The discussions revealed that there was little common ground between the Congress and the Government.

The Congress reaction to the peace feelers threw into sharp relief the gulf between the Congress and the British. In Britain,

Winston Churchill was carrying on a crusade against handing over the people of India to 'an oligarchy of lawyers, politicians, fanatics and greedy merchants'. 'We ought to make it perfectly clear,' he said, 'that we intend to remain rulers of India for a very long and indefinite period and though we welcome co-operation from loyal Indians, we will have no truck with lawlessness and treason'. Ramsay MacDonald's Labour Government continued in office with the support of the Liberals; it was in no position, even if it had the intention, to make a radical concession to India. In India, Lord Irwin's advisers were confident of crushing Gandhi's rebellion and carrying on the administration with the help of the moderates and the Muslims. The majority in the Viceroy's Executive Council and almost all the Governors and senior civil servants were for further tightening of the screws on the Congress.

Meanwhile the constitutional caravan had moved on. The report of the Simon Commission, published during the summer, made an elaborate survey of the Indian constitutional problem and meticulously catalogued the difficulties which hampered a substantial advance. Its recommendations were so low-pitched that they did not evoke the enthusiasm of even conservative opinion in India. The first Round Table Conference met in London in 1930. The Congress was not represented on it but some of the delegates, who had left their country in turmoil, were anxious to return with some tangible result and pleaded for a conciliatory policy towards the Congress. In his farewell address (January 19, 1931) Ramsay MacDonald expressed the hope that the Congress would participate in the next session of the conference. A little earlier, Lord Irwin's speech in the Central Legislature had included a surprisingly chivalrous reference to the 'spiritual force which impels Mr Gandhi to count no sacrifice too great in the cause, as he believes, of the India he loves'. Irwin had already decided not to interfere with a meeting of the Congress leaders in Allahabad. He released Gandhi and the members of the Congress Working Committee on January 25, 1931—the eve of Independence Day—to the accompaniment of a conciliatory statement.

The unconditional release of members of the Congress Working Committee had not by itself brought the Congress any nearer to the Government. The members of the Congress Working Committee as they congregated in Allahabad—where Motilal Nehru lay on his death-bed—saw no warrant to call off civil disobedience, but they withheld this decision from the

Press on receipt of a telegram from Sapru and Sastri, who were on their way back home and were anxious to give the Congress leaders first-hand impressions of the Round Table Conference. Gandhi was not impressed by the achievements of the conference; nor did he feel optimistic about the possibilities of an understanding with the Government. Nevertheless he wrote to Lord Irwin and asked for an interview. His argument was that as a Satyagrahi he had a moral obligation to make a response to the Viceroy's gesture in releasing the Congress Working Committee.

The Gandhi-Irwin parleys began on the afternoon of February 17, 1931. They lasted for a total of twenty-four hours, spread over eight meetings. There were long intervals during which hopes of a settlement alternately receded and revived, but finally, on the morning of March 4th, an agreement was reached. The Delhi Pact, or, to give it its popular name, the Gandhi-Irwin Pact, provided for discontinuance of civil disobedience on the part of the Congress, and the revocation of the ordinances and the release of civil disobedience prisoners on the part of the Government. The amnesty did not cover political prisoners detained without trial or convicted for covert or open violence; nor did it cover the Garhwali soldiers who had declined to fire at an unarmed crowd in Peshawar. The restitution of lands sold to third parties and the reinstatement of those who had lost their jobs during the non-co-operation movement were also not included in the agreement.

There was a concession in a small way to poor people on the sea-coast, to manufacture salt, and the recognition of picketing of foreign cloth. There was to be no inquiry into the allegations of excesses by the police; this was a crucial point on which both the Congress and the Government were very sensitive, and negotiations nearly broke down on it. Gandhi did not insist on the inquiry when Irwin told him that though he had the right to ask for an inquiry, it was wise to let bygones be bygones and not rake up bitterness afresh.

On the constitutional issue the Delhi Pact accepted safeguards 'in the interest of India' for such matters as defence, external affairs, minorities and finance. This was the clause which dealt Jawaharlal Nehru a 'tremendous shock', and which seemed so obviously at variance with 'complete independence,' to which the Congress was pledged. The agreement did not even guarantee dominion status; its terms fell manifestly short of those which the Congress leaders had considered as the minimum for a truce in August 1930 during the negotiations initiated by Sapru and Jayakar.

Alan Campbell Johnson was not wrong in reaching the conclusion that in the Delhi Pact Gandhi's gains were consolation prizes, and Irwin's only surrender was in agreeing to enter into negotiations. Lord Irwin's stock with Indian nationalists fluctuated from time to time. It was at its highest immediately after the Gandhi-Irwin Pact, and touched its nadir a year later when the Pact had gone to pieces and the Congress was in opposition and outlawed. The impression among Congressmen was that the Gandhi-Irwin Pact had been a clever manoeuvre, and that Irwin had led the Mahatma up the garden path of the Viceroy's House. A fellow-prisoner read to Gandhi, in July 1932, B. G. Horniman's description of Lord Irwin as 'an agile opportunist who endeavoured to cover his inconsistencies and change of principle and policy with a thick veneer of unctuous rectitude and hypocritical professions of sincerity'.[1] Gandhi's comment was that the description did less than justice to the Viceroy, who, though loyal to the British Empire, had meant well by India. Indeed it was his belief in Lord Irwin's sincerity that had made Gandhi give way during the negotiations on several points of detail. He saw in Irwin a kindred spirit. 'The two Mahatmas', Sarojini Naidu's epithet for the two negotiators, was apt in so far as it emphasized their religious make-up.

So far as Gandhi was concerned, there is little doubt that he took the Delhi Pact as the beginning of a new chapter in Congress-Government relations. In a letter dated March 6, 1931 from the house of his host at Delhi, Dr Ansari, to the Private Secretary to the Viceroy, he wrote:

'I must ask for one favour. I told you that it would be a point of honour with the Working Committee to see that there was a cent per cent fulfilment of the conditions obligatory on the Congress. You will help me to implement this obligation if you will draw my prompt attention by wire, where necessary, to any irregularity on our part, that may come under your notice . . .

'I pray to God that the friendship at which the settlement is an attempt will become a permanent fact.'

That Gandhi should have agreed to attend a Round Table Conference without any definite commitment from the Government, on which he and Motilal Nehru had insisted in December 1929, was itself surprising. Gandhi's reasons for signing the pact

[1] Mahadev Desai: *Diaries* (entry dated July 19, 1932).

should be sought, however, not in its clauses, but in the logic of Satyagraha. His speech at the Karachi session of the Indian National Congress gave a peep into the working of his mind.

'I have often wondered myself what we are going to do at the conference when we know that there is such a gulf between what we want and what has been as yet offered at the conference. But considerations of a Satyagrahi decided me. There comes a stage when he may no longer refuse to negotiate with his opponent. His object is always to convert his opponent by love. The stage of negotiation arrived when the Working Committee was released after the Premier's declaration. The Viceroy also made an appeal to us to lay down arms and to indicate what we want.'

To the suggestion that there was no need for a truce with the Government when the Congress was in a position to continue civil disobedience for at least another year, Gandhi's answer was: 'Well, for that matter, we might be capable of carrying on the struggle for twenty years, and a true Satyagrahi fights to the last, even if the rest are tired into submission. But the truce was made not because we were tired out, but because it was imperative. He who will fight on because he can fight on is no Satyagrahi but a conceited person guilty before God.'[1]

The obvious inconsistencies in Gandhi's position can thus be explained only in terms of his own technique. The Satyagraha movements were commonly described as 'struggles', 'rebellions', and 'wars without violence'. Owing to the common connotation of these words, however, they seemed to lay a disproportionate emphasis on the negative aspect of the movements, namely opposition and conflict. But the object of Satyagraha was not to achieve the physical elimination or moral breakdown of an adversary but, through suffering at his hands, to initiate those psychological processes which could make it possible for minds and hearts to meet. In such a struggle a compromise with the opponent was neither heresy nor treason, but a natural and a necessary step. And if it turned out that the compromise was premature and the adversary was unrepentant, there was nothing to prevent the Satyagrahi from returning to non-violent battle. It is true that national feeling could not be made to reach a high watermark at will, but Gandhi did not set much store by political freedom on the crest of a passing wave of emotion; he believed that India would be independent when she

[1] Tendulkar: *Mahatma*, Vol. III, p. 109.

came of age, and then no Power would be able to keep her in bondage.

The Karachi Congress, held in March 1931, approved of the Delhi Pact, though it put an interpretation on it which seemed more consistent with the ideals of the Congress than with the clauses of the Pact.

In April Gandhi was in Bombay and bade farewell to Lord Irwin. The new Viceroy, Lord Willingdon, was already in Bombay but did not send for Gandhi. The hard-headed officials at Delhi and in the provincial capitals, to whom the Delhi Pact had been a bitter pill, had now a sympathetic chief. The friction began within a few days of the signing of the Pact. *Young India* of July 9, 1931 came out with an editorial listing breaches of the Pact with the startling title: 'Is it crumbling?'

The Government accused the Congress of having acted in a spirit contrary to the Delhi Pact, which thus verged on repudiation by both sides. Negotiations were resumed, however, and a compromise—'the second settlement'—was patched up. It was agreed that the Congress would participate in the Round Table Conference, and that its sole representative would be Gandhi.

A special train was arranged from Simla to Kalka, and other trains were held up to enable Gandhi to reach Bombay in time to sail on August 29th, in the ss *Rajputana*.

# CHAPTER XXVIII

# The Round Table Conference

'HE is perhaps the best sailor on board the ss *Rajputana*,' wrote Mahadev Desai, the Mahatma's secretary. Gandhi, who travelled second class—the lowest—on the ship, spent most of the day and the whole of the night on deck, rose and retired at his usual hours, and followed the Ashram routine of prayers, spinning and studies. Little boys and girls of the home-going English passengers became his friends; they watched him ply the spinning-wheel, and when they peeped into his cabin in the morning or in the evening they were rewarded with armfuls of grapes and dates. At Aden the Indian community presented him an address. Messages of good wishes came from Madame Zagloul Pasha, the widow of the Egyptian patriot, and from leaders of the Wafd Party. At Marseilles he was greeted by Madeleine Rolland, the sister of the French savant, and was given a warm welcome by French students, who hailed him as the 'spiritual ambassador of India'.

On September 12, 1931, he arrived in London. He had accepted Muriel Lester's invitation to stay in Kingsley Hall in the East End, in order to be 'among the same sort of people to whom I have given my life'. Friends had pleaded with him that his residence was inconvenient for his fellow delegates and colleagues attending the Conference. He agreed to have an office at 88, Knightsbridge, but every evening, late though it was, he returned to sleep in Bow. Sometimes he returned from committee meetings after midnight, but the light still appeared in his room at 4 a.m. for the morning prayer. He had his morning walk in the mean streets of the east end; he visited his neighbours in Bow; he made friends with the children. 'Here I am,' he would say, 'doing the real round table work, getting to know the people of England.'

Gandhi was the sole representative of the Congress at the Round Table Conference. The British Press and politicians made out that Gandhi, however eminent as an individual, was only one of the Indian delegates, and the Congress was just one of the numerous parties of which a cross-section had been brought together at the Conference. All the delegates were nominees of the Government; they had a sprinkling of able individuals, but the majority of them were drawn from the princely order, the landlords, the titled gentry and the leaders of communal groups and vested interests, big and small. Many delegates were only too willing to become pawns in the political intrigues, the jockeying for position, the scramble for jobs and seats in legislatures and in services, to which the Conference gradually reduced itself.

What with its composition and what with its procedure, which the British Government controlled, the Conference sidetracked its energies into secondary issues and particularly the communal problems. Gandhi saw through this game and did some plain speaking in public as well as in private. Surely, he asked, the British Government had not invited the Indian delegates from six thousand miles to London to settle the communal question. He pointed out that the various communities had been led to place an undue emphasis on the communal question as a condition precedent to constitutional advance; this had turned them virtually into hungry wolves prowling about for prey under the new constitution. The problem had been presented to the Conference in an inverted way; it had been called upon to divide a cake the size of which was not known. 'Let us know what we are going to get,' he demanded, 'so that on that basis I might endeavour to bring about unity even in the present ill-assorted group. I could tell them they are dashing a precious thing to pieces.'

He pleaded for an honourable and equal partnership between Britain and India, held not by force but 'by the silken cord of love'. The Congress had accepted the principle of federation, as also the principle that there should be 'safeguards', but the safeguards had to be devised in the interest of India and not to reduce self-government to a mockery. If all the safeguards which were being proposed were incorporated in the new constitution, the responsible government which India would enjoy could be no better than 'the responsible government prisoners have in their cells; the prisoners too have complete independence immediately after the cell door is locked up'. He admitted that the British had more organizing ability, but Indians knew their country better. He was against any special treatment for European business interests, but he assured them that there would be no discrimination against them either. He advocated adult suffrage, a single-chamber legislature and indirect elections. He even envisaged the possibility of British troops remaining in India for some time after the grant of independence; he explained that it was for the British to initiate Indians into the mysteries of defence. 'Having clipped our wings it is their duty to give us wings wherewith we can fly.'

All this homely eloquence was wasted on the Conference. There was a financial crisis and a change of Government in Britain; in the new Government the Conservatives were heavily represented. The British public was preoccupied with domestic issues; for it the financial crisis was a more urgent issue than the niceties of an Indian Constitution. Inevitably, even if imperceptibly, there was a change in emphasis. Sir Samuel Hoare, the new Secretary of State, told Gandhi that he sincerely believed that Indians were unfit for complete self-government. Meanwhile, the Round Table delegates were busy with the bargains and counter-bargains of the communal problem. In these squabbles they were encouraged by the vested interests from India and the 'diehard' elements from Britain to expose to the world that it was Indian disunity and not British reluctance which barred the path to Indian self-government. Gandhi was prepared to give a 'blank cheque' to Muslims and other minorities to remove all their legitimate fears, provided they were willing to press the national demand for freedom. The Hindu delegates were not ready for this generous gesture, and the Muslim nationalists were not represented at the Conference. Gandhi realized that he had underrated the forces arrayed against him and the Congress. It was almost with a sense of relief that he saw the Conference tail off to a formal conclusion. The British Premier, Ramsay MacDonald, in his concluding address promised to impose a solution of the communal problem, and to appoint a committee to go to India for further investigation so that an 'all-embracing statute' could be framed.

In London's East End, among the poor of London, 'uncle Gandhi' had become a popular figure with the children. He answered their innocent and often penetrating questions. He told them stories of his childhood. He explained to them why he had chosen to stay in the East End and why he wore his meagre dress. He advised them to return good for evil. There was an interesting sequel to this advice when the father of a four-year-old girl told the Mahatma that he had a bone to pick with him. 'And what is it?' asked Gandhi. 'Well my little Jane comes every morning to me, hits me and wakes me up and says, "Now, don't you hit back, for Gandhi told us not to hit back." ' On October 2nd, his birthday, the children presented him with 'two woolly dogs, three pink birthday candles, a tin plate, a blue pencil and some jelly sweets'—gifts which he especially treasured and took to India. 'Thousands and thousands of children in England will have seen Gandhiji,' wrote Mahadev Desai, 'before he leaves the English shores. And who knows, it may be this generation with whom we may have to settle accounts?'

One of the most pleasant surprises of the tour was the courtesy and even affection Gandhi received from the cotton operatives of Lancashire, which had been hit the hardest by the Congress boycott of British goods. He listened with obvious attention and sympathy to the tale of woe of those who were jobless. Many of them saw the background of the boycott which he had sponsored when he told them: 'You have three million unemployed, but we have nearly 300 million unemployed for half the year. Your average unemployment dole is seventy shillings. Our average income is 7s 6d a month.'

Some of his English friends felt that by staying in the East End he was ignoring the middle and upper classes of England, who really determined the political future of India. So they arranged for him to meet the best minds of Britain in politics, religion, science and literature. He met George Bernard Shaw, who found in him 'a kindred spirit'. He addressed Members of Parliament in committee rooms. He met Bishops and Church dignitaries. He spoke to the boys at Eton and to the students of the London School of Economics. At Oxford, where he stayed at the invitation of Dr Lindsay, the Master of Balliol, he had talks with Dr Gilbert Murray, Gilbert Salter, Professor Coupland, Edward Thompson and others, and spoke at a meeting organized by the Indian students. He went to see Lloyd George; Charlie Chaplin, of whom he had never heard before, came to see him.

It is difficult to assess the results of these informal contacts. The Englishman's courtesy to the distinguished guest often concealed the real impact of his personality. It was apparent that the gulf between Congress aims and the prevalent British view was almost unbridgeable; only a tiny minority was prepared to go the whole hog with the Mahatma in his claim for an equal partnership between India and Britain. He was unable to carry immediate conviction; it appeared to most British statesmen and thinkers that he wanted India to travel too far and too fast on the difficult road to self-government. Nevertheless, the homely logic and the transparent sincerity of the man left an indelible impression on some of those whom he met. They formed clearer impressions of him than the loin cloth and goat's milk version with which the popular Press regaled them. While his opinions might appear utopian or revolutionary, he could no longer be dismissed as 'humbug', the appellation with which *Truth* had heralded his arrival in England.

The news from India was far from reassuring. The compromise which had been patched up between the Congress and Government, just before his departure for England, had virtually broken down. The Mahatma was anxious to return home; he declined invitations to prolong his itinerary in Europe and to visit America, but he decided to spend a few days with Romain Rolland in Switzerland on his way back to India.

Accompanied by Mahadev Desai and Pyarelal, his secretaries, Mirabehn (Miss Slade) and his son, Devadas, Gandhi arrived at Villeneuve on December 6th. In his book *Mahatma Gandhi*, published soon after the first non-co-operation movement in the early nineteen-twenties, Rolland had interpreted Gandhi's life and message with remarkable insight, and expressed the hope that the message of non-violence and self-sacrifice might yet save violence-ridden Europe from self-destruction: 'One thing is certain; either Gandhi's spirit will triumph or it will manifest itself again, as were manifested, centuries before, the Messiah and Buddha, till there finally is manifested in a mortal half-god the perfect incarnation of the principle of life which will lead a new humanity on to a new path.'

Gandhi and Rolland were closeted together for hours daily. A glimpse into their conversations, which ranged over a wide field, has been given by Rolland's sister:

'My brother describes for Gandhi the tragic situation of Europe; the sufferings of the people oppressed by dictators: the drama of the proletariat, who in their desperate effort to break the shackles of an anonymous ruthless capitalism and pushed forward by their legitimate aspiration for justice and freedom see only one way out, that of rebellion and violence. For man in the West is by education, by tradition and by temperament unprepared for the religion of *ahimsa*.

'. . . Gandhi listens; reflects. He reaffirms his unshakable faith in non-violence. Yet he understands that to convince sceptical Europe the concrete example of a successful experiment in non-violence would be necessary. Will India furnish it? He hopes so.'[1]

[1] Shukla (Editor): *Incidents of Gandhiji's Life*, p. 294.

Gandhi's visit to Switzerland evoked a good deal of local enthusiasm. The Syndicate of the Milkmen of Lemen telephoned Gandhi's host that they would like to supply milk to the 'King of India'; a Japanese artist hurried from Paris to make sketches of the Indian leader; a young musician played a violin under his window. Correspondents from Italy asked the Indian saint to indicate the ten lucky numbers for the next drawing of the national lottery; school children brought him flowers. He addressed private gatherings of pacifists.

Gandhi had planned to spend a day in Rome on his way back. Romain Rolland warned him to be on his guard against the wiles of the Fascists and arranged for him to stay with a friend whose integrity was beyond doubt. In Rome he walked through the Vatican galleries; in the Sistine Chapel he was spell-bound: 'I saw a figure of Christ there. It was wonderful. I could not tear myself away. The tears sprang to my eyes as I gazed.'

The Pope did not grant him an audience, but Mussolini did. Of the latter, a prison official said in Yeravda gaol five months later that he was an attractive personality. 'Yes,' said the Mahatma, 'but he looks like the executioner. How long will a rule based on bayonets last?'[1]

After he had boarded the Italian liner *Pilsna* for Brindisi, Gandhi learnt that the *Giornale d'Italia* had published an interview with him in which he was supposed to have announced that he was returning to India to resume the civil disobedience movement. He had given no interview in Rome and cabled to London that the report was a complete fabrication. In spite of this denial several British papers and politicians persisted in the insinuation that Mr Gandhi was lying. It seemed as if the *Giornale d'Italia* provided just the excuse for which diehard politicians in England and British bureaucrats in India were looking to revert to the time-honoured policy of 'no truck with the Congress', to which the Gandhi-Irwin Pact had been a temporary aberration.

[1] Diaries of Mahadev Desai. (Entry 26th May, 1932.

# CHAPTER XXIX

# Total War

GANDHI landed at Bombay on December 28, 1931. Within a week he was in gaol and civil disobedience was resumed; the Indian National Congress was practically outlawed and the Gandhi-Irwin Pact had gone to pieces. The explanation for this swift and somewhat unexpected turn in the political scene is to be sought not only in the incidents of that crucial week which spanned Gandhi's return and rearrest, but in the undercurrent of antagonism between the Congress and the Government which the Gandhi-Irwin Pact had failed to eradicate.

The Government had already perfected its plans for an offensive against the Congress. For months the Government of India and the Provincial Governments had been working out the details of the special powers with which executive officers were to be armed to deal a knock-out blow to the Congress if civil disobedience was resumed. The ordinances had been drafted and circulated to Provincial Governments; civil disobedience 'manuals' had been drawn up. On December 19, 1931, when Gandhi was on the high seas, the Government of India by a circular letter alerted the Provincial Governments regarding the anticipated struggle with the Congress. The temper of the official world may be gauged from a letter which the Bombay Government addressed to their superiors in Delhi on December 21st, pointing out the inconvenience of lodging Mr Gandhi in gaol in Bombay Presidency: 'If the Government of India still consider it essential that the place selected should be on the mainland of India . . . Coimbatore might be a suitable place. I am, however, to say that the Governor-in-Council considers that the moral effect of Mr Gandhi's internment would be far greater and that it would have a more valuable effect in showing the determination and power of Government to crush the civil disobedience movement, if Mr Gandhi were removed to the Andamans, or possibly Aden might be considered in order to place him beyond reach of political exploitation.'

The proposal was not considered a practical proposition by

the Government of India, but Gandhi's arrest under Bombay Regulation XXV of 1827 was a foregone conclusion. Lord Willingdon had evidently decided not to repeat that hesitation which his three predecessors, Lords Chelmsford, Reading and Irwin, had exhibited in arresting the author of civil disobedience. Many senior officers in the Central and Provincial Secretariats believed that Gandhi's movements of defiance of authority had thriven on the initial indecision or leniency of the Government and that a more resolute policy could have nipped the evil in the bud. For many of them the Gandhi-Irwin Pact had been a bitter pill; the Pact did not alter the basic fact that the Congress was pledged to liquidate the Indian Empire, which the servants of the Crown had sworn to serve and defend. The fact that the Congress, under Gandhi's leadership, eschewed the use of force did not seem to make much difference to those who considered non-violence a mere mask. Those British officials who did not doubt Gandhi's bona fides questioned his ability to control the popular feeling once it had been worked up.

When Gandhi landed at Bombay on December 28, 1931, after four months absence from India, he was far from being optimistic but he certainly did not expect to be confronted with a first-class political crisis. The arrest of Jawaharlal Nehru and Abdul Ghaffar Khan in the promulgation of ordinances in the United Provinces and the North-West Frontier had brought matters to a head. 'I take it,' Gandhi told a mass meeting of the citizens of Bombay, 'that these (ordinances) are Christmas gifts from Lord Willingdon, our Christian Viceroy.' The Congress Working Committee came to the conclusion that the Government had decided on a showdown and that the only answer to the Government was a revival of civil disobedience.

Gandhi was anxious, however, to ascertain the Government's point of view and to seek a peaceful solution so long as there was a single ray of hope; he could not lightly plunge the country into another ordeal. Gandhi telegraphed to the Viceroy seeking an interview. He offered to go to these two provinces to study both the official and the popular versions of recent events, and, if the enquiries proved the Congress to have been in the wrong, to correct his colleagues and co-workers. It is true that the Congress Working Committee had already sketched a plan of civil disobedience; but this plan was not to be enforced until Gandhi had explored with the Viceroy all avenues of maintaining peace. The Viceroy's reaction was sharp: he accused Gandhi of holding out threats of civil disobedience and warned him that

he and the Congress would be responsible 'for all the consequences which may follow from the action which the Congress
have proclaimed as their intention of taking'. Only the intervention of His Majesty's Government could possibly have staved off
the crisis. Sir Samuel Hoare, the Secretary of State, had impressed Gandhi during the Round Table Conference with his
extreme frankness; he had warned Gandhi that if the Congress
tried to force the pace by 'direct action' the Government would
crush it with all the force at its command. Gandhi had begged
him to reconsider his position: 'It would be such a tremendous
strain on both the communities, yours and ours, if you set yourselves to do it . . . But Sir Samuel, what do you mean by a
rebellion like this? Rebellion is not so terrible when it is completely peaceful.'

Sir Samuel knew how unhappy Gandhi had been with the
results of the Round Table Conference; Gandhi had assured him,
however, that after his return to India he would strain every
nerve to avoid a breach with the Government. The fabricated
interview with Gandhi which Signor Gayada of the *Giornale
d'Italia* had broadcast from Rome had surprised Sir Samuel,
but he had sought and obtained a repudiation from Gandhi
while he was still on the high seas. Sir Samuel may have preferred peace to hostilities with Gandhi; but he had neither the
will nor perhaps the strength to oppose the combined weight of
official opinion in India; already he had approved plans for an
offensive against the Congress; now he gave permission to press
the button that was to unleash a *blitzkrieg* against the Congress.

'In the last fight,' Gandhi warned a mass meeting in Bombay soon after his return from England, 'the people had to face
*lathis*, but this time they will have to face bullets.' He had
sensed the mood of the Government, even though he did not
know the thoroughness of its preparations to crush the Congress.
Lord Willingdon had the reputation of a firm and hard-headed
administrator, and had every intention of living up to it. The
Governors in the Provinces shared his resolution to put trouble-
makers in their proper places; many of them were ready, even
impatient, to teach a lesson to an organization which they believed had flourished on half-hearted measures by the Government. The plans for dealing with civil disobedience were
pulled out of the 'top secret' pigeon-holes of the Secretariat
and put into execution with lightning speed. Within a few hours
of the arrest of Gandhi and the members of the Congress Work-

ing Committee on January 4, 1932, a series of ordinances were promulgated. Not only the Working Committee, but the Provincial Committee and innumerable local committees were declared illegal; a number of organizations allied with or sympathetic to the Congress, such as Youth Leagues, National Schools, Congress Libraries and Hospitals were also outlawed. Congress funds were confiscated; Congress buildings were occupied and almost every possible measure was taken to prevent the Congress from functioning. That the Ordinances were drastic and severe and covered almost every activity of Indian life was admitted in so many words by the Secretary of State in the House of Commons in March 1932.

By skimming off its leadership and freezing its funds, the Government hoped to demoralize the Congress. The powers acquired through the Ordinances included those which permitted the administration to control or forefeit any funds 'which were suspected of being held or used for the purposes of an unlawful association'; officials were authorized to examine account books, make inquiries or order searches. The Government went so far as to seek the intervention of the Secretary of State for India to stop the payment of royalties from Columbia Gramophone Company to the All-India Spinners Association for the sale of a record of a talk given by Gandhi during his stay in England.

Gaol administration hardened perceptibly. The first Congress campaign in 1930-1 had received a great impetus from the participation of women. In the second campaign (1932-4) treatment in gaols seemed almost to have been designed to scare away women. Mirabehn, Gandhi's disciple and the daughter of a former Admiral of the British Fleet, gave an account of the conditions in Arthur Road gaol which was a severe indictment of conditions in women's prisons. She noticed that women political prisoners were allowed to interview their children through iron bars. Her neighbours in this gaol were three criminals, two thieves and a prostitute; these criminals were not locked up for the night, while the political prisoners were.

One of the greatest anxieties of the Government during the truce period had been the penetration of Congress influence in the countryside; difficult as it was to fight middle-class nationalism in the towns, the possibility of disaffection spreading to the peasantry seemed to the Government a more sinister threat. This is the most plausible explanation of the severity with which 'no-tax campaigns' in the rural areas were handled. These campaigns were conspicuous in Allahabad and Rae-Bareilly districts of the United Provinces and a few districts of Bombay, Bengal and Bihar and North-West Frontier Province.

A similar firmness guided the Government in its dealings with the Press. The initial success of the Salt Satyagraha campaign in 1930 was partly attributed in official circles to the publicity it had received. In 1932, by a series of drastic measures, the freedom of the Press was curtailed. Apart from the prosecution of Press correspondents, the forfeiture of securities from newspapers was used as a deterrent. On July 4, 1932, just six months after the resumption of civil disobedience, the Secretary of State for India stated in the House of Commons that action had been taken under the Press Laws against 109 journalists and 98 printing presses.

Gandhi had meanwhile been lodged in the Yeravda Prison in Poona. The Bombay Government had not been able to persuade the Government of India to deport him from the Indian mainland nor to transfer him to some other province. Two of his closest colleagues, Vallabhbhai Patel and Mahadev Desai, were lodged with him. The latter's diaries are a very full and lively record of Gandhi's life in gaol. The Mahatma knew enough to gauge the scale of the official offensive against his movement. Repression, he wrote to Sir Samuel Hoare, 'was crossing all legitimate limits'. Suffering, however, was an essential part of Satyagraha, to purify those who invited it and to convert those who inflicted it. If the ordeal through which the country was passing was fiery enough, Gandhi hoped it would only burn out the dross. If people remained true to their pledge of resistance, no repression, however severe, could possibly crush them. From the new constitution that was being forged in England by British experts and Indian observers, Gandhi did not expect much. 'Why don't you accept half the loaf today?' asked Thomas, Home Secretary to the Government of Bombay, who came to see him in gaol. 'I would,' replied the Mahatma, 'if it was bread and not stone.'

Gandhi was as busy in gaol as he had been outside. Prayers and spinning figured in the daily routine. He washed his clothes, dictated or wrote his heavy mail—one day he wrote as many as forty-nine letters—most of it to his 'family' in the Ashram. He warned his correspondents not to give publicity to his letters from gaol, which were to be treated as private. He read copiously, developed a keen interest in astronomy, and often gazed into the sky to decipher the 'mysterious universe'. He had his moments of relaxation, particularly when he exchanged sallies with the irrepressible Vallabhbhai Patel, whose barbed wit made him a delightful companion.

The Government had acted with lightning speed not only in applying its carefully planned repression but in blocking publicity, which alone could sustain popular morale and boost a nationalist movement. In spite of this initial handicap, no less than 61,551 convictions for civil disobedience took place in the first nine months of the movement in 1932; this figure was a little higher than that of the campaign in 1930-1. For the first four months the movement functioned with vigour; after that the number of convictions declined and except occasionally, such as in April 1932, when Congress attempted to hold an annual session with Pt Malaviya as president, the stream of civil resisters became a mere trickle.

By the end of 1932 the Provincial Governments and the Government of India were exchanging mutual felicitations on having attained victory over Congress; they would not, however, shed the special powers assumed under the ordinances earlier in the year. There was to be no drawn battle this time, and for years to come Lord Willingdon was resolved not to accept from Gandhi and the Congress anything less than an unconditional surrender. He had decided to keep the Mahatma under a political quarantine. At the end of 1932, when Tej Bahadur Sapru and M. R. Jayakar were returning from the constitutional discussions in London, the Secretary of State suggested to the Viceroy that they should be allowed to see Gandhi in gaol. In a long cable dated January 4, 1933 the Viceroy opposed the suggestion:

'We (Governors and the Executive Council) recognize that the chief object of such an interview would be to show that we are not unreasonable and that we are giving Gandhi and the Congress every opportunity of co-operating in the new constitution; but we are of the opinion that such an interview could not fail to have very embarrassing results and would tend to destroy the favourable position achieved partly by the consistent policy followed during the last year and partly by the success of the last Round Table Conference.'

The Viceroy's view of Gandhi's personality and politics did not err on the side of generosity. In a letter dated July 1, 1933 to the Secretary of State, he wrote: 'The leadership of Gandhi is being openly attacked both from the left and from the right, as having led Congress after fourteen years of constant struggle to a position perilously near failure. There are profound differences in Congress ranks as to the policy to be pursued and a general sense of despondency. The only man who might pull the Congress together is Gandhi. He realizes very clearly that his influence depends virtually on his relations with the Government. If he could produce the impression that the Government are prepared to treat with him, his influence will rise at once one hundred per cent.'

The idea of Gandhi as a Machiavellian politician with the Congress as his pliable tool, extending his influence over the ignorant Indian public by contriving an interview with the Viceroy, was an incredible misreading of the Mahatma and the millions who obeyed his slightest nod. In his *Nine Troubled Years*, Sir Samuel Hoare (later Lord Templewood) rightly observes, 'If I made any criticism, it would be that Lord Willingdon did not, like Irwin, understand Gandhi's personality and on that score underrated his power.' Lord Willingdon's past experience as an administrator seems to have been more of a liability than an asset to him in his role as Viceroy. The Indian problem struck him primarily as an administrative one, requiring timely and judicious use of coercion to crush trouble-makers. He was almost incapable of understanding the deep intellectual and emotional roots of the movement for political liberation: the enthusiasm it evoked struck him as a variant of ignorant fanaticism. Little as he understood the springs of Indian nationalism, he understood Gandhi even less. Civil disobedience was a part of the Gandhian technique of Satyagraha, which sought to achieve changes in political as well as social spheres by organizing the masses non-violently, by offering resistance without retaliation, and non-co-operation without hatred. To Gandhi the non-violent basis of the movement was its most significant one; to Willingdon not only was the conscious moral superiority of Gandhi and his followers irritating, but a non-violent movement was the more insidious for the odium it brought on those who had the responsibility for keeping law and order.

Gandhi was often driven to the verge of despair by the wall of prejudice behind which British statesmen entrenched themselves. When he criticized their actions he was denounced as a demagogue; when he claimed to be their friend he was accused of hypocrisy. When he applied for an interview he was suspected of out-manoeuvring the Government; when he launched a campaign he was irreconcilable; when he circumscribed its scope or withdrew it he was alleged to have lost credit with his followers.

It was the object of Satyagraha—of which civil disobedience was one form—to penetrate this wall of prejudice. When reasoning failed voluntary suffering at the hands of the opponent was intended to melt his heart and to release the springs which hindered understanding. In practice this method of 'attack' on the opponent was not always easy, nor quick in producing results. With their moral defences exposed, the British officials answered the challenge to their position with increased assertion and self-complacency. The successive civil disobedience movements, however, furthered the cause of Indian nationalism at least in two ways. They lifted the spell of fear which had enveloped the Indian masses for nearly a century and a half, and they wore down, however slowly, British rigidity into scepticism and scepticism into fatigue. Administering a sub-continent in the best of conditions was for many civil servants an arduous enough task; in the face of tenacious opposition from vocal sections of the population, the task ultimately became almost an impossible one.

But we are anticipating events. By August 1932 Lord Willingdon and his advisers felt that under the hammer-blows of the Government civil disobedience had wilted. The announcement of a fast by Gandhi, as a protest against the grant of separate electorates to untouchables, was to stir public opinion powerfully, but it was to divert it into non-political channels.

# CHAPTER XXX

# Harijans

On September 13, 1932, newspapers all over India carried a sensational announcement: Gandhi, still a prisoner in Yeravda Gaol, had decided to fast to death from September 20th, as a protest against the grant of separate electorates to the depressed (untouchable) classes in the new constitution.

When the Communal Award was published on August 17, 1932, it confirmed Gandhi's worst fears. In spite of the double vote given to the depressed classes, for their own separate constituencies as well as for the general (Hindu) constituencies, the fact remained that separate electorates were to be set up for these classes. Gandhi immediately wrote to the British Premier that he would embark on 'a perpetual fast unto death', which could only end 'if during its progress the British Government, of its motion or under pressure of public opinion, revised their decision and withdrew their scheme of communal electorates for the depressed classes'. The fast was to continue even if he was released.

The British Premier and his advisers were unable to appreciate Gandhi's deeply emotional and religious approach to the problem. Their first impulse was to scent a political motive in the fast: Gandhi was trying a stunt to recover the prestige he had lost through the decline of civil disobedience. If the British ministers failed to fathom the depth of Gandhi's feeling on this subject they were even less able to see the ethics of fasting for the solution of what was to them a political problem. Fasting struck them as a thinly-disguised method of coercion. The British reaction to Gandhi's fasts was well exemplified in Low's cartoon as a 'Prophecy for 1933', in which Lord Willingdon was shown going on hunger strike at the instance of 10 Downing Street 'to force Mr Gandhi to admit the new constitution as touchable'.

Gandhi, however, did not have to justify his fast to anybody except to his own conscience, or, as he put it, to his Maker. Fasting had a definite place in his discipline of life. A fast was sometimes the only way out for the agony of his soul. It could not be used without the deepest searching of the heart; not until 'the still small voice' had spoken in clear, unmistakable accents. But was it not possible that he could be mistaken? Could not his own conceit masquerade as an inner voice? Gandhi did not deny that he might be mistaken, but if he was, his death from voluntary starvation would be, he argued, a good riddance for those who had fallen under his false spell.

Was not the fast a form of coercion? Gandhi was aware that his fast did exercise a moral pressure, but the pressure was directed not against those who disagreed with him but against those who loved him and believed in him; he sought to prick the conscience of the latter and to convey to them something of his own inner anguish at a monstrous tyranny. He did not expect his critics to react in the same way as his friends and co-workers, but if his self-crucifixion could demonstrate his sincerity to them, the battle would be more than half-won. The fast dramatized the issue at stake; ostensibly it suppressed reason, but in fact it was designed to free reason from that mixture of inertia and prejudice which had permitted gross social iniquities to exist for centuries.

The news that Gandhi was about to fast shook India from one end to the other. September 20th, when the fast began, was observed all over India as a day of fasting and prayer. At Santiniketan, Rabindranath Tagore, dressed in black, spoke to a large gathering on the significance of the fast and the urgency of fighting an age-old evil. There was a spontaneous upsurge of feeling; temples, wells and public places were thrown open to the depressed classes. A conference of leaders of caste Hindus and depressed classes was summoned to devise alternative electoral arrangements to replace those provisions of the British Award that had provoked Gandhi to offer the supreme sacrifice.

Meanwhile, the sands of time were running out. The Government were willing to remove Gandhi to a private residence in Poona under certain restrictions; but Gandhi preferred to fast in gaol. He took his last meal of lemon juice and honey with hot water at 11 a.m. on September 20th; an hour later the fast began.

The Hindu Leaders' Conference met at Bombay. The leaders, who included Madan Mohan Malaviya, Tej Bahadur Sapru, M. R. Jayaker, Rajagopaladhari, N. C. Kelkar, Rajendra Prasad and Moonje, were anxious for a quick solution. They had to carry with them, however, the leaders of the depressed classes, particularly Ambedkar, who was not only a stubborn advocate of separate electorates but fully conscious of his pivotal position: no solution to which he did not agree was likely to commend itself to the Government. What with the progress of the fast and the strain of the negotiations, Gandhi's strength began to ebb quickly. Ambedkar bargained hard; he was reluctant to give up separate electorates, which the Communal Award gave to his community, unless he received some counter-balancing advantages. Eventually an agreement, popularly known as the Poona Pact, was reached; it doubled the representation of the depressed classes in the provincial legislatures but revised the electoral system. Voters from the depressed classes were to hold a primary election and choose a panel of four candidates for each seat; these four candidates were then to submit to a joint electorate of caste Hindus and untouchables. Reservation of seats was to continue until it was ended by mutual agreement. But the method of primary election was to lapse after ten years.

The British Cabinet accepted the Poona Pact and Gandhi broke the fast. The Poona Pact substituted one scheme of electoral representation of the depressed classes for another. The fast had at least one good result; it did away with separate electorates for the depressed classes. The insidious influence of this mode of representation as a wedge in Indian politics was to become fully visible in the next decade, and it was well that at least one crack in national life was closed in time. But more important than these constitutional arrangements, which incidentally did not come into force for nearly four and a half years, was the emotional catharsis through which the Hindu community had passed. The fast had been intended, as Gandhi had avowed, 'to sting the conscience of the Hindu community into right religious action'. The scrapping of separate electorates was only the beginning of the end of untouchability.

One of the greatest campaigns of social reform in history was thus launched by a state prisoner. Nobody knew better than Gandhi that an ancient tyranny could not be blasted overnight and that the results of the fast had to be followed up by work in the field and by propaganda. Under his inspiration an all-India organization was established with G. D. Birla as President and the indefatigable A. V. Thakkar as Secretary. From his prison cell Gandhi issued a series of Press statements and a stream of letters to his numerous correspondents to educate the public on the evils of untouchability. He arranged for the publication of a weekly paper, *Harijan,* to promote this campaign.

*Harijan* means 'Children of God'; it was Gandhi's name for the untouchables.

As Gandhi threw himself into the movement, he discovered that the evil was of much greater magnitude than he had thought at first. The task of the reformer was stupendous. How was he to fight this age-old evil? How was he to convince his co-workers that he was in dead earnest? How was he to acquire greater application and dedication for this great mission? Gandhi's anguish was brought to an end by 'a call from within' to embark on a twenty-one day fast from May 8, 1933.

The civil disobedience movement had been suspended for six weeks immediately after Gandhi's release and on his advice. As soon as he recovered some strength, he telegraphed to the Viceroy a request for an interview 'to explore the possibilities of peace'. Lord Willingdon's reply was a polite rebuff. Gandhi was again arrested on August 1st, and sent back to Yeravda prison. He was released three days later but confined within the limits of Poona City. He defied the order, was rearrested and sentenced to a year's imprisonment. Back in gaol, he commenced a fast on August 16th, to protest against the denial of facilities for the promotion of the campaign against untouchability which he had been receiving during his earlier incarceration. His condition deteriorated rapidly and he was released.

He was now faced with a curious dilemma. If he went back to gaol, the Government was likely to refuse him facilities for Harijan work; if he undertook a fast the Government might release him. This was a 'cat and mouse' game, to which he decided not to be a party. He announced his intention not to offer civil disobedience during the unexpired portion of his sentence of a year's imprisonment.

With this self-denying ordinance on his political activities, his energies were directed exclusively towards the abolition of untouchablity. In September 1933 he moved to Wardha and announced the gift of the Sabarmati Ashram to the Harijan Sevak Sangh. On November 7th he set out on a countrywide tour to promote the Harijan cause. During the next nine months he covered 12,500 miles, penetrating into some of the remotest parts of the country, which were off the beaten track of national leaders. He called on caste Hindus to purge themselves of prejudice against the Harijans, and he urged the Harijans to shake off the vices (drugs and drink) which hindered their absorption into Hindu society. He pleaded for the opening of temples to Harijans: 'Temples are for sinners, not for saints;

but who is to judge where no man is without sin?' He ridiculed the superstition that anybody could be unclean by birth, or that the shadow or touch of one human being could defile another human being. Bathing was all very well, he told a village audience, but even buffaloes had long daily baths.

He wore himself out in making his collections for the Harijan Fund. In ten months he received eight lakhs of rupees. He could, if he had wished, have obtained this amount as a gift from a Maharaja or a millionaire, but he did not set much store by money as such. The millions of men, women and children who contributed to his begging-bowl became fellow-soldiers in the campaign against untouchability.

The Harijan tour was by no means a triumphal progress. Gandhi was attacking an age-old tyranny and long-established vested interests, which did not stick at anything to preserve themselves. The *Sanatanists* (orthodox Hindus) accused him of a dangerous heresy: they organized black-flag demonstrations; they tried to heckle him and disrupt the meetings he addressed. On June 25th, while he was on his way to the municipal hall in Poona, a bomb was thrown at his party; seven persons, including the chief officer of the municipal committee, were injured, but Gandhi was unhurt. He expressed his 'deep pity' for the unknown thrower of the bomb. 'I am not aching for martyrdom,' he said, 'but if it comes in my way in the prosecution of what I consider to be the supreme duty in defence of the faith I hold in common with millions of Hindus, I shall have well earned it.'

Even though the opposition of the *Sanatanists* died hard, and even though militant Harijan leaders were critical, Gandhi succeeded in piercing an ancient sore. In an article entitled 'The Revolution is Over', Rajagopalachari, the well-known Congress leader from Madras, wrote: 'Untouchability is not yet gone. But the revolution is really over and what remains is but the removal of the debris.' This was probably an optimistic verdict, but there is no doubt that the reformists had made a good beginning. The Congress Ministries in 1937-9 removed some of the legal disabilities of the Harijans, and untouchability itself became illegal in the constitution of free India. A social tyranny which had deep roots needed a continuous war on all fronts, legal, social and economic, and for many years to come.

# CHAPTER XXXI

# Rural Economics

THE civil disobedience movement was at a low ebb even in the autumn of 1932 when Gandhi's fast on untouchability diverted attention from it. The Harijan work opened safer channels for activity, which not a few Congressmen were glad to use. The temporary suspension of mass civil disobedience in May 1933 nearly killed it; the revival of individual civil disobedience was to the Government little more than a minor nuisance. The harsh repression by the Government had temporarily numbed the country, but many Congressmen felt that if their leader's strategy had been determined less by moral and more by political considerations, the Government could have been embarrassed to a greater extent. Congressmen had accepted non-violence as a policy for wresting self-government from the British; they had agreed to eschew the use of physical force, but they chafed at the innumerable limitations with which the Mahatma encumbered himself. In May 1933 he had unambiguously condemned secrecy as inconsistent with Satyagraha. Yet so pervasive was the repressive apparatus of the Government that the alternative to functioning secretly was not to function at all.

The conviction grew upon Gandhi that some of his followers had tired of his methods and views and that they pretended to accept policies with which they really differed; that his personality was unfairly dominating the Congress and interfering with its democratic spirit. He felt that he owed it to himself and to his followers not to strain their loyalty unduly. The suspension of civil disobedience was not the only issue. There were other differences of outlook which were glossed over or bridged temporarily during the mass struggle against the Government. His renewed emphasis on the spinning-wheel as 'the second lung of the nation' seemed as misplaced to many as was his moral and religious approach to the removal of untouchability. He himself viewed with misgivings the nascent Socialist group, which he described as a body of 'men in a hurry'.

It was on the crucial issue of non-violence, however, that he felt most deeply the difference between himself and the intelligentsia in Congress. After fifteen years of preaching and practising non-violence, it almost hurt him to see how little it was understood by those who professed to follow him. Mass civil disobedience had struck the imagination of Congressmen, but this was only one aspect of his non-violent technique. There was another aspect, the constructive programme, which he now stressed, and which seemed strangely unpolitical to many Congressmen.

It was this divergence in outlook that drove Gandhi to retire from Congress in October 1934. 'I do not leave the Congress in anger or in huff nor yet in disappointment,' he wrote to Vallabhbhai Patel. He was restoring freedom to the Congress; he was also regaining freedom of action for himself. Henceforth, at least for the next three years, not politics but village economics were to be his dominant interest.

The Bombay session of the Indian National Congress in October 1934, which formally registered Gandhi's retirement from that organization, also authorized the formation, under his guidance, of the All-India Village Industries Association. This Association, 'unaffected by and independent of the political activities of the Congress', was to work for the revival and encouragement of village industries and the moral and physical advancement of the village. The resolution was an index of the new orientation that Gandhi was giving to his own activities and those of Congress.

Ever since Gandhi had entered Indian public life in 1915, he had been pleading for a new deal for the village. The acute pressure on land and the absence of supplementary industries had caused chronic unemployment and under-employment among the peasants, whose appalling poverty never ceased to weigh upon Gandhi's mind. His advocacy of the spinning-wheel derived from its immediate practical value as a palliative. The All-India Spinners Association, to which he had given a good deal of his time during the years of political quiescence, had in a period of ten years extended its activities to 5,300 villages, and provided employment to 220,000 spinners, 20,000 weavers and 20,000 carders, and disbursed more than two crores of rupees in Indian villages. These figures may not seem impressive today in the context of large-scale state-sponsored planning, but they represented solid work on the part of an organization often against heavy odds.

Nobody knew better than Gandhi that the All-India Spinners Association had only scratched the surface of the problem of rural poverty, but he began to think and plan for the revival of the village economy as a whole. His Harijan tour had revealed to him how, with the decay of village industries, Harijans had sunk deeper and deeper into poverty; the reform of untouchability was thus linked with the economic amelioration of these unfortunate people. The revival of village industries thus acquired a new urgency. The *Swadeshi* cult, which insisted on the use of articles made in India and had swayed the country during periods of intense political excitement, received a new twist in the nineteen-thirties. It was not enough, argued Gandhi, that an article should be of Indian origin; it was equally important that it should be made in a village. He appealed to town-dwellers to examine each article of daily consumption which was manufactured in India or abroad, and to find a substitute for it from the village. The broom could do duty for a brush; a 'kikar' tooth-stick for a tooth brush; hand-pounded rice for factory-polished rice; 'gur' for factory sugar, and hand-made paper for the products of the paper mills. Village products might sometimes cost more, but they distributed wages and profits among those whose need was the direst. For nearly 150 years, the cities had drained the villages of wealth and talent. 'For the city dweller,' wrote Gandhi, 'the villages have become untouchable. He does not know them; he will not live in them, and if he finds himself in a village he will want to reproduce city life there. This would be tolerable, if we could bring into being cities which would accommodate thirty crores of human beings.'[1]

Since eighty-five per cent of the population of India lived in villages, their economic and social resuscitation was a *sine qua non* for freedom from foreign rule. Gandhi described the exploitation of the village in the interest of the town as a species of violence. The growing gap in economic standards and social amenities between village and town had to be bridged. This could best be done by volunteers from the towns, who would spread themselves in the countryside to help revive dead or dying rural industries and improve standards of nutrition, education and sanitation. Gandhi expected these public-spirited men and women to support themselves on 'a village scale'; if they put on their work a price which villages could not sustain, village economy would face bankruptcy.

It was not Gandhi's habit to preach what he did not practise;

[1] Gandhi, M. K.: *Cent per Cent Swadeshi*, p. 18.

he decided to settle in a village. His choice fell upon Segaon, which was also situated near Wardha but had only a population of 600 and lacked such bare amenities as a *pucca* road, a shop and a post office. Here, on land owned by his friend and disciple Jamnalal Bajaj, Gandhi occupied a one-room hut. Those who came to see him during the rains had to wade through ankle-deep mud. The climate was inhospitable; there was not an inhabitant of the village who had not suffered from dysentery or malaria. Gandhi himself fell sick, but was resolved not to leave Segaon. He had come alone; he would not allow even his wife to join him. He hoped he would draw his team for village uplift from Segaon itself, but he could not prevent his disciples, old and new, from collecting round him. When Dr John Mott interviewed him in 1937, Gandhi's was the solitary hut; before long a colony of mud and bamboo houses grew up. Among its residents were Prof. Bhansali, who had roamed the forests naked and with sealed lips, subsisting on *neem* leaves; Maurice Frydman, a Pole, who became a convert to the Gandhian conception of a handicraft civilization based on non-violence; a Sanskrit scholar who was a leper and was housed next to Gandhi's hut so that he could tend him; a Japanese monk who, in Mahadev Desai's words, worked like a horse and lived like a hermit. No wonder that Vallabhbhai Patel called Segaon a 'menagerie'. Gandhi referred to it as the 'House For Invalids'.

Sevagram, as Segaon was renamed, was not planned as an Ashram; Gandhi never conceived it as such and did not impose any formal discipline upon it. This motley group of men and women of vastly dissimilar temperaments and attainments, bound to him by varying degrees of respect or affection and by the common ideal of service to the village, constituted a human laboratory which gave him, in the words of Mahadev Desai, 'enough exercise in the practice of ahimsa (non-violence) in the domestic field. Its successful practice would mean its automatic extension to the political field. That is why he always longs to get back to his laboratory in order to be free for more self-examination and more experimentation. The difficult instruments make his immediate task more difficult it is true, but it is also true that they make him all the fitter for the larger task'.

Before long, Sevagram became a centre of the Gandhian scheme of village welfare. A number of institutions grew up in and around it to take up the various strands of economic and social uplift. The All-Indian Village Industries Association, with its headquarters at Maganwadi, supported and developed such industries as could easily be fostered in the villages, required little capital and did not need help from outside the village. The Association set up a school for training village workers and published its own periodical, *Gram Udyog Patrika.* There were other organizations, such as the Goseva Sangh, which sought to improve the condition and breed of cows, and the Hindustani Talimi Sangh, which experimented in Gandhi's ideas on education.

To rid India's seven hundred thousand villages of poverty, disease and ignorance was a colossal task and required a multi-sided effort. Fostering village industries could create employment and pump purchasing power into the villages; it could also shake the villagers out of their lethargy. 'The 400 adults of Segaon,' wrote Gandhi, 'can easily put ten thousand rupees annually into their pockets if only they would work as I ask them. But they won't. They lack co-operation; they do not know the art of intelligent labour, they refuse to learn anything new.'

Nutrition was a problem on which Gandhi wrote and spoke frequently. Ever since his student days he had experimented on himself with food and fasting. Nutrition took on a new urgency as a problem of the Indian masses when he realized, with something of a shock, that apart from their poverty their food habits were responsible for their undernourishment. The deficiency in vitamins was inexcusable when green leaves were available for the picking. He appealed to Indian scientists to pursue research into Indian diets in the context of Indian conditions. 'As a practised cook,' he wrote on the modes of cooking which did not destroy the nutritive value of foods and on the superiority of hand-ground wheat and hand-polished rice to the factory products. 'The textile mills,' he explained, 'had brought unemployment in their wake, but rice and flour mills have also brought in undernourishment and disease.'

It was obvious to Gandhi that rural India could not be transformed without the help of the urban intelligentsia. To make the country village-conscious he advised Congress to hold its annual sessions in villages. The first to be so held was the Faizpur Congress; Gandhi noted that the session was free from the scramble and hustle inevitable in big towns, that village hedges could do duty for barbed wire, and exhibitions of village handicrafts could entertain as well as instruct.

He interpreted every problem in terms of the needs of the village. The educational system had always struck him as inadequate and wasteful. The vast majority of people had been denied the rudiments of education; but even those who went to village primary schools soon unlearnt what was taught them because it had little to do with their daily lives and environment.

The medium of a foreign language at the high school standard had created a barrier between the millions in the villages and the few thousands of the upper crust of society. It was to evolve a system of education which suited the real needs of the people that Gandhi summoned a meeting of educationists and the education ministers from the Congress-governed provinces. The system of 'Basic Education' which evolved from these discussions was to evoke much controversy, but it definitely provided a corrective to the stereotyped ideas along which education departments were working in India.[1]

Work in the villages was an arduous and slow affair; it was 'plodder's work', as Gandhi put it. It did not earn banner headlines in the Press and did not seem to embarrass the Government. Many of Gandhi's colleagues did not see how this innocuous activity could help India in advancing to the real goal—that of political freedom. Gandhi was accused of sidetracking the main political issue; his answer was: 'I do not see how thinking of these necessary problems (of village uplift) and finding a solution for them is of no political significance and how any examination of the financial policy of the Government has necessarily a political bearing.'[2]

A more serious criticism of Gandhi's village work was that he was turning his back on science and industry and advocating a primitive economy which would perpetuate poverty. In *Hind Swaraj*, Gandhi had mercilessly criticized machinery, mills and industrial civilization, but during the next forty years of his life he further elaborated his ideas on machinery, relating them to his fundamental doctrine of non-violence. His principal objection to mechanization was that it tended to concentrate the production of wealth in a few hands. In a country where the hands were too many and the work too little, machinery could only add to unemployment and poverty. 'I would favour,' he had written in 1921, 'the use of the most elaborate machinery if thereby India's pauperism and resulting idleness could be avoided.' There was a distinction in his mind, however, between mass production and production for the masses; the former under free enterprise often made the rich richer and the poor poorer. He was not opposed

[1] For details of Basic Education, see the following chapter, 'Congress in Office'.
[2] *Harijan*, January 11, 1936.

to machinery as such. Even his beloved spinning-wheel was machinery, but it was 'machinery reduced to the terms of the masses'. He welcomed simple tools and instruments which 'lightened the burden of the millions of cottages' without atrophying the limbs of man. He also recognized that some of these comparatively simple machines, such as sewing machines, required factories for their manufacture. 'I am socialist enough to say,' he added, 'that such factories should be nationalized or state-controlled. They ought only to be working under the most attractive and ideal conditions, not for profit but for the benefit of humanity, love taking the place of greed as motive.'

Gandhi's picture of the ideal Indian village was of a 'republic', independent of its neighbours for its vital wants, yet interdependent in other ways, growing its own food and cotton and if surplus land was available, money crops. As many of its activities as possible were to be on a co-operative basis; it was to have its own theatre, school and public hall; elementary education was to be free and compulsory; an elected 'panchayat' was to decide disputes; guards selected by rotation from a register were to police the village.

The image of this 'perfect democracy based on individual freedom' could be dismissed as utopian, but to Gandhi it was the only form a non-violent society could take. He did not care what label was applied to his ideas. Indian socialists, who by 1935 were a strong wing within the Congress, sometimes criticized him. Gandhi claimed that he was a socialist long before many Indian socialists had avowed the creed. 'But my socialism,' he wrote, 'was natural to me, and not adopted from any books. It came out of my unshakable belief in non-violence. No man could be actively non-violent and not rise against social injustice wherever it occurred.'

He did not accept the inevitability of class war or of violence; he believed his non-violent technique could end social injustice no less than foreign rule. By eschewing force, his socialism did not become a pious futility; in spite of its humanitarian and ostensibly gentle methods, it had revolutionary implications. How were the propertied few to be persuaded to subordinate their own greed to the good of the community as a whole? The first step was to reason with the rich; if argument failed non-violent non-co-operation was to be invoked. Just as no government could survive for long without the co-operation, willing or forced, of the people, economic exploitation was impossible without the active or passive acquiescence of the exploited. Gandhi did not seek refuge from hard realities in the safety of a rigid doctrine. His ideas were evolved in response to the social and economic conditions around him.

The central idea in Gandhi's mind was to relieve the grinding poverty which stalked the villages; he shrank from the idea of further pauperizing the village for the greater prosperity of a few big towns. Rather than turn the wheels of a few gigantic plants, he wished the hundreds of thousands of cottages in the countryside to hum with activity, to cater for their needs, as well as to send their wares to the towns. If in Switzerland and Japan work and wages could be carried to thousands of cottages, why could it not be done in India?

In one important respect conditions in India differed from those in other countries; an alien government had neither the incentive nor the organization to undertake radical changes in the country's economy. When Gandhi had torn himself away from politics to work in the villages, the Government even suspected him of an astute and deeply-laid plan to prepare the rural masses for a country-wide civil disobedience campaign.

Two and a half years later, the wheel was to come full circle; the new constitution was scheduled to come into force from April 1, 1937. Gandhi had seen the new constitution being beaten into shape and had never had a high opinion of it. But as the elections drew near, he wondered whether this constitution, its limitations notwithstanding, could not be used to improve the lot of the people.

# CHAPTER XXXII

# Congress in Office

---

In 1937, with the coming into force of the new constitution in the provinces, a new field opened for constructive work for the Indian National Congress under Gandhi's inspiration.

The new constitution, which was enacted by the British Parliament in 1935 and came into force in 1937, embodied the policy of self-government for India by measured stages. The Indian Reforms Act of 1919 had contained a provision for a review of the constitutional field after ten years. Though discussions were initiated two years earlier than scheduled, with the appointment of the Simon Commission in 1927, nearly a decade was to lapse before the next instalment of reforms was actually granted. For ten years Indian politics were rocked by nationalist discontent and witnessed two major civil disobedience campaigns, while a series of official conferences and commissions hammered out the details of a constitution.

In Britain the 'Indian Question' aroused fierce political controversy. Winston Churchill led the opposition to Indian self-government, which he denounced not only as a betrayal of the British Empire but of the Indian peoples, whose future was, in his view, safer in the hands of British officials then those of Indian politicians. He had poured scorn on Lord Irwin for parleying with Gandhi. Lord Willingdon's strong-arm policy pleased him, but he wanted the Government to consolidate its 'victory' over the nationalists by refusing to relax the Imperial authority in India. Sir Samuel Hoare, who as Secretary of State for India in the British Cabinet had to pilot the new constitution through Parliament and bear the brunt of Churchill's opposition, had analysed its springs: 'The splendid memories gathered round the Indian Empire blinded him to the changes that had come about since the days of Clive, Wellington, Lawrence and Kipling. The India that he had served in the Fourth Hussars was the India of polo and pigsticking, of dashing frontier expeditions, of paternal government freely accepted and the great white Empress revered as a mysterious goddess.'[1]

The India of the nineteen-thirties was not the same as the India of the eighteen-nineties, not only because of the passage of time but because of the imprint of Gandhi's personality on Indian politics. This was something that Churchill with all his sense of history could not understand. The reasons are not far to seek. Gandhi's religious make-up and doctrines of truth and non-violence sounded only hypocritical nonsense to Churchill, the military strategist and politician, while Gandhi's challenge to Britain's moral right to govern India touched him in a particularly tender spot.

Faced with a solid bloc of opposition in the Press and Parliament, spokesmen of the British Government had in England to defend the very features of the new constitution which were most repugnant to Indian opinion: the 'safeguards' or the overriding powers retained in the hands of the Viceroy and the Governors to prevent Indian democracy from running amuck. The British dilemma was aptly summed up in a comment by the *Manchester Guardian*, that since the British could neither govern nor get out of India, it was necessary 'to devise a constitution that seems like self-government in India and at Westminster like British *Raj*'.

The new constitution, as it finally emerged, was as impressive for the powers it conferred on the elected representatives of the people as for those it withheld. It was as if a motor vehicle had been set in motion in low gear with the brakes on. The Indian Federation, when it came into being, was to incorporate Provinces as well as Princely States. The latter were allotted nearly one-third of the total seats in the federal legislature, and since their representatives, because of the absence of elective bodies, were likely to be nominees of the princes, who in turn were dependent for their very existence on the British Government, Indian nationalists viewed the new constitution with a feeling bordering on dismay. The powers of the federal legislature were circumscribed; a substantial part of the budget, that relating for instance to the military, the services, the interest charges, etc., was outside its purview. In the Provinces a wider field was permitted to ministers responsible to elected legislatures, but even here their powers had been restricted in financial and other matters, on which the Governors had been invested with overriding and preventive authority.

These limitations led Jawaharlal Nehru to describe the Indian

[1] Templewood, Lord (Sir Samuel Hoare): *Nine Troubled Years*, p. 98.

Reforms Act of 1935 as 'a Charter of Slavery'. At the Lucknow session of the Indian National Congress he declared that the new constitution offered Indians responsibility without power. The Congress decided, however, to contest the elections under the new constitution. The Congress election manifesto reaffirmed the rejection 'in entirety' of the new constitution, and demanded its replacement by another constitution based on political freedom for India and framed by a constituent assembly. However, the decision to contest the elections was taken partly because it was considered unwise to leave the field clear to anti-national elements, and partly because there was a powerful wing within the Congress which saw possibilities of constructive work in the Provinces even within the limited framework of the new constitution.

The results of the general election were known in February 1937. The Congress won clear majorities in U.P., Bihar, Orissa, C.P., and Madras. In Bombay it won nearly half the seats, and with allied groups could form a government. It was the largest party in the N.W.F.P. and Assam.

The Congress Manifesto had not given any clear lead as to what Congress was to do if it won majorities in the provincial legislatures. The subject was one on which opinion was sharply divided. Those who opposed the formation of ministries felt that nothing could be got out of the new constitution, that Congress would have to bear all the odium for the apparatus of imperialism without securing real relief to the people, and, worst of all, Congress would go the way of 'moderate' parties by ceasing to be a militant organization and getting out of touch with the masses from whom it derived its real strength. Those who favoured the assumption of responsibility for administering the provinces recognized the limitations of the new constitution, but were unwilling to yield any vantage point to the Government or to the political parties subservient to it; many of them were also convinced that the new constitution could be used for the service of the masses. As a compromise between these two opposing views, it was decided by a convention of Congress members of provincial legislatures, and of the All-India Congress Committee in March 1937, that Congress would agree to form ministries, provided the leader of the Congress party in the provincial legislature was satisfied, and was able to state publicly that the Governor would not use his special powers of interference or set aside the advice of the ministers 'in regard to their constitutional activities'.

Gandhi's own attitude to legislatures and to office acceptance was ultimately to prove crucial. In 1937, when the controversy on office acceptance was at its height, he wrote: 'The boycott of legislatures, let me tell you, is not an eternal principle like that of truth and non-violence. My opposition to them has lessened but that does not mean that I am going back on my former position. The question is of strategy and I can only say what is most needed at a particular moment.'[1]

The need of the moment was constructive work. Since the suspension of civil disobedience, Gandhi had been preoccupied with activities which though non-political in common parlance were nevertheless important, such as a clean water supply, a cheap and nutritious diet, a sound educational system and a healthy and self-sufficient economy for Indian villages. He wondered whether, with all its deficiencies, the new constitution could not further this programme of village uplift. There was no reason why Congress ministries in the provinces could not encourage village industries, introduce prohibition, reduce the burdens on the peasantry, promote the use of home-spun cloth, extend education and combat untouchability.

The Congress offer of March 1937 to accept office, provided the Governors gave assurances of non-interference in day-to-day administration, was thus influenced by Gandhi's desire to glean something constructive out of the new constitution and not lay traps for the Government. Official spokesmen at first took the line that any such assurance, or 'gentleman's agreement' would do violence to the constitution. Lord Linlithgow had told an Indian visitor in August 1936 that he could not change even a comma of the Government of India Act.[2] The debate on the assurances from the Governors was brought to an end by a long statement issued by the Viceroy, which was so phrased as to allay the fears of Congress without surrendering any constitutional ground.

The formation of Congress ministries in six provinces—Bombay, United Provinces, Bihar, Central Provinces, Orissa and Madras—was a significant event; a political party which was committed to the liquidation of the British Empire had agreed to run the administration in these provinces. The experiment was not as explosive as it was feared. The Congress ministers were preoccupied most of the time not with the best means of precipitating crises, but with those of fulfilling the social and

[1] *Harijan*, May 1, 1937.
[2] Birla, G. D.: *In the Shadow of the Mahatma*, p. 207.

economic programme enunciated in the Congress Election Manifesto. It was in this programme that Gandhi was interested and
by which he judged the work of Congress ministers. He advised
them to set an example of simplicity and frugality in their personal lives in line with the poverty of the people whom they
governed; he urged them to cultivate 'industry, ability, integrity,
impartiality, and an infinite capacity for mastering details'.

Two items in the legislative programme of the Congress
ministries appeared particularly important to Gandhi; these were
prohibition and education. Himself a total abstainer, Gandhi's
advocacy of prohibition derived not only from his own puritan-
ism, but from solicitude for the half-starved peasants and industrial workers who dissipated part of their meagre earnings
on drink, which would have been better spent on milk for their
children. On education, Gandhi had ideas based on his own
experience. At Phoenix and Tolstoy farms in South Africa, he
had helped run schools for children. The conviction grew upon
him that the value of academic instruction had been over-
rated and that character-building and the acquisition of practical
skills had not been given due recognition. In October 1937,
Gandhi placed his ideas before an educational conference which
met at Wardha and included, besides the Congress ministers, a
number of prominent educationists. A detailed scheme of elementary education based on these ideas was prepared by a
committee of educationists headed by Dr Zakir Husain.

The Wardha Scheme of Education, as these proposals came
to be known, stirred the stagnant pools of Indian education and
stimulated administrators and educationists to think along new
and progressive lines. The scheme had its critics. Did it not
sacrifice academic training to manual work? Were teachers in
schools to be turned into slave-drivers? Gandhi explained that the
object of the scheme was not primarily to produce craftsmen
but to exploit for educative purposes the resources implicit in
craft work. Nor was mass production of shoddy articles in
schools intended; a certain degree of skill, however, was inevitable, and it was enough if the sale of handicrafts covered the
teachers' salaries. The idea was to substitute a co-ordinated
training in the use of hand and eye for a notoriously bookish
and volatile learning which most village children unlearnt after
leaving school, or found of little use in their daily lives.

When the Congress ministries accepted office, neither the
Congress leaders nor the Government knew exactly how the
new partnership in the provinces would actually work out. It

was not easy for either side to leave the history of its long conflict behind, but association in day-to-day problems seemed to break some barriers. 'Fancy,' wrote Mahadev Desai, Gandhi's secretary, to G. D. Birla, 'Garret, the Commissioner of Ahmedabad, now going to the station to receive Minister Morarji and travelling a fair distance with him in third class.'[1] Of the I.C.S. officers serving in the provinces nearly half were Europeans. Though their salaries were a charge on the revenues of the provinces, and their careers were protected by the constitution, many of them tried to adapt themselves to provincial autonomy and to their new bosses. The tempo seemed to have quickened all round; in the provincial secretariats, the new democratic structure made increasing demands upon the time of the executive officers. There was some meddling in day-to-day administration by local politicians. The British officers had been able to adapt themselves to dyarchy during the twenties; in the thirties they tried to adjust their step to provincial autonomy, even if it required a visibly greater effort. The régime of the benevolent despots in the districts, conferring titles and lands and jobs for loyalty to the British *Raj*, was no longer unquestioned. Here was something that was not easy to accept by those who had been reared in the Imperial tradition. As Philip Mason, a former member of the I.C.S., sums it up, 'it is hard to serve where you have ruled'.[2]

A breach between the Congress and the Government may have been inevitable in the long run, but it might have been postponed, if not averted, in the ardour of Congress for social and economic reform and the anxiety of the Government not to disturb stable administration in the provinces in a period of acute international uncertainty.

The outbreak of war precipitated the crisis and brought the brief partnership between the Congress and the Government to a sudden end. It would be well at this stage to refer to the communal problem, which was in a sense to dominate and even distort Indian politics during the war and post-war years.

[1] Birla, G. D.: *In the Shadow of the Mahatma*, p. 243.
[2] Woodruff, Philip: *The Guardian*, London, 1955, p. 244.

# CHAPTER XXXIII

# The Genesis of Pakistan

THE session of the Round Table Conference in 1931, which was attended by Gandhi, failed to bring about a solution acceptable to the motley group of delegates whom the Government had assembled in London. Since constitution-making seemed to founder on lack of agreement, the Government decided to impose a solution. The British Premier issued a Communal Award to determine the quantum and mode of representation in legislatures, and the new constitution based on this Award came into force in April 1937. The Award had conceded the principal demands of Muslim spokesmen. The perpetuation of the communal franchise (separate electorates) in the Award was repugnant to the Indian National Congress, but Congress decided not to reject it until some better solution, acceptable to all the communities, could emerge. Whatever the shortcomings of the Communal Award as a 'package solution' of the communal problem, it might have been expected to end the communal controversy and to release the energies of the people for more constructive work.

Events were to show that the communal controversy, far from being suppressed, was to rage like a hurricane during the next ten years and pull down many familiar landmarks. The history of this decade cannot be understood without reference to the personality and politics of Mr M. A. Jinnah. That communal antagonisms should have reached a new peak in the closing years of British rule was perhaps natural; it was, in political terms, a war of succession. However, it is doubtful if the communal problem would have dominated Indian politics in the way it did without Jinnah's impact on it.

Six years younger than Gandhi, Jinnah had also studied law in England, but unlike Gandhi his main interest outside legal studies had been in politics and not in religion. Jinnah had in his youth come under the influence of Dadabhai Naoriji; he was a friend of Gokhale and took to law and politics in Bombay. In his early forties he was a front-rank politician and took a prominent part in the conclusion of the Lucknow Pact in 1916, which brought the National Congress and the Muslim league on to a common platform. These were the years when he was described as 'the ambassador of Hindu-Muslim unity.'

Whether in the Imperial Legislative Council, of which he was an elected member, or outside Jinnah's stand on most political problems reflected a spirit of nationalism. He joined the Home Rule movement and supported the demand for Indian self-government as a condition precedent to wholehearted Indian support to the British Government in the war against Germany. In 1919 Jinnah condemned the Rowlatt Bills, which had hastened Gandhi's conversion from a loyalist into a rebel. He criticized the Government for its policy in the Punjab and towards Turkey, but he did not join Gandhi's movement; in fact he left the Indian National Congress just as Gandhi began to dominate its counsels. Like many another 'moderate' leader, Jinnah would have liked Congress to remain an unofficial parliament of the Indian intelligentsia in which well-educated—and well-dressed—gentlemen debated current affairs in the King's English, and passed resolutions for the information of the Indian Press and the British Government. Jinnah had once (December 1918) led a demonstration to foil a public meeting in honour of the retiring Governor of Bombay, Lord Willingdon. But this was perhaps the solitary lapse from that lofty, almost Olympian, dignity with which Jinnah loved to play the game of politics in those years. When Gandhi broadened the scope of his movement to embrace the illiterate millions in towns and villages, Jinnah feared that the march to disaster had begun. 'What the consequences of this may be,' he wrote, 'I shudder to contemplate.'

It was not only Gandhi's politics which jarred upon Jinnah. Gandhi's religious frame of mind, his habit of self-analysis, his emphasis on such abstractions as truth and non-violence, his conscious humility, his voluntary poverty—all these were alien to Jinnah's own make-up and struck him either as a political irrelevance or as downright hypocrisy. There are indications that Jinnah even suffered from a feeling that he had been unfairly edged out of the forefront of the political stage by Gandhi. Louis Fischer records that Jinnah told him: 'Nehru worked under me in the Home Rule Society. Gandhi worked under me at the time of the Lucknow Pact.' It is doubtless true that in 1916 Jinnah was in the limelight and in 1920 he had almost ceased to be a political force. Several other leaders had a similar experience, which is to be attributed to the intensity with which Gandhi's personality and doctrines appealed to millions of Indians who had so far been little affected by politics.

In the nineteen-twenties, Jinnah headed an independent group in the Central Legislative Assembly, where he held the balance between the Government and the Congress. This was a role which he could play with masterly skill. He did not align himself with the Government or the Congress, and though he pleaded for communal unity his price for co-operation continued to rise. His opposition to the solution of the communal problem in the Nehru Report went a long way to kill it in 1928. To Gandhi's civil disobedience movements in the early thirties he took no more kindly than he had done ten years earlier to the non-co-operation movement. At the Round Table Conference he ploughed a lonely furrow; as Sir Samuel Hoare puts it, 'he never seemed to wish to work with anyone'. After the Conference he almost bade good-bye to Indian politics and settled down in England. But as the time came for the general elections under the new constitution, he returned to India and led the Muslim League to the polls. The League did not get more than five per cent of the Muslim vote, but within four years of this disastrous defeat Jinnah was able to build up his position so skilfully that he was accused of placing a veto on India's constitutional progress.

We have already seen that Congress had agreed, with Gandhi's blessing, to form governments in the summer of 1937 in provinces where its adherents commanded majorities in the legislatures. Congress decided not to form coalition ministries; it had comfortable majorities and did not require the support of other parties to remain in office. Congress leaders were also influenced by the fear that coalition cabinets might lead to compromise and conflict and thus weaken Congress, which had yet to win political freedom for the country. Against these considerations was the fact that out of the 450 Muslim seats in the provincial legislatures, Congress had contested only fifty-eight and won twenty-six. Congress did take Muslim legislators into the cabinets, but only after they had signed the Congress pledge. Whatever the justification for this decision, which was taken against Gandhi's advice, it cut the leaders of the Muslim League, particularly Jinnah, to the quick. The separate electorates on which they had banked all these years had only helped to keep Muslims out of Congress and failed to bring them an effective share in political power.

From 1937 onwards a new exacerbation enters Jinnah's

speeches and writings; a new desperation leads him from one tactical position to the other until he reaches the edge of the abyss. The Congress ministries without representatives of the Muslim League offered him the handiest pegs on which he could deposit all the grievances of Muslims, real or fancied. 'The fact is,' he declared, 'the Congress wants domination of India under shelter of British bayonets.' The Congress was he alleged, 'encircling' the Muslim League and trying to 'break up its solidarity'. He ridiculed the Congress proposal for a Constituent Assembly, which Gandhi had endorsed as a solution of the political and communal problems. 'It is puerile to ask the British Government in the first instance to call a Constituent Assembly of another nation and afterwards have the honour and privilege of placing the constitution framed by this supreme assembly of India on the statute-book of British Parliament.' Gandhi was Jinnah's chosen target. He was the 'sole dictator and interpreter of the Congress'. Light had 'not yet dawned within the territories of Segaon'; Gandhi was trying 'to subjugate and vassalize the Muslims under a Hindu Raj and annihilate the Muslims'.

Jinnah's campaign against the Congress steadily rose in tempo. In the spring of 1939 he declared that the provincial part of the new constitution had utterly failed to safeguard Muslim rights. A few months later he questioned the suitability of a democratic system of government 'in such a vast country with different nationalities'. He blamed the Governors and the Viceroy for not exercising their special powers to protect the interests of the Muslims in Congress-governed provinces. When the Congress ministries resigned in November 1939, as a protest against India's participation in the war without her consent, Jinnah announced the celebration of 'a day of deliverance' of Muslims 'from tyranny, oppression and injustice' during two and a half years of Congress rule, in which Muslim opinion was alleged to have been flouted, Muslim culture destroyed, Muslim religious and social life attacked, and Muslim economic and political rights trampled upon.

Under the constitution, the Governors had special responsibilities for the protection of the minorities. One of them, Sir Harry Haig (Governor of the United Provinces), wrote after his retirement: 'In dealing with communal issues, the Ministers in my judgment normally acted with impartiality and a desire to do what was fair. Indeed towards the end of their time they were seriously criticized by the Hindu Mahasabha on the ground that they were not being fair to the Hindus, though there was in fact no justification for such a criticism.[1]

Early in 1940 the Congress President, Dr Rajendra Prasad, wrote to Jinnah suggesting that the charges against the Congress ministries should be investigated by a judge of the Federal Court. Jinnah turned down the suggestion and called for a Royal Commission. A Royal Commission in wartime and for raking up such a controversy was hardly likely to be appointed, but it looked as if Jinnah wanted to keep the controversy alive as long as he could. His propaganda was directed not so much at the Congress or the British Government as at his own community; it was, to use a contemporary phrase, 'for home consumption'. Anything which widened the gulf between Hindus and Muslims and indicated that the differences between the two communities were irreconcilable proved his thesis that a democratic set-up was impossible for India.

Jinnah began to develop his two-nation theory; the differences between Hindus and Muslims were not just confined to religion, but covered the whole range of their social, cultural and economic life. In March 1940, the two-nation theory was officially accepted by the All-India Muslim League, which declared that no constitutional plan for India would be workable or acceptable to Muslims unless it was based on a demarcation of Muslim majority areas in the north-west and the east as independent states. Pakistan, which Muslim spokesmen had dismissed during the Round Table Conference as a 'students' scheme', had now become the goal of the Muslim League.

Gandhi's first reaction to the two-nation theory and the demand for Pakistan was one of bewilderment, almost of incredulity. Was it the function of religion to separate men or to unite them? He described the two-nation theory as an untruth; in his dictionary there was no stronger word. He discussed the attributes of nationality. A change of religion did not change nationality; the religious divisions did not coincide with cultural differences. A Bengali Muslim, he wrote, 'speaks the same tongue as a Bengali Hindu does, eats the same food, has the same amusements as his Hindu neighbour. They dress alike. His (Jinnah's name) name could be that of any Hindu. When I first met him, I did not know he was a Muslim'.

To divide India was to undo the centuries of work done by Hindus and Muslims; Gandhi's soul rebelled against the idea that Hinduism and Islam represented antagonistic cultures and

[1] *Asiatic Review*, July 1940.

doctrines, and that eighty million Muslims had really nothing in common with their Hindu neighbours. And even if there were religious and cultural differences, what clash of interests could there be on such matters as revenue, industry, sanitation or justice? The differences could only be in religious usage and observances, with which a secular state should have no concern.

'Vivisect me before you vivisect India,' was Gandhi's anguished comment; but however strongly he felt on Pakistan, he was the last man to force his views down the throat of a single individual. 'I know,' he confessed in *Harijan*, April 6, 1940, 'no non-violent method of compelling the obedience of eight crores of Muslims to the will of the rest of India, however powerful the majority the rest may represent. The Muslims must have the same rights of self-determination that the rest of India has. We are at present a joint family. Any member may claim a division.'

This was the only possible attitude for a man of non-violence, though it may have encouraged Jinnah in the belief that if the Muslim League persisted in its demand and could carry Muslim public opinion, Pakistan would become a reality. Until almost the last stage, Jinnah did not define the boundaries or fill in the outlines of his Pakistan proposal; each of his followers was thus free to see Pakistan in his own image. The orthodox dreamed of a state reproducing the purity of pristine Islam, a community living in conformity with the teachings of the holy Prophet. Those with a secular outlook hoped for tangible benefits from their 'own' state.

Though it came like a bolt from the blue to Indian nationalists, the Pakistan idea sold fast with the Muslim community, particularly with its middle class. There were several reasons for this development. The Muslim middle class, which for historical reasons had been left behind in the race for the plums of government service, trade, and industry, was attracted by the idea of a Muslim state. In a competitive society anything which promised a short-cut to success was welcome. Muslim landlords in Bengal and Punjab saw the prospects of deliverance from the 'progressive politicians' who indulged in dangerous talk of abolishing *zamindari*. Muslim officials were glad of the new vistas which were expected to open to them a new state, without Hindu seniors hovering over their heads. Muslim traders and industrialists began to cherish visions of free fields for prosperous ventures without the intrusion of Hindu competitors.

Pakistan seemed to fulfil a psychological need of the Indian Muslims. As W. C. Smith explained in 1946:

'The Muslim League, then, has been becoming the organ of a surging nationalism; at its centre a hard core of business interests intent on power, but beginning to be supported also by an awakening peasantry and surrounded by a nationalism's complete paraphernalia, of poetry, and a whole cultural renascence of youthful idealism and open-hearted devotion.'[1]

The outbreak of the world war helped the propagation of the separatist ideology. The resignation of the Congress ministries allowed the League to occupy the political stage. If the Congress ministries had remained in office, the atrocity stories against them could not have been repeated without being challenged. As it was, the Governors could hardly be expected to give a 'clearance certificate' to those who had now become their political opponents. The war itself was an important consideration for not alienating the Muslim League. The Viceroy and his advisers were anxious not to do anything which would offend Jinnah. The demand for Pakistan probably surprised the British Government as much as it surprised Congress. Initially, its significance in British eyes was that it confirmed their stock thesis that constitutional progress in India was barred not by British hesitation but by Indian discord. The declaration in August 1940 that 'it goes without saying that they (the British Government) could not contemplate transfer of their present responsibilities for the peace and welfare of India to any system of government whose authority is directly denied by large and powerful elements in India's national life' was the first tacit recognition that the British Government were prepared to consider even such drastic solutions as Jinnah had propounded. The Pakistan resolution of the All-India Muslim League had only been passed in March 1940. But for the war, it is doubtful if even an indirect endorsement of the Pakistan proposal would have been publicly made so soon. The war, however, was dictating the pace of events, which neither the British Government nor the Indian leaders could entirely foresee or control.

---

[1] Smith, Wilfred Cantwell: *Modern Islam in India*, London, 1946, p. 275.

# CHAPTER XXXIV

# India and the War

In the two decades between the first and second World Wars, Gandhi's faith in the British Empire had been irrevocably shaken; but his own belief in the power of non-violence had grown with greater reflection and experience, and the people of India, thanks to three major Satyagraha campaigns and his extensive countrywide tours, had become familiar with the cult of non-violence. Such was the emphasis which Gandhi had placed on non-violence in the struggle for political freedom that it sometimes looked as if he regarded the means as more important than the goal. In November 1931 he had gone so far as to say: 'And I would like to repeat to the world, times without number, that I will not purchase my country's freedom at the cost of non-violence.'

As the threat of war grew in 1938 and 1939, and the forces of violence gathered momentum, Gandhi reasserted his faith in the efficacy of non-violence. He felt more strongly than ever that at that moment of crisis in world history he had a message for India and India had a message for bewildered humanity. Through the pages of *Harijan* he expounded the non-violent approach to military aggression and political tyranny. He advised the weaker nations to defend themselves not by seeking protection from better armed States, nor by increasing their own fighting potential, but by non-violent resistance to the aggressor. A non-violent Abyssinia, he explained, needed no arms and no succour from the League of Nations; if every Abyssinian man, woman, and child refused co-operation with the Italians, willing or forced, the latter would have to walk to victory over the dead bodies of their victims and to occupy the country without the people.

It may be argued that Gandhi was making a heavy demand upon human endurance. It required supreme courage for a whole people to die to the last man, woman and child, rather than surrender to the enemy. Gandhi's non-violent resistance was thus not a soft doctrine—a convenient refuge from a dangerous situation. Nor was it an offer on a silver platter to the dictators of what they plotted to wrest by force. Those who offered non-violent resistance had to be prepared for the extreme sacrifice.

Non-violence, moreover, was not merely a method of meeting aggression; it represented a way of life. The motive power of Nazi and Fascist militarism was the desire to carve new empires, and behind it all was a ruthless competition to annex new sources of raw materials and fresh markets. Wars were thus rooted in the overweening greeds of men, as also in the purblind tribalism which enthroned nationalism above humanity. If the world was to get rid of this recurring menace of war, it had to shake off not only militarism, but the competitive greed and fear and hatred which fed it.

In an article in the *Aryan Path* in September 1938, John Middleton Murry described Gandhi as the greatest Christian teacher in the modern world and wrote: 'Assuredly I see absolutely no hope for western civilization except the kindling of a vast and consuming flame of Christian Love. The choice appears to be between that or a mass-murder on a scale at which the imagination sickens.'

In fact there was no kindling of a flame of Christian Love. The lights went out one by one until the war broke out.

On September 3, 1939, the Gazette of India carried the grave announcement: 'I, Victor Alexander John, Marquess of Linlithgow, Governor-General of India and ex-officio Admiral, therein being satisfied thereof by information received by me, do hereby proclaim that war has broken out between His Majesty and Germany.'

One man, and he a foreigner, writes Jawaharlal Nehru in the *Discovery of India*, plunged four hundred million human beings into war without the slightest reference to them. Since the federal part of the Government of India Act of 1935 had not get become operative, and ultimate responsibility for the governance of India was vested in the British Parliament, the declaration of Lord Linlithgow was unexceptionable from the constitutional point of view; but tactically it was a great blunder. That this should have happened was the more unfortunate because the sympathy of the Indian National Congress was overwhelmingly in favour of the Allies. The 'foreign policy' of Congress was largely shaped by Nehru, whose opposition to totalitarian régimes admitted of no compromise. Gandhi, too, briefed by Nehru in international affairs, naturally sympathized with the victims of aggresson.

There was thus a great reservoir of sympathy for the Allied

cause on which the British Government could have drawn. The Viceroy had failed to take Indian leaders into his confidence before declaring India a belligerent, but he endeavoured to make up for this omission soon afterwards. He telegraphed to Gandhi to see him. Gandhi took the first train to Simla. He told Linlithgow that his sympathies were with England and France. As a man of non-violence, the utmost he could offer to the Allied cause was his moral support. As he discussed the war and pictured the possible destruction of the House of Commons and Westminster Abbey be broke down. Violence seemed triumphantly on the march.

His heart, under the first impact of war, was heavy: 'I have become disconsolate. In the secret of my heart I am in perpetual quarrel with God that He should allow such things to go on. My non-violence seems almost impotent. But the answer comes at the end of the daily quarrel that neither God nor non-violence is impotent. Impotence is in men.' He saw the futility of violence in countering violence. His line was cast: 'Whether I act as a guide of the Working Committee, or if I may use the same expression, without offence, of the Government, my guidance will be for the deliberate purpose of taking either or both along the path of non-violence, be the step ever so imperceptible.'[1]

The Indian National Congress, however, was not a body of pacifists; it had accepted non-violence in the struggle for freedom, but not as a creed for all times and in all situations. Prominent Congressmen, including Motilal Nehru, had interested themselves in the Indianization of the officers' cadre of the British Indian army, and few of them had imagined that an independent India would be able to dispense with the police and the military. Most Congressmen viewed the war, not from the angle of non-violence, but from that of Indian self-government. In the First World War, Tilak, Annie Besant and other ardent nationalists had demanded political freedom as a condition precedent to India's unreserved participation in the war effort. A quarter of a century later, with greater awakening in the country, it was scarcely to be expected that nationalists would ask for less. There was an obvious contradiction in Indians fighting to hold aloft the banner of freedom and democracy in Czechoslovakia or Poland, while their own country was in bondage. There was yet another consideration which weighed with those who felt keenly for the Allied cause. Wars were no longer bouts between professional armies in distant battlefields; whole nations

[1] *Harijan*, September 30, 1939.

had to be mobilized as workers or soldiers; unless Britain released India's energies by treating her as an equal partner in a common fight, it was hardly possible for her to play her full part in the world struggle.

In its resolution of September 14, 1939, the Congress Working Committee expressed its sympathy for those who were resisting Nazi aggression and offered its co-operation in the war against Nazism. Co-operation however, was to be 'between equals by mutual consent for a cause which both consider to be worthy'. The committee invited the British Government to declare in unequivocal language its war-aims in regard to democracy and imperialism, and in particular how these aims were going to apply to India: 'The real test of any declaration is its application in the present, for it is the present that will govern action today and give shape to the future.' Congress thus posed two basic problems to Britain: to define the shape of the order for which the war was being waged, and to give India a foretaste of that freedom and democracy for which she was being called upon to fight.

In the summer of 1940, Nazi armies overran Western Europe. The spectacle of the island of Britain, fighting single-handed against heavy odds, evoked widespread sympathy as well as admiration in India. It was also evident that if Britain failed to stem the German tide of conquest, nothing could stop Hitler from dominating the Mediterranean and marching into India. The imminence of the peril dictated a new approach, and the Congress Working Committee declared that if the British Government made an unequivocal declaration of Indian independence after the war, Congress would immediately join in a provisional National Government for the effective defence of the country. That Congress was in dead earnest is shown by the fact that in making this offer of co-operation to the British Government it agreed to part company with Gandhi. In spite of his detestation of the regimentation and violence which Nazism represented, in spite of his sympathy for the Allies, Gandhi believed that violence could only be effectively neutralized by non-violence; he wished Congress to declare that it would meet even armed aggression with non-violent resistance. When Congress offered to enter a provisional government for the better prosecution of the war, Gandhi felt he could not associate himself with a policy in which he did not believe.

# CHAPTER XXXV

# The Widening Rift

THE Congress leaders believed in that critical summer of 1940 that they had brought down their terms for co-operation with the Government to the lowest pitch. They had gone the length of forgoing the leadership of Gandhi. In return, they expected a bold and imaginative gesture by the British Government—'a pleasant psychological shock'—which would wipe out past suspicion and generate a new enthusiasm among the people.

They looked in vain for this gesture in the announcement which the Viceroy made on August 8th on behalf of His Majesty's Government. The view that the framing of the new constitutional scheme should be primarily the responsibility of the people of India was conceded, but with the qualification that this could not be undertaken at a time when Britain was engaged in a struggle for existence. There were the familiar references to the responsibilities which Britain's long association with India had imposed upon her and of which she could not divest herself. There was the significant statement that the British Government 'could not contemplate transfer of their present responsibilities for the peace and welfare of India to any system of government whose authority is directly denied by large and powerful elements in India's national life. Nor could they be parties to the coercion of such elements to such a government'. An affirmation of this kind was hardly called for; nobody expected the Government to coerce 'large and powerful elements' in the country's national life. To use such phraseology, whether its authors willed it or not, was calculated only to increase the intransigence of the Muslim League, and to make more difficult a Congress-League concord, which the Government professed was a *sine qua non* for the transfer of substantial authority to Indians.

The immediate constitutional changes included the expansion of the Viceroy's Council to include some 'representative Indians', and the establishment of a War Advisory Council consisting of representatives from the Provinces and the States and other interests 'in the national life of India as a whole'.

The 'August Offer' was the maximum which the British Government felt able to make to India in the summer of 1940, but it fell short of the minimum which Congress was prepared to accept. That even in a supreme crisis the Government should fail to respond to appeals for co-operation stung Congress leaders. Their disappointment was all the greater because many of them were really anxious to co-operate in the emergency which faced the Government and the country.

Gandhi was genuinely anxious not to embarrass the Government during the war, and Congress leaders were so apprehensive about the fate of the Allied cause that a mass movement at this stage was not on the cards. Nevertheless, such was the profound frustration among Congressmen at the attitude of the Government as disclosed in the 'August Offer' that there was a powerful impulse for action of some kind.

An eloquent expression of this frustration was given by Jawaharlal Nehru in an article entitled 'The Parting of the Ways'. 'The declaration of the British Government,' he wrote, 'means the final breaking of such slender bonds as held our minds together.' The All-India Congress Committee met in September 1940 at Bombay and affirmed its total rejection of the Government's proposals. Since there was no prospect of co-operation with the Government in furtherance of the war-effort, the argument as to whether this co-operation could or could not be based on non-violence became irrelevant. There was now no occasion for Gandhi and the Congress to pursue divergent ways; Congress therefore called upon him to resume its leadership. Congress wanted to lodge a protest against the policy of the Government and looked to Gandhi for guidance.

It was a political issue—the refusal of the British Government to give adequate assurances of Indian freedom in the future, and practical evidence of its intentions in the present—which had widened the gulf between the Government and the Congress. But it was not on a political but a pacifistic plank that Gandhi initiated his campaign of protest. His argument was that if the British could not grant or guarantee independence to the people of India, they could at least grant the right of free speech, including the right to preach against India's participation in the World War, and indeed against all wars.

Gandhi resisted the pressure exerted by some of his colleagues and left-wing Congressmen for the launching of a mass movement. He decided to confine civil disobedience to selected individuals. The instructions which he issued for the Satyagrahis and sportingly communicated to the Viceroy ruled out public excitement and harassment of the authorities. The movement began on October 17, 1940 with an anti-war speech by Acharya Vinoba Bhave at Paunar, a village near Wardha; he was arrested four days later. Jawaharlal Nehru had been chosen to follow Vinoba Bhave on November 7th, but he had been arrested a week earlier on his way to Allahabad and sentenced to four years' imprisonment. In the middle of November the second stage of the campaign began, with what Gandhi called the 'representative Satyagraha'. Satyagrahis were selected from groups such as the Congress Working Committee, the All-India Congress Committee and the Congress members of the Central and Provincial Legislatures.

By the end of the year nearly 400 Congress legislators, including twenty-nine ex-ministers, were in gaol. Early in January 1941 the third stage in the campaign was initiated, with lists of Satyagrahis prepared by the local Congress Committees and approved by Gandhi. The fourth stage of the campaign in April 1941 witnessed the enrolment of rank and file Congressmen. By May 15, 1941, according to official records, 25,069 convictions had been made for individual civil disobedience. There was very little excitement, however, thanks to the manner in which Gandhi had conducted this 'symbolic' campaign; he would not agree to its extension into a mass civil disobedience movement: 'There is neither warrant nor atmosphere for mass action. That would be naked embarrassment and a betrayal of non-violence.'

When the *Hindu* pointed out that the movement had produced no appreciable impression on the war-effort, Gandhi replied that it was not intended to hamper the war-effort. The Secretary of State for India, Mr Amery, said the movement was 'as regrettable as it is irrational', and described it as proceeding 'languidly and without evoking much interest'. Three days before the Japanese attack on Pearl Harbour, the Government of India, to quote from the official communiqué, 'confident in the determination of all responsible opinion in India to support the war-effort until victory is secured', announced that it had decided to release those convicted for individual civil disobedience.

The entry of Japan into the war brought it almost to India's door. With the American fleet crippled, the Japanese swept quickly through the Western Pacific. On February 15, 1942 Singapore fell and the Bay of Bengal lay exposed to the Japanese

fleet. The British command of the sea had gone. The tide of
Japanese conquest, after overwhelming Malaya and Burma, threatened to engulf eastern and southern India. The rapidity with
which the Japanese advanced was evidence not only of their
superiority in numbers and strategy, but also of the lack of will
to resist in the countries invaded by them.

Gandhi had condemned the Japanese slogan of 'Asia for
Asiatics' and even favoured the boycott of Japanese goods as a
mark of sympathy with China. Nehru's sympathy for China was
well known. The danger, therefore, was not so much of active
collaboration by sections of Indians with the Japanese, as of
defeatism and passivity on the part of the people, which might
enable the Japanese to consolidate themselves if they managed
to land and win an initial battle or two. The demand of the
Indian National Congress that the people should be given a
stake in an all-out resistance to the Axis Powers acquired a new
urgency.

Gandhi's first reaction to the Viceroy's gesture in releasing
prisoners convicted for individual civil disobedience at the beginning of December 1941 had been far from enthusiastic; it did
not, he declared, 'evoke a single responsive or appreciative
chord' in him. Events, however, moved fast, faster than anticipated by Congress and the Government. In the winter of 1941-2
the war situation was as critical for the Allies as it had been
in the summer of 1940 after the fall of France. Once again, a section of Congressmen led by Rajagopalachari favoured an immediate settlement with the British Government for a united front
against the Japanese. Most of the Congress leaders were prepared to throw the weight of Congress against the Japanese
peril, provided the Government made a reciprocal gesture.

Meanwhile, the war situation had made its impact upon the
British Government. Prime Minister Churchill's views on Indian
independence have already been discussed;[1] in 1941 they were no
different from those he had held in 1931. In December 1941,
when Churchill visited Washington, President Roosevelt referred
to the Indian problem. 'I reacted so strongly,' Churchill has recorded, 'and at such length that he never raised it verbally
again.' It was not only American pressure but the pace of the
Japanese advance which was to persuade Churchill to seek a way
out of the Indian political deadlock. On February 25th, ten days
after the fall of Singapore, he appointed a sub-committee of the
War Cabinet to study the Indian problem and to suggest a solu-

[1] Chapter XXVII.

tion. Of the members of this study group Simon and Attlee
had been members of the Statutory Commission, James Grigg
and John Anderson had held high office in India, Stafford Cripps
was well acquainted with Indian leaders and politics, and Amery
was the Secretary of State for India. On March 11th Churchill
was able to report to the House of Commons that the war Cabinet had come to a unanimous decision on the Indian question,
and that Stafford Cripps, the leader of the House of Commons,
was proceeding to India to discuss the proposals with Indian
leaders.

No better choice could have been made than that of Stafford
Cripps for this momentous mission. His sympathies with the
cause of Indian freedom were known and he personally knew
the front-rank leaders of Indian opinion. He had thus good
reason to be optimistic when he arrived at New Delhi on March
22nd. The 'Draft Declaration' which Cripps brought with him
and discussed with prominent officials and leaders contained the
British Government's proposals for the solution of the Indian
political problem. Immediately after the war elections were to be
held to provincial legislatures, and members of the lower houses
of these legislatures were to elect a constitution-making body.
The Indian States were to be invited to nominate representatives to this assembly, which was to be charged with framing
a constitution for a 'Union of India', a full-fledged Dominion
'with the same full status as the other Dominions'. The Union
of India was to have the right to opt out of the British Common-
wealth. The British Government undertook to implement this
constitution subject to '. . . the right of any Province of British
India that is not prepared to accept the new Constitution to
retain its present constitutional position, provision being made
for its subsequent accession if it so decides.' Mr Attlee has
recorded in his memoirs that the Draft Declaration was a bold
plan, and 'reflected credit on those members of the Government
who were not sanguine as to the feasibility of Indian self-
government and especially upon the Prime Minister whose views
were very strong'.

Against this exuberant confidence of the British leaders may
be set the grave misgivings with which the plan was received
by Indian leaders. Gandhi, whom Cripps had summoned from
Wardha by telegram, after reading the proposals advised Cripps
to take the next plane home. Jawaharlal Nehru confessed to
a 'profound depression' when he read the proposals for the first
time; the more he read them and pondered over them, the more

depressed he felt. It was true that India's right to self-determination had been definitely conceded by the British Government for the first time, and both the time and the machinery for exercising this right had been clearly specified. But the right of non-accession reserved to the Provinces and the Indian States threatened to convert the country into a political chequerboard containing scores of 'independent states', which could make short work of India as a political and economic entity. The right of non-accession was evidently given to the Provinces to meet half-way the Muslim League's demand for Pakistan. 'If you want,' Cripps said in one of his broadcasts 'to persuade a number of people who are inclined to be antagonistic to enter the same room, it is unwise to tell them that once they go in there is no way out.' Congress leaders felt that the Cripps' offer in 1942 had gone one step further than Linlithgow's August offer of 1940 to encourage Jinnah to persist in his separatist line. In March 1940 Pakistan had seemed a phantom; by March 1942 it had become a political possibility.

Even though Cripps had presented his proposals as a 'package deal', and even though the long-term proposals were the 'bold' part of the plan, Congress leaders suggested that the long-term proposals be shelved for the time being and an agreement sought on immediate arrangements for the defence of India. There were a series of discussions between the Indian leaders on the one hand and Cripps and the Viceroy on the other, regarding the functions of an Indian Defence Member of the Viceroy's Council. These discussions, in which Colonel Louis Johnson, the personal envoy of President Roosevelt, also joined, broke down not on the demarcation of duties between the Indian Defence Member and the British Commander-in-Chief, but on a much wider issue—the nature and authority of the interim government as a whole.

On his return to England, Cripps asserted that from the outset he had made it clear to all those whom he had seen that it was not possible to make any constitutional changes—except of the most insignificant kind—prior to the new constitution, which was to come into operation as a result of the labours of the constitution-making body after the war. This may have been Cripps's intention from the outset, but the Congress leaders nevertheless received a contrary impression. During the negotiations he had used such terms as 'National Government' and 'Cabinet', which had led Congress leaders to hope that the new Government would function, by convention if not by law, as a Cabinet with full powers, and with the Viceroy as constitutional head. The misunderstanding may have been due to assumptions which the Draft Declaration did not justify; as Nehru wrote later, the Congress leaders' eagerness for a settlement may have fed their optimism.

The comment of an Indian paper, the *National Herald* of April 24, 1942, that 'the Cripps mission was the result of American pressure. It was a stage-managed show to buy off world opinion and to foist preconcerted failure on the people of India' was an index to Indian frustration at the failure of the Cripps Mission, but did less than justice to the British Government. For the first time that Government had recognized unequivocally India's right to self-government, and this, coming from a Government led by a Premier who made no secret of his distrust of Indian nationalism was certainly a step forward. Unfortunately, the constitutional proposals were framed as a halfway house between two irreconcilable objectives, the creation of a free and democratic India and its fragmentation into endless segments in deference to Muslim separatism and the vested interests of the Princes. Thanks to Jinnah's ideology and tactics, the Indian political problem had become too complicated to be solved by a formula hurriedly hammered out in London by a sub-committee of the War Cabinet. The fact that the proposals were not subject to any major amendment—the 'take it or leave' condition attached to them—made chances of success still more remote.

Such was the gravity of the war situation that in spite of serious objections to the long-term constitutional proposals, nationalist India was willing to put that complicated problem into cold storage and concentrate on the immediate task of mobilizing the country against the Japanese peril. Unfortunately, the critical war situation which had provided the main impulse for the despatch of the Cripps Mission was also responsible for wrecking it. Congress leaders, who had parted company with Gandhi on the non-violent defence of India, were thinking in terms of a last ditch fight against the Japanese, of building up new armies, militia and home guards.

Roosevelt, who had been anxiously watching the progress of Cripps's negotiations and was receiving first-hand reports from his personal envoy at New Delhi, sent a mesage to Churchill through Hopkins that the American public could not understand why, if there was willingness on the part of the British Government to permit the component parts of India to secede from the

British Empire after the war, the British Government was unwilling to permit Indians to enjoy during the war what was
tantamount to self-government. Roosevelt suggested that another
effort should be made to set up a nationalist government 'in
essence similar to our own form of government'. 'I was thankful,'
writes Churchill, 'that events had made such an act of madness
impossible.' Cripps had already left for India.

'To us and to all Indians,' the Congress President had written
to Cripps 'the dominant consideration is the defence and safety
of India.' Paradoxically, the consideration which made Congress
leaders call for a National Government weighed with the British
in their determination that there should be no substantial transfer of power to Indian political parties during the war. Many
senior officers in the Government of India and the provinces felt,
to quote Philip Woodruff[1], that 'not another shell, not another pair of boots, not another recruit,' could be contributed by
Congress support of the war-effort. As early as January 1942,
Churchill had written that the idea that the British Government
could get more out of India by putting Congress in charge at
that juncture was ill-founded. 'Bringing hostile elements into
the defence machine,' he added. 'will paralyse action.' In March
1942 the British Premier had been persuaded to agree to the
Cripps proposals as a long-term solution of the Indian political
problem, but his distrust of Congress—and Congress's distrust
of him—persisted. Turning down President Roosevelt's last-
minute plea for yet another effort by Cripps for reconciliation
with Congress, Churchill recorded that he could not take responsibility for the defence of India 'if everything had again to
be thrown into the melting pot at this critical juncture'.

On his return to England Cripps blamed the failure of his
mission on Gandhi. He went so far as to suggest that the Congress Working Committee had passed a resolution accepting the
Cripps proposals, but that Gandhi had intervened and the resolution was reversed. Gandhi had been reluctant to come to
Delhi. He had agreed to meet Cripps at the latter's insistence.
He had made no secret of his misgivings; but he had left Delhi
at an early stage of the negotiations. The final decisions were
taken by the Working Committee; its members were aware
of Gandhi's unfavourable reactions, but the Committee also
knew that Gandhi would not stand in the way of any decision
it took.

Gandhi had been quoted as having remarked that the Cripps
[1] Woodruff, Philip: *The Guardian*, p. 305.

offer was a post-dated cheque on a crashing bank. 'I had of course', Gandhi told a friend, 'said nothing of the kind. But the criticism on the score of its being a post-dated cheque is absolutely correct.' The whole approach, the reluctance to rectify the present and the emphasis on the future left him cold. And he had his own way of judging a policy by its results in the present. If the British had really accepted India's right to freedom, or, to use Gandhi's terminology, if they had undergone a change of heart, he expected to see it not only in state documents but in day-to-day administration. Of this he saw no sign.

# CHAPTER XXXVI

# Quit India

GANDHI had taken little interest in the Cripps Mission, but its failure was a great disappointment to him. That even a friend of India like Stafford Cripps could have misunderstood or misinterpreted the position of Congress was something of a shock. It was clear that there was little prospect of a political settlement as long as the war lasted. The Government were preoccupied with the critical war situation. The Indian army was being rapidly expanded and reinforced with troops and military equipment from Britain and America.

What defence in depth could do in a vast sub-continent had been learnt, at heavy cost, by Japan in China and by Germany in Russia. India was also a vast country, not easy to occupy quickly. In India, however, unlike China and Russia, the war had not evoked an upsurge of patriotism. There was hardly any unity of purpose between the Government and the people. The distrust of the British had become almost pathological. While the Government were in touch with the small minority which had thrived on the new avenues of employment and contracts opened by the war, Gandhi's hand was on the pulse of the people. He noted that their mood in the face of grave peril was not one of resolute defiance, but of panic, frustration and helplessness. If India was not to go the way of Malaya and Burma, something had to be done and done quickly. Gandhi became convinced that only an immediate declaration of Indian independence by the British Government could give the people a stake in the defence of their country.

Lord Hardinge, who was Viceroy of India during the years 1910-16, has recorded in his memoirs that on one occasion he had asked Gokhale, 'How would you like it if I were to tell you that all the British officials and troops would leave India within a month?' 'I would be very pleased to hear that news,' replied Gokhale, 'but before you had all reached Aden, we would be telegraphing you to return.' Public opinion had advanced much since the days of Hardinge and Gokhale, but a total British withdrawal in the midst of a global war was certainly a startling suggestion. Gandhi was asking not for the physical withdrawal of every Briton from India, but for the transfer of political power from British to Indian hands. To those who said that the time was inopportune for such a step, his answer was: 'This is the psychological moment for recognition (of Indian independence). For then and then alone can there be irresistible opposition to Japanese aggression.'

For more than twenty years Gandhi had argued that the independence of India was impossible without Hindu-Muslim unity. However, he had seen communalism raise its ugly head higher and higher, and was driven to the conclusion that only in a climate of freedom could the antagonistic claims of the communities be reconciled. 'Quit India' was thus Gandhi's solution for the two perils of Japanese invasion and internal disunity which confronted India in the summer of 1942. The charge that this solution was 'defeatist' and a homage to the rising sun of Japan arose from a complete misunderstanding of his views. In February 1942, when the Japanese were advancing in the Far East with lightning speed, he had publicly discounted fears of a British collapse. Britain had, he wrote, suffered reverses in several wars, but she had a knack of surviving them and turning them into stepping stones to success. In unambiguous language he declared himself against a change of masters: 'I have no desire to exchange the British for any other rule. Better the enemy I know that the one I do not. I have never attached the slightest importance or weight to the friendly professions of the Axis powers.'

Clearly, if the Axis Powers had any collaborators in India, actual or potential, Gandhi was not one of them. It was pointed out to him by some foreign correspondents that the sudden withdrawal of British troops would have the inevitable result of exposing India to a Japanese invasion and of immeasurably weakening the defence of China. He recognized that he 'could not guarantee fool-proof non-violent action to keep the Japanese at bay'; subsequent discussions with Jawaharlal Nehru led him to elaborate the proposal for the withdrawal of British power, so as to fit it into the realities of the international situation. He agreed that Allied troops should remain on Indian soil during the war, and one of the first acts of a National Indian Government should be to enter into a treaty with the United Nations for defensive operations against the Axis Powers. This was a striking departure from the position Gandhi had consistently held since September 1939.

Ever since the outbreak of war, Gandhi had been commending to his countrymen non-violent resistance even to an invading army; he wished Congress to adhere to the same method for the defence of the country which it had employed in the struggle for freedom. Twice he had parted company on this issue with the majority in the Congress Working Committee. When, therefore, he agreed to the whole-hearted participation of Congress in the Second World War, he did something which went deeply against the grain. Only the critical turn which the war had taken, and his passion for Indian freedom, reconciled him to this deviation from a principle which was dearer to him than life itself.

'British Rule in India must end immediately,' the Congress Working Committee declared after a meeting at Wardha on July 14, 1942. The Committee pointed out that the failure of the Cripps Mission had resulted in a rapid and widespread increase in ill-will against Britain and a growing satisfaction at the success of Japanese arms. In order to make India 'a willing partner in a joint enterprise', the Committee considered it essential that Indians should feel 'a glow of freedom'.

If there was no response to the appeal for the immediate withdrawal of British Rule, the Committee forecast a civil disobedience movement 'which would inevitably be under the leadership of Mahatma Gandhi'. The final decision on this momentous issue was taken by the All-India Congress Committee at Bombay on August 7th.

In August 1942 the mood of the Government of India was no less desperate than that of Congress. From his own point of view, Lord Linlithgow had been patient for three long years; in December 1941 he had made a gesture to Congress by releases from gaol, but he had failed to win its co-operation. The 'Quit India' proposal had already raised the political temperature; if a mass civil disobedience movement was actually launched, it might paralyse civil administration and endanger the war-effort. For strong preventive action the Viceroy had the full support of the British Cabinet.

Gandhi, Jawaharlal Nehru, Maulana Azad and other Congress leaders were arrested in the early hours of August 9, 1942. The news of these arrests produced violent reactions. In several provinces, particularly in Bihar, U.P., Bengal and Bombay, the fury of the people burst the dykes and turned on the instruments

and symbols of British rule. Post offices, police stations and courts
were burnt; railway lines, buildings and rolling stock were
damaged, telephone and telegraph wires were cut. In his last
speech before the All-India Congress Committee Gandhi had
stressed non-violence as the basic premise of the struggle which
he proposed to launch, but this advice remained unheeded between the frenzy of the people and the hammer blows of the
Government. Though many British officials and non-officials recalled the Mutiny of 1857, the outbreak in 1942 was the result
of a violence as spontaneous as it was suicidal. The Government hit back with all its might; mobs were dispersed by firing
and even machine-gunned from the air.

'The Congress Party,' Churchill told the House of Commons,
'has now abandoned the policy in many respects of non-violence
which Mr Gandhi has so long inculcated in theory and has come
into the open as a revolutionary movement.' In India and abroad
official propaganda attributed violence to a plot carefully laid by
Congress leaders. Within a week of his imprisonment in the Aga
Khan Palace at Poona, which had been improvised as a gaol for
him, Gandhi wrote to the Viceroy complaining of the 'slaughter
of truth' in the official version of the sequence of events. He
would have strained every nerve, he said, to reach a settlement
with the Government if he had not been arrested; neither he
nor his colleagues had at any stage envisaged violence as part of
the campaign. He charged the Government with precipitating
the crisis by the wholesale arrests of the leaders. Gandhi was
arrested before he could unfold his detailed plans to the All-
India Congress Committee. He had been trying hard to balance
his passion for Indian freedom with his desire not to embarrass
the Government during the war. If he had not been arrested
it is likely that his programme would have been conditioned
by the latter consideration. It is certain that his weight
would have been thrown against any violent outbreak. He
knew how to bring unruly mobs to order; when appeals
failed he could bring them back to sanity by undertaking a
fast.

Responsibility for the '1942 disturbances' formed the subject
of a long and somewhat acrimonious correspondence between
Gandhi, still a prisoner, on the one hand and the Viceroy and
his advisers on the other. That Lord Linlithgow, whom Gandhi
considered a friend, should have questioned his *bona fides*, and
even his belief in non-violence, was more than the Mahatma could
bear. He sought 'a soothing balm' for his pain in a twenty-one

day fast which began on February 10, 1943. The fast, which the Government of India had dreaded so long had come, but it is an index to their hardened attitude that they took a risk which they had never taken before—that of Gandhi's death in prison. There was an emotional upheaval in the country, as the doctors' bulletins grew gloomier; three members of the Viceroy's Executive Council resigned; leaders of various parties, whatever their other differences, united in appeals to the Government to release Gandhi and save his life. But the Viceroy, backed by the authorities at home, did not budge an inch; he described the fast as 'political blackmail'; whatever satisfaction such an epithet may have given him, it only stung Indian public opinion the more.

That Gandhi 'put the match to the train carefully laid beforehand by himself and his colleagues, That he was forced to do so prematurely was not his fault but our fortune'—this charge by Sir Reginald Maxwell, the Home Member of the Viceroy's Executive Council, was part of the official indictment which represented Gandhi and the Congress as saboteurs of the Allied struggle against Japan. This propaganda held the field for a time, but not for long. 'It is sheer nonsense,' Field Marshal Smuts told a Press Conference in London in November 1942, 'to talk of Mahatma Gandhi as a fifth columnist. He is a great man. He is one of the great men of the world.' The attempt to erase him from political life by excluding his photographs and even mention of his name from the Press was doomed to failure. The courage with which he stood up to the Government, the indomitable faith which he asserted in non-violence at a time when violence seemed to have triumphed all round him, the tenacity with which he attacked the cobwebs which official propagandists spun round the events of 1942—all this raised him further in the esteem and affection of millions of Indians. He became the symbol of a nationalism bloody but unbowed.

Now that the deep emotion aroused by the events of 1942 have somewhat faded, it should be possible to see those events in clearer perspective. When we recall the emphasis which Gandhi had placed on the training of the people for non-violence since 1934, when we recall his anxiety at the growth in the prewar years of indiscipline and the spirit of violence, and his studied restraint in conducting the individual civil disobedience movement of 1940-1, we wonder how he could have permitted what was certainly a dangerous plunge in the surcharged atmosphere of that period. He knew the risks inherent in a mass movement in the midst of a global war which had brought the Japanese to the gates of India. But he also saw the passivity of the people and the possibility that they might succumb to the Japanese invader. To rouse them to a final assertion of their national self-respect without hatred or violence required a miracle, but miracles had happened before. Within a few months in 1930 Gandhi had succeeded in electrifying political India, with remarkably little racial bitterness and violence. Twelve years later, however, the conditions were different; both the people and the Government were keyed up to a high pitch of tension. With the fortunes of the war trembling in the balance, the Government were less inclined to wait on events, while large sectors of the population were seething with discontent. The political situation in 1942 bore greater resemblance to that of 1919 than to that of 1930. In 1919, as in 1942, Gandhi had sensed the temper of the people, but he was hopeful that he could purge it of hatred and violence through a Satyagraha movement. Satyagraha, however, had no chance in the face of the popular terrorism and official counter-terrorism which followed the arrest of Congress leaders.

Gandhi had no right to expect the Government to play the game according to his rules, but the Government equally had no right to blame him for the consequences of the policy it adopted. Lord Linlithgow had acted in accordance with the viewpoint common among experienced British Administrators, that the only means of mastering Gandhi's movements was to deliver telling blows in the initial stages. This was the policy which Lord Willingdon was believed to have adopted with signal success. The ostensible gains of such a policy, however, tended to be transient; repression, with its resultant bitterness, recoiled on those who practised it. In 1932 Lord Willingdon inflicted what he believed to be a crushing defeat on Congress; five years later Congress swept the polls in the first elections under the Government of India Act of 1935. In 1942 Lord Linlithgow won what was, from his point of view, a decisive victory over Congress; in 1947 British rule came formally and finally to an end. It is a strange irony of history that Lords Willingdon and Linlithgow, who dealt the strongest blows to the Indian National movement, unwittingly served as catalytic agents in the political liberation of India.

From the nationalist point of view, the events of 1942 were to prove an embarrassing legacy. It was almost the first large-scale outbreak in which wrecking and burning were indulged in in a spirit of misconceived patriotism. It lowered the standards of mass behaviour and set a dangerous precedent when in 1946-47 communal feeling replaced patriotism as the principal ingredient in the popular ferment.

# CHAPTER XXXVII

# No Defeat

WITHIN a week of his imprisonment in the Aga Khan Palace, Gandhi lost his private secretary, Mahadev Desai. Competent, industrious and modest, the ever-smiling 'M.D.' had been for twenty-five years the Mahatma's inseparable assistant. 'Son, secretary and lover rolled into one'—this was how the Mahatma once described Mahadev, who had joined him in 1917, after graduating in law from Bombay University and trying his hand at a few odd jobs. Mahadev's fine handwriting, alert mind, and undivided loyalty made him an efficient secretary; but Gandhi's secretary had to be something more than an amanuensis. In the years preceding the first non-co-operation movement, when Gandhi was not so well known, Mahadev Desai was often his sole companion during his country-wide tours; he made his bed, cooked his food and washed his clothes, besides performing secretarial functions. As public life increased its demands on Gandhi, Mahadev Desai's burden grew too; he sorted and dealt with an enormous mail, received and looked after guests, warded off unwelcome visitors, kept accounts, pored over railway guides and maps to arrange itineraries, recorded speeches and conversations and edited journals. As a good deal of his writing was done in third-class compartments of moving trains, he carried candles with him so that if lights failed in the compartment the dispatch of the 'copy' to the press was not held up.

He constituted a perfect one-man secretariat, expounding and implementing Gandhi's instructions, keeping in touch with hundreds of public workers, and doing all that he could to save the Mahatma from any avoidable strain. He drove himself too hard in the process; his sudden death in August 1942 was due not only to the terrific strain of the months which preceded the passage of the 'Quit India' resolution, but also to a gnawing fear that the Mahatma would fast unto death in gaol.

Another shadow fell upon the Aga Khan's Palace. Kasturbai's health had been causing concern for some time; she was treated by the 'family doctors', Gilder, Dinshaw and Sushila Nayar, and then by Sriv Sharma, an Ayurvedic physician from the Punjab, but she did not rally. On February 22, 1944 she passed away in the lap of her husband. 'I am going now,' she said to him, 'we have known many joys and many sorrows.' One of her last wishes was that she should be cremated in a *sari* made from yarn spun by him.

'We were,' wrote Gandhi in reply to a letter of condolence from Lord Wavell, 'a couple outside the ordinary.' The sixty-two years of their married life had been a period of continual growth. In spite of the immense intellectual gap between them, he had learnt to respect her opinions and to let her take her own decisions. In South Africa she had chosen to go to gaol in the last phase of the Satyagraha struggle. In India she had sought imprisonment during the civil disobedience movements; but her last imprisonment was to end with her death.

It was not in the political field, however, that her real work was done. To a vast circle of disciples and co-workers of her husband she was 'Ba', the mother; they were her family and the Ashram was her home. She was the picture of contentment when she sat in her husband's hut, fanning him while he ate his lunch, or when she massaged his feet as he dozed off to sleep. She could read and write in Gujerati and had picked up scraps of spoken English in South Africa, which she occasionally practised with more innocence than expertness. 'I know my husband,' she told a European Superintendent of Prisons when he protested that Gandhi himself was responsible for his under-feeding, 'he always mischiefs.' In the Aga Khan Palace, Gandhi resumed his efforts to fill up gaps in her education. It was amusing to see this lady of seventy-four pace up and down her room committing elements of geography and general knowledge to memory. But when the time came for the lessons her memory played her tricks. 'Lahore,' she would say, 'is the capital of Calcutta.'

After the death of his beloved secretary and wife, the Aga Khan Palace had sombre associations for Gandhi. His health began to cause concern to the Government early in 1944. He had contracted malaria and had been running a high tempera-ture. The tide of the war had already turned in favour of the Allies, and the risks of his release seemed to the Government immeasurably less than those of his possible death in gaol. His release on May 6, 1944, did not please Gandhi; he even felt ashamed that he should have fallen ill in gaol. He was taken to

Juhu, a sea-side resort near Bombay. It turned out that he was suffering not only from the after-effects of malaria, but from hookworm and amoebic infections, which had resulted in acute anaemia. He ascribed all illness to lack of faith in God, the 'Master-Physician'; his known antipathy to drugs did not make it easy to treat him. Nevertheless, before many weeks were over he was well enough to attend to the problems which faced the country.

Gandhi knew that his stock in official circles was not high, that his own *bona fides* and those of the Congress were questioned, that with a British Cabinet presided over by Churchill the scales were heavily tipped against him. In spite of this he took the initiative in an attempt to break the political deadlock between the Government and Congress. On June 17, 1944, he wrote to Lord Wavell seeking permission to see members of the Congress Working Committee. The Viceroy turned down this request; nor did he see any advantage in a meeting with Gandhi 'in consideration of radical differences' in their view-points. In an interview with Stuart Gelder of the *News Chronicle,* Gandhi suggested the formation of a National Government at the centre, chosen by the elected members of the Central Legislative Assembly; this proposal was described by the Viceroy as 'quite unacceptable to His Majesty's Government'.

Having failed to break the deadlock between the Government and the Congress after his release from gaol, Gandhi sought an accord with Jinnah. The Mahatma did not accept the two-nation theory, but he was prepared to recognize the psychology which had commended this theory to the Muslim intelligentsia. The basis on which he proposed to negotiate with Jinnah was the 'Rajaji formula', devised by Rajagopalachari, the ex-Premier of Madras, and one of the keenest intellects in Congress. Rajagoplachari had suggested that if the Muslim League endorsed the Congress demand for national independence and for the formation of a provisional government during the war, Congress would agree to a demarcation of contiguous Muslim majority districts in the north-west and north-east of India, and to a plebiscite of all adult inhabitants in these areas to decide whether they would prefer to remain in a free United India or in separate states. And if ultimately separation was agreed upon, the two states were to devise mutual agreements for defence, communications and other essential matters.

The Gandhi-Jinnah talks began on September 9, 1944 and concluded on September 27th. The optimism which they aroused at

the time did not derive from any real prospects of an agreement
between the two leaders, but only reflected public weariness of
the political deadlock, and an almost universal desire for concord
between the League and the Congress. On his return from the
first interview, Gandhi was asked if he had brought anything
from Jinnah. 'Only flowers,' he replied. The subsequent meetings
registered no more tangible gains. Jinnah questioned Gandhi's
credentials; it was true that the Mahatma since 1943 had ceased
to be a member of Congress, but Jinnah knew very well that
Gandhi's weight in the counsels of Congress did not depend
upon a membership card or on the holding of any office. The
Muslim League leader's approach was doctrinaire. He wanted
Gandhi to recognize that the All-India Muslim League had the
exclusive right to speak on behalf of Indian Muslims. He wanted
the principle of Pakistan to be conceded before he would define
its geographical boundaries or discuss its details. He would not
hear of non-Muslims in Muslim majority provinces participa-
ing in the plebiscite which was to determine their future; the
right of self-determination in these areas could only be exercised by Muslims.

Gandhi suggested that while the principle for the demarcation
of boundaries and the plebiscite could be decided in advance,
the actual partition, if it became inevitable, should follow and
not precede the transfer of power from Britain to India. He
hoped that after the departure of the British the communities
would learn, in the bracing climate of freedom, to make mutual
adjustments, and the need for partition of the country might
never arise. What was Gandhi's hope was Jinnah's fear; the Muslim League leader did not want to take any risks and so made
partition the pre-condition of Indian independence. Jinnah also
rejected the proposal for treaty arrangements between the two
states for defence, communications and foreign affairs as affecting the sovereignty of the new states. To Gandhi the prospect of
two states carved out on the basis of religious affiliation, 'with
nothing but enmity in common between them', was disconcerting; the search for cultural and economic autonomy was legitimate enough, but some safeguards were necessary to prevent an
armament race and an armed conflict between the two states.

While these conversations were no more than a kind of re-
education for Gandhi, to Jinnah they brought an accession of
political strength. The fact that Gandhi had knocked at his door
raised Jinnah's prestige. For four years the Muslim League
leader had not swerved an inch from the position he had adopted

in March 1940; events had shown that intransigence paid dividends. The 'Rajaji formula', which had formed the initial basis of the negotiations, did not concede all that Jinnah demanded, but at least it recognized the possibility of the partition of the country. The fact that the Mahatma, who had once described the division of India as a sin, had relented so far as to discuss the machinery for the exercise of the right of self-determination was a feather in Jinnah's cap. Viewed in the long-term strategy of the campaign for Pakistan, the Gandhi-Jinnah talks were another milestone, marking further progress from the offer of Lord Linlithgow in August 1940, and the Cripps Mission in March 1942.

In the summer of 1945, Lord Wavell, who had recently returned from England with the concurrence of the British Cabinet to a proposal for the reconstitution of his Executive Council in consultation with Indian leaders, convened a conference in Simla to discuss the Viceroy's proposal. Gandhi was not a delegate to the Conference, though he was consulted by the Viceroy and the Congress Working Committee. Lord Wavell had suggested parity of representation in the Executive Council between the 'caste Hindus' and Muslims, but by the time the conference was over Jinnah was demanding parity between Muslims and all the other communities. The conference actually broke down on the insistence of Jinnah that the Muslim League should have an exclusive right to nominate Muslim members of the Viceroy's Executive Council. This was something which Congress could not concede without repudiating its national composition and outlook. The conclusion is inescapable that at this time Jinnah was not interested in a compromise; he did not think the time for agreement was opportune; in any case, an understanding with Congress had little attraction for him when he hoped to get better terms from the Government.

As the war drew to a close, the need for a fresh move in India was keenly felt. The Simla Conference was a recognition of this need. The war in Europe had ended in May and Japan surrendered in August. The first post-war elections in Britain returned the Labour Party to power. The new Secretary of State for India, Lord Pethick-Lawrence, spoke of equal partnership between Britain and India. The Viceroy had already announced that elections would be held 'as soon as possible' to the Central Legislative Assembly and the Provincial Legislatures, which had been in existence since 1934 and 1937 respectively. In September 1945, after a visit to London, the Viceroy announced that in the spirit of the Cripps offer the Government proposed to convene a constitution-making body. The announcement did not arouse much enthusiasm. The Labour Government decided to send an all-party British Parliamentary Delegation to study the situation in India and convince her people that self-government was within their grasp.

# CHAPTER XXXVIII

# The Coming of Independence

In January 1946, when Gandhi visited Srinivasa Sastri, the veteran Liberal leader, the conversation turned to the British Parliamentary Delegation which was touring India. 'We know,' commented Sastri, who was on his death-bed, 'nothing can come out of it. Labour or Conservative, so far as India is concerned, they are all one and the same.' That this melancholy judgment should have been passed at a time when the transfer of power was about to take place, and by one who had always been considered a friend of the British connection, was significant and showed that the representatives of the British *Raj* in India gave hardly any inkling of an early departure.

On a superficial view, the British position in India at the close of the Second World War could not have been stronger. There had never been more British troops on Indian soil. The Congress organization was banned and with the exception of Gandhi almost all nationalist leaders were in gaol. The Muslim League was campaigning for Pakistan, but its target was Congress, not the British Government. In six provinces constitutional government was in abeyance; in the remaining five provinces ministries more or less friendly to the Government were in power. The repressive measures adopted in 1942 had brought a welcome respite to the British officers who had slogged at their desks for six years. The civil servants were hard-working men who did their duty according to their lights, but, as Gokhale put it, 'their lights are dim. And even as regards efficiency my own conviction is that it is impossible for the present system to produce more than a certain very limited amount of efficiency and that standard has now been reached'. Gokhale had spoken in 1905; forty years later the dynamics of national awakening and economic change had accentuated these deficiencies. Few of these conscientious civil servants could see in 1945 that the old order, which they had known and shaped and loved, had been largely, even if imperceptibly, eroded.

The war had accelerated this process of erosion. It had

brought easy money to a few, but in the minds of millions of
Indians it was synonymous with scarcity and high prices. A
terrible famine, to the making of which man and nature con-
spired, had ravaged Bengal; the people did not know and perhaps did not care how far the tragedy was due to ministerial
neglect and corruption in Bengal and how far to the constitutional
propriety or inertia which prevented timely intervention by the
Central Government. Shortages of food and cloth were endemic
almost throughout the country, and efforts to control and ration
supplies had brought corruption in their wake. The war had
lowered moral standards; it tempted too many people to make
hay while the brief sun of war-time prosperity shone.

In any case, the transition from war to peace was going to be
a necessarily slow and painful process. The demobilization of
an army which had swelled in number from 189,000 to 2,250,000
was a stupendous task. The Indian soldier was no longer the raw
peasant whom the recruiting officers had picked up from the
village; he had fought in the battle-fronts of Malaya, Burma,
the Middle East and Italy; he had seen empires topple and he
had learnt to ask awkward questions.

It must be stated, however, that whatever their difficulties the
morale of the majority of the British officers in India was high,
and that they had not lost confidence in their ability to govern
India for many years to come. If within a year of the end of the
war, large strides had been taken towards Indian independence, it
was due not so much to any weakening on the part of representatives of the *Raj* as to the change of political climate in Britain,
and the determination of the Attlee Government to come to terms
with Indian nationalism.

British historians are inclined to regard the events of 1947
as a logical climax of the policy outlined in the declaration of
August 1917. Lord Chelmsford, who as Viceroy of India had
pleaded for this declaration, had himself suggested that 'it should
be accompanied by a very clear declaration that this is a distant
goal'. One is reminded of Morley's comment on his talks with
Gokhale: 'He made no secret of his ultimate hope and design—
India to be on the footing of a self-governing colony—I equally
made no secret of my conviction that for many a day to come—
long beyond the short span of time that may be left to us—this
was a mere dream.' 'Not in my lifetime', seems to have been the
verdict on Indian independence of Lloyd George and Montagu,
MacDonald and Benn, Baldwin and Hoare, Churchill and Amery.
British statesmen were conscious of the long process of conflict

and evolution through which parliamentary government had passed in Great Britain, and of the time taken by Canada and Australia to attain political maturity. That this process should have taken even longer in an Oriental country, with its variety of creeds and cultures, was axiomatic to them.

From 1917 the policy of successive British Governments towards India was 'self-government by stages'. The trouble about this mode of advance was that each instalment tended to become out of date by the time it was actually granted. The Reforms of 1919 might well have appeased political India in 1909; the Reforms of 1935 would have evoked enthusiasm in 1919, and an equivalent of the Cripps offer in 1940 could have opened a new chapter in Indo-British relations, and halted the process of estrangement between Congress and the Government and between Hindus and Muslims.

To this step-by-step advance Gandhi dealt a mortal blow in 1920. His promise of 'Swaraj in one year' was no make-believe; since slavery was in his view essentially a state of mind, a nation began to liberate itself the moment it resolved to be free. Satyagraha, his technique of non-violent resistance posed a difficult problem for the British. If they ignored it, it gathered momentum. If they attacked it, it enlisted sympathy in India and abroad. Repression was not only ineffective in the long run; it was also repugnant to the democratic conscience of England. The British people took only a fitful interest in Indian affairs, but they were too proud of their liberal tradition to agree to 400 millions of Indians being governed against their will. As each successive Satyagraha campaign revealed the strength of the nationalist opposition in India, it weakened the plea of the official apologists that only a minority of malcontents was against the *Raj*.

It was World War II which helped to mature British public opinion on India. The war changed the map of the world and the balance of power, but it also changed the minds of men. The intellectual and social ferment, of which the Labour Party's triumph in 1945 was an expression, helped in reassessing the merits of the traditional policies. Ideologically, the Labour Government was prepared for a new policy, but the facts of the Indian situation also drove it in the same direction. Speaking on March 6, 1947 in the House of Commons on the condition of India in November and December 1945, Mr Alexander, a member of the Labour Cabinet who was closely associated with the process of transferring power, observed: 'It might be said that the

Indian authorities were literally sitting on the top of a volcano, and as a result of the situation which had arisen after the war, the outbreak of revolution might be expected at any time.'

The opening months of 1946 confirmed the correctness of this estimate. Such was the irascibility of the popular temper that there were violent outbreaks at the slightest provocation, and sometimes without any provocation. In February 1946, a Muslim demonstration at Calcutta against a court-martial verdict on a Muslim officer of the Indian National Army degenerated into general lawlessness, in which shops were ransacked and tramcars and buses burnt. There were instances of indiscipline in the Air Force and a major naval mutiny in Bombay. In several Provinces there were signs of disaffection spreading to the police. The instruments of law and order, on which British rule ultimately depended, were proving broken reeds.

In face of this diminishing respect for authority what was needed was an immediate strengthening of the administration, but the war had, from the British point of view, led to a lamentable dilution of the 'superior services'. There had been a tremendous expansion in the sphere of governmental activity, while recruitment to the Indian Civil Service and the Indian Police Service had been kept in abeyance during the war. Not only were there fewer Europeans to man key jobs; their ranks were likely to thin yet further in the next few years as the senior officers retired.

That the run-down condition of the administration should have figured prominently in the explanations of British ministers was only to be expected; but the emphasis on this factor seems to have derived from the habit of empiricism, which makes the British stress the practical rather than the ideological aspect of a solution. The transfer of power from Britain to India would not, however, have been a significant event in world history if it had been only a recognition of a political necessity. Not merely the compulsion of events, but a measure of idealism went into the policy which Prime Minister Attlee initiated and carried through during the years 1946-7. And in so far as the British Government was impelled by this idealism, by a desire to open a fresh chapter in Indo-British relations, it was a victory for Gandhi, who had pleaded for nearly thirty years for a transformation of the relationship between the two countries. Among the advocates of this transformation were several English men and women, Hume and Wedderburn, C. F. Andrews and Horace Alexander, Brailsford and Brockway, Laski and Carl Heath, Muriel Lester and Agatha Harrison, who never wavered in their sympathy for the Indian cause. In their own day they represented a tiny and not-too-influential minority, but in the fulness of time their opinions became the national policies of their country.

Whatever the reasons for the change in British policy, the arrival of the Cabinet Mission in March 1946 went a long way to convince India that the British Government was in earnest. Of the three Cabinet Ministers of the Mission, Lord Pethick-Lawrence and Sir Stafford Cripps were well known to Gandhi. The Mission consulted him frequently during their stay, both formally and informally. They interviewed no less than 472 'leaders', though it was clear from the outset that the only parties which mattered were the Congress and the Muslim League, and the crucial question was whether India was to remain united or to be split up. Congress was opposed to partition of the country but was prepared to go to the farthest limits in conceding cultural, economic and regional autonomy. A conference at Simla failed to resolve the Congress-League differences. The Cabinet Mission then offered a compromise plan in their statement of May 16th. They sketched a three-tier constitutional structure for India. At the top was to be a Union of India embracing British India as well as the Indian States, but dealing only with foreign affairs, defence and communications. The bottom tier was to consist of Provinces and States, in which were to vest all residuary powers. The intermediate tier was to comprise groups to be formed by Provinces, if they chose, to deal with certain common subjects. It was laid down that the Constituent Assembly (consisting of representatives of Provinces and States), after a preliminary meeting, was to divide up into three sections; Section A consisting of Madras, Bombay, United Provinces, Bihar and Orissa; Section B comprising Punjab, Sind and North-West Frontier Province; and Section C consisting of Bengal and Assam. Each section was to decide whether the Provinces covered by it were to form a group, and if so, what were to be the subjects which were to fall within the jurisdiction of the group executive and legislature.

To understand the shifting and somewhat confused political situation which developed after the departure of the Cabinet Mission, it is useful to sum up briefly the attitudes of the British Government and the two major parties on the eve of the transfer of power. Mr Attlee was anxious to retain the initiative he had so boldy taken; his one anxiety was to make the transfer of power not only speedy but smooth. To the British Government the Indian constitutional problem was a political problem which was capable of solution by compromise and a spirit of 'give and take'. They were thus committed to no one solution; they were prepared to accept any workable arrangement on which the Congress and the League could agree.

Gandhi's view was different; the transfer of power was not a problem of expediency or power politics, but one which called for and admitted of a just and moral solution. He wanted the majorities to go far to meet the anxieties of the minorities, but he was not prepared to be stampeded into partition, which in the long run might do more harm than good to India and the two communities themselves. He was disturbed by the understandable anxiety of the British Government not to alienate Jinnah. He advised Congress not to accept any arrangement in a hurry which they might have to repent at leisure; at the worst, Congressmen were to be prepared to go once again into the wilderness. This advice did not appeal to Congress leaders, who like the British, tended to judge the situation in terms of political necessity, and feared a drift to civil war through vacillation or delay.

It seemed to Gandhi that, the declaration of the British Government notwithstanding, quite a few people in India seemed to think and behave as if the British were really not going. Only a dramatic gesture, such as the immediate withdrawal of British troops, or the immediate revocation of the Paramountcy of the crown, from the States, could jolt the various political parties and interests out of the grooves in which they had moved too long. Ever since it became apparent to him that the British had decided to quit, the one question which had exercised Gandhi incessantly was: how would the people of India, after centuries of servitude, react to the shock of freedom? He told Brailsford, a British journalist, in April 1946: 'This time, I believe the British mean business. But the offer has come suddenly. Will India be jerked into independence? I feel today like a passenger who has been hoisted in a basket chair on a ship's deck in a stormy sea and has not found his feet.'

Gandhi was worried at the growing indiscipline, which was partly a hangover from 1942 and partly a symptom of the post-war malaise. In February 1946, in an editorial in *Harijan* on 'How to canalize hatred', he wrote: 'Hatred is in the air and the impatient lovers of the country will gladly take advantage of it if they can through violence further the cause of independence.' The prime dangers, as Gandhi saw, were hatred and violence, which were finding expression in anti-British feeling or in the communal riots that were again beginning to disfigure the towns. For the riots the Hindus blamed the Muslims, the Muslims blamed the Hindus, and both blamed the hooligans. 'Who are the hooligans?' Gandhi asked and replied, 'We are the makers of the brand.' It was when the intelligentsia spilled venom and whipped up excitement that the hooligans got their chance. He revived the suggestion he had made in the late thirties for the formation of 'peace brigades', consisting of men sworn to non-violence and ready to die in the noble task of restoring the rioters to sanity. Meanwhile, the one thing which was needed was restraint in speech and writing, so that the great changes which were imminent could be ushered in peacefully.

Unfortunately, the very reasons which impelled Gandhi and Congress to seek a lowering of the political temperature led Jinnah and the Muslim League in the opposite direction. For the latter it was a question of 'now or never'. The long negotiations with the Cabinet Mission had revealed that not only was Congress opposed to Pakistan but the Labour Government seemed to prefer a solution which kept the Congress and the League within the framework of a single constitution. Only a civil war, or the threat of a civil war, seemed likely to beat down the objections of the Congress and the scepticism of the British Government towards partition. The Cabinet Mission plan was a compromise, but it did not really bring the two parties together. The result was that questions presumed to have been settled by the Cabinet Mission were reopened soon after the return of its three members to England.

Controversy rose to fever pitch on two crucial questions, that of the grouping of Provinces and the composition of the interim government. On July 27, 1946, the Muslim League Council withdrew its acceptance of the Cabinet Mission Plan, decided to boycott the Constituent Assembly and announced a programme of 'direct action' to achieve Pakistan. Jinnah declared that Muslims had bid good-bye to constitutional methods. 'We have forged a pistol,' he said, 'and are in a position to use it.' When asked whether the movement would be violent or non-violent, he refused to 'discuss ethics'. Some of his lieutenants in the League were even more forthright. Angry words and impatient gestures, however, were a poor preparation for 'direct action', if the object was a peaceful agitation.

At a time when tension was mounting it was imperative that

the country should have a strong and stable government at the centre. The Cabinet Mission had failed to secure the formation of a national interim government. In July the Viceroy, Lord Wavell, once again took the initiative and asked Nehru to form the Government. Jinnah, who was approached by Nehru but refused to co-operate, was bitterly critical of what he described as 'the caste Hindu Fascist Congress and their henchmen' who sought 'to dominate and rule over the Mussalmans and other minority communities of India with the aid of British bayonets'.

This bitterness boded ill at a time when exemplary restraint was necessary to pull the country through a critical period. The 'Direct Action Day' which was celebrated by the Muslim League on August 16th touched off a chain reaction of violent explosions which in the succeeding twelve months shook the country.

# CHAPTER XXXIX

## Quenching the Flames

THE Muslim League observed August 16, 1946, as 'Direct Action Day'. On that day Calcutta witnessed a communal riot the scale and intensity of which had never been known in living memory. For four days, bands of hooligans armed with sticks, spears, hatchets and even fire-arms, roamed the town, robbing and killing at will. The 'Great Calcutta Killing'—to use the grim epithet coined by the *Statesman*—took a toll of more than five thousand lives besides the fifteen thousand or more who were injured.

Bengal was ruled by a Muslim League ministry led by H. S. Suhrawardy. 'In retrospect,' wrote the *Statesman* 'it is the Muslim League's conduct before the riots that stands open to inference—not only by its political opponents—that it was divided in mind on whether rioting of some sort would be good or bad.' Charges were in fact levelled against the Provincial Government that it did not provide against the outbreak, which it might well have anticipated, and that Suhrawardy deliberately prevented the police from acting promptly and impartially when the riots broke out.

If, as was suggested at the time, the outbreak was intended to serve as a demonstration of the strength of Muslim feeling on Pakistan, it proved a double-edged weapon. The non-Muslims of Calcutta reeled under the initial impact, but then, taking advantage of their numerical superiority, hit back savagely. The prevalent impression was that, in spite of a Muslim League ministry in Bengal, the Hindus had won in this 'trial of strength' in Calcutta. Two months later reprisals followed in the Muslim-majority district of Noakhali in East Bengal where, taking advantage of poor communications and encouraged by fanatical priests and ambitious politicians, local hooligans burnt the Hindus' property, looted their crops and desecrated their temples. A shocking innovation was the forcible conversion of Hindus and the kidnapping of Hindu women. Thousands of Hindus fled from their homes. In that year of growing lawlessness. East Bengal did for rural India what Calcutta had done for the towns; it showed what inhumanities could be practised in the name of religion and ostensibly for political ends.

Gandhi was in Delhi when the news from East Bengal came through. He was particularly hurt by the crimes against women. He cancelled all his plans and decided to leave for East Bengal. Friends tried to dissuade him. His health was poor; important political developments on which his advice would be required were imminent. 'I do not know,' he said, 'what I shall be able to do there. All that I know is that I won't be at peace unless I go.'

At Calcutta he saw the ravages of the August riots and confessed to a 'sinking feeling at the mass madness which can turn man into less than a brute.' The atmosphere in East Bengal was charged with fear, hatred and violence. In a statement, Gandhi declared that he found himself in the midst of exaggeration and falsehood: 'I am unable to discover the truth. There is a terrible mutual distrust. Oldest friendships have snapped. Truth and *Ahimsa*, by which I swear and which have, to my knowledge, sustained me for sixty years, seem to fail to show the attributes I have ascribed to them. To test them or better to test myself I am going to a village, Srirampur . . .'

Of the 200 Hindu families of Srirampur village in Noakhali district, only three had remained after the recent disturbances. He dispersed his entourage in the neighbouring villages. Pyarelal, Sushila Nayar, Abha, Manu Gandhi and Sucheta Kripalani—each of them settled in a village. At Srirampur Gandhi's only companions were his stenographer Parsuram, his Bengali interpreter, Prof. Nirmal Kumar Bose, and Manu Gandhi. For the next six weeks a wooden bedstead, covered with a mattress, served as his office by day and his bed by night. His working day extended to sixteen and sometimes twenty hours. He slept little and ate little, made his bed, mended his clothes, cooked his food, attended to his enormous mail, received callers and visited local Muslims. For several years he had been maligned in the Muslim League Press as the 'enemy number one' of Indian Muslims. He let the Muslims of Srirampur judge for themselves.

The restoration of confidence between the two communities was, however, a slow and difficult process. Nevertheless, Gandhi's presence acted as a soothing balm on the villages of East Bengal; it eased tension, assuaged anger and softened tempers. His success would have been more spectacular were it not for the sustained propaganda against him in the Muslim Press, which continued to suspect a 'deep political game' in his mission. Under pressure from local party bosses, and perhaps from the League High Command, Premier Suhrawardy became critical of Gandhi's tour, and joined the outcry that Gandhi should quit Bengal. Gandhi was not dismayed by this perverse opposition; he argued that, if he could not command the confidence of the Muslim League leaders, the responsibility was his own. He was in a mood of self-examination, almost of self-castigation. An entry in his diary dated January 2, 1947, reads: 'Have been awake since 2 a.m. God's grace alone is sustaining me. I can see there is some grave defect in me somewhere which is the cause of all this. All round me is utter darkness. When will God take me out of this darkness into His light?'[1]

The same day he left Srirampur on a village-to-village tour. At Chandipur village he discarded his sandals, and like the pilgrims of old, walked bare-foot. The village tracks were slippery and sometimes maliciously strewn with brambles and broken glass; the fragile bamboo bridges were tricky to negotiate. He saw gaping walls, gutted roofs, charred ruins and the remnants of skeletons in the debris—the handiwork of religious frenzy. A song from Tagore that he liked to hear expressed some of his anguish:

Walk Alone.
If they answer not to thy call, walk alone;
If they are afraid and cower mutely facing the wall,
O thou of evil luck,
Open thy mind and speak out alone.
If they turn away and desert you when crossing the
     wilderness,
O thou of evil luck,
Trample the thorns under thy tread
And along the blood-lined track travel alone.
If they do not hold up the light when the night is
     troubled with storm,
O thou of evil luck,
With the thunder-flame of pain ignite thine own heart,
And let it burn alone.

On March 2, 1947, he left for Bihar, where the Hindu peasants had wreaked terrible vengeance on the Muslim minority for the events in Noakhali. Gandhi had first heard of the Bihar riots when he was on his way to Noakhali in the last week of October 1946. He made it known that if peace did not return at once

[1] Pyarelal: *Mahatma Gandhi, The Last Phase*, Vol. I, p. 470.

he would embark on a fast unto death. This warning, coupled with the stern measures adopted by the Bihar Government and a visit by Jawaharlal Nehru, helped in restoring order quickly.

In Bihar Gandhi's refrain was the same as in East Bengal; the majority must repent and make amends; the minority must forgive and make a fresh start. He would not accept any apology for what had happened, and chided those who sought in the misdeeds of the rioters in East Bengal a justification for what had happened in Bihar. Civilized conduct, he argued, was the duty of every individual and every community irrespective of what others did. Conditions in Bihar began to improve; they would have improved more quickly but for the fact that communal tension in 1946-7 was a reflection of the political situation, which continued to oscillate continually and violently.

While Gandhi had 'buried' himself in the villages of East Bengal and Bihar, the political landscape had undergone bewildering changes. The Cabinet Mission's Plan, prepared with such infinite patience and skill had, soon after its departure failed to work. The Muslim League withdrew its acceptance of the Plan, and launched a 'direct action campaign' to achieve Pakistan. The savage rioting in Calcutta touched off a chain reaction in East Bengal and Bihar. Minor riots went on in most provinces. Alarmed by this increasing lawlessness, Lord Wavell brought the Muslim League into the Interim Government, but the formation of this coalition—which for seven years had been talked of as a panacea for India's political ills—fanned political controversy instead of putting it out. The Constituent Assembly was summoned to meet on December 9th, but the Muslim League had declared that its representatives would not participate. The constitutional impasse looked complete when, in the last week of November 1946, in an eleventh-hour bid to bring the parties together, the British Government invited the Viceroy, Nehru, Jinnah, Liaquat Ali Khan, and Baldev Singh to London. The discussions proved abortive, but the British Government issued a statement on December 6, 1946 to clarify the disputed clauses about the grouping of provinces in the Cabinet Mission Plan. Though this clarification largely met its objections, the Muslim League did not remove its boycott of the Constituent Assembly.

The year 1947 dawned with the darkest possible prospects on the political horizon. India seemed to be sliding into an undeclared, albeit confused, civil war, with the battle lines passing through almost every town and village. The Central Government, split from top to bottom, was unable to set an example of cohesion or firmness to the governments in the Provinces. The Viceroy, Lord Wavell, seemed to have been completely outplayed in the face of divergent pressures which he could neither reconcile nor control; he even suggested the desperate expedient of a British evacuation of India province by province. To check the drift to chaos, Premier Attlee came to the conclusion that what was needed was a new policy and a new Viceroy to carry it out. He announced in the House of Commons on February 20, 1947 that the British Government definitely intended to quit India by June 1948, and if by that date the Indian parties had not agreed on an All-India constitution, power would be transferred to 'some form of Central Government in British India or in some areas to the existing Provincial Governments or in such other ways as may seem most reasonable and in the best interest of the Indian people'. Simultaneously, it was announced that Lord Mountbatten would succeed Lord Wavell as Viceroy.

'Wise and courageous' was Jawaharlal Nehru's comment on the statement of February 20th. Jinnah, however, was impressed not so much by the bold sweep and the abounding faith which inspired this historic declaration as by the possibility envisaged in it of transferring power in June 1948 'to existing Provincial Governments'. Apparently the Muslim League could, by staying out of the Constituent Assembly, frustrate an All-India constitution, and get power for the Provinces in the east and west which it claimed for Pakistan. Of these Provinces, Bengal and Sind had already Muslim League ministries and Baluchistan was centrally administered. There were Congress ministries in Assam and the North-West Frontier Province, and a Congress-Akali Unionist coalition in Punjab; the immediate Muslim League strategy was to dislodge these three ministries and replace them by Muslim League governments. 'Direct Action' campaigns were launched or intensified in these three provinces. The results, particularly in the Punjab, were disastrous. The Hindu and Sikh minorities in the West Punjab went through the same horrors as those suffered by the Hindu minority in East Bengal and the Muslim minority in Bihar.

Gandhi was in Bihar when he received news of the trouble in the Punjab. Since October 1946 he had been wandering from one Province to another in a vain attempt to stem the tide of violence. While his work was unfinished in one Province, there was an outbreak in another. There were some who shrugged their shoulders and said that anarchy was only to be expected with the departure of the British, who alone had prevented Hindus and Muslims from flying at each other's throats.

To Gandhi the violence of 1946-7 was a shocking and even a bewildering phenomenon. All his life he had worked for the day when India would set an example of non-violence to the world. The chasm between what he had cherished in his heart and what he saw was so great that he could not help feeling a deep sense of failure. His first impulse was to blame himself. Was his technique faulty? Had he been unobservant, careless, indifferent, impatient? Had he failed to detect in time that while the people had, on the whole, refrained from overt violence in the struggle against foreign rule, they had continued to harbour ill feeling against the British? Was communal violence only an expression of the violence which had smouldered in the breasts of those who had paid lip service to non-violence?

It was only natural that he should have sought an explanation of this tragedy in terms of his own philosophy and of his part in India's political struggle. In retrospect, it would appear that he was exaggerating his own responsibility and the failure of non-violence. It would have been too much to expect that even in thirty-one years one single leader, however great, could have purged completely the hate and violence of 400 million people inhabiting a vast continent. It was remarkable enough that in the several Satyagraha campaigns he had led, violence had been reduced to negligible proportions, and India's millions had received a nationalist awakening without that dose of hatred which is usually associated with resurgent nationalisms.

While it is possible that the lawlessness which followed the arrests of Congress leaders in August 1942 lowered standards of mass behaviour, the real explanation for the violence of 1946-7 is to be sought in the tensions which the movement for Pakistan aroused, both in its protagonists and antagonists. The basic premise of this movement was that Hindus and Muslims had nothing in common in the past, present or future. Large sections of the population were seized with vague hopes or equally vague fears. No one could say with certainty whether India would remain united or be divided into two or more states, whether the Punjab or Bengal would retain their boundaries or be split, whether Indian states would be integrated into an independent India or become autonomous. The Adivasis of Central India and the Nagas of Assam found champions for an independence which they had never claimed before; there was talk of a Dravidistan in the south and a thousand-mile corridor to link the two wings of future Pakistan. The 'balkanization of India', once an ominous phrase, had become a real danger. All this excited popular fantasy; the turbulent elements in society saw in the coming transfer of power a period of vacuum, such as had occurred in the eighteenth century during the twilight of the Mogul Empire.

In the face of these perils, the Central Government was a house divided against itself, and the Provincial Governments were facing increasing demoralization. The impending termination of their careers had embittered some British officers; moreover, few of them had the will or the ability to cope with the volcanic violence which erupted everywhere. Indian officers, when themselves free from prejudice, were not always able to restrain their subordinates from petty tyranny. The growth of private armies, the Muslim League National Guards, the Rashtriya Swayamsevak Sangh, and others, showed that popular faith in the instruments of law and order had been shaken.

Gandhi had sensed the explosive possibilities of this situation. 'We are not yet in the midst of a civil war,' he had commented on the Great Calcutta Killing, 'but we are nearing it.' From the end of October 1946, when he had left Delhi for Noakhali, he had made the assuaging of communal fanaticism his primary mission. He knew as well as anybody else that a settlement between the political parties could help in restoring stability. But he also saw that not only was political settlement not in sight, but violence might influence the nature of the political settlement. He wondered whether the people might be persuaded to agree, if their leaders could not. His tours of Bengal and Bihar succeeded in re-educating the masses, but he was handicapped by the fact that his voice did not carry the weight with the Muslim middle classes which it once had done. The Hindus were also restive and critical of what they believed to be his policy of 'unilateral disarmament', but he could still sway them. If Jinnah had toured East Bengal or West Punjab, he might have helped in stopping the rot. Such a suggestion, however, would have been simply laughed away by the Muslim League leader, whose political instinct rebelled against fasts and walking tours.

Lawyer and parliamentarian as he was, it is difficult to believe that Jinnah could have believed in force. But he seemed to have believed in threats of force. After the 'Great Calcutta Killing' and the disturbances in Bengal and Bihar, communal violence became the strongest argument in his brief for Pakistan; if

India was not divided, he warned, worse things would happen. Though he obliged Wavell and Mountbatten by signing appeals for peace, he did little to restrain his bellicose lieutenants; he himself issued doubled-edged statements which extenuated the violence they purported to condemn.

# Victory of the Vanquished

FROM Mr Attlee's window in Downing Street, the darkest aspect of the Indian horizon was the threat of civil war. He has recorded in his memoirs that though he did not think the chances of an orderly change-over were very good he felt there was one man who 'might pull it off'. The man was Rear-Admiral Lord Mountbatten, who succeeded Lord Wavell in March 1947.

One of the first acts of the new Viceroy was to invite Gandhi for a discussion. The Mahatma interrupted his peace mission in Bihar and travelled by train to New Delhi. He advised Mountbatten to dissolve the Congress-League coalition government and to ask Jinnah to form a cabinet. Evidently, Gandhi's object was to disarm Jinnah's suspicion of Congress and the Hindus with one supreme gesture. To the British Government, however, the suggestion looked far-fetched. The Congress leaders had lately seen enough of their Muslim League colleagues in the Interim Government not to want to give them *carte blanche;* the time for gestures was past. When Jinnah met Mountbatten he reiterated his demand for the division of India.

The Viceroy's task was made easier by a reorientation of the Congress attitude to partition. Hitherto Congress had insisted that partition should, if at all, follow and not precede political liberation, that—to use a famous expression of Maulana Azad—there could be no divorce before marriage. But a few months of stormy courtship in the Interim Government had cured Congress leaders of all desire for a closer union. In the spring of 1947 the choice seemed to them to be between anarchy and partition; they resigned themselves to the latter in order to salvage three-fourths of India from the chaos which threatened the whole.

The stage was thus set for the June 3rd Plan, under which power was to be transferred by the British to two successor states on August 15, 1947. The final proposals, which took the Viceroy ten weeks of tireless negotiation and taxed to the full his ingenuity and diplomatic skill, represented the lowest common denominator of agreement between the Congress and the

League; though they left the ultimate decision to democratic processes—voting by members of provincial legislatures or by referendum—the partition of India, as also the partition of the Punjab and Bengal, were foregone conclusions.

What Gandhi had feared had come to pass. India was to be divided, but partition was not to be imposed; it had been accepted by Jawaharlal Nehru, Vallabhbhai Patel and a majority of the Congress Working Committee. Gandhi had no hand in the final negotiations, but his opposition to partition was an open secret. His reasons were the same as those he had given several times before: 'We are unable to think coherently whilst the British power is still functioning in India. Its function is not to change the map of India. All it has to do is to withdraw and leave India, carrying out the withdrawal, if possible, in an orderly manner, maybe even in chaos, on or before the promised date.' The very violence which in the opinion of his Congress colleagues and that of the British Government provided a compelling motive for partition was for him an irresistible argument against it; to accept partition because of the fear of civil war was to acknowledge that 'everything was to be got if mad violence was perpetrated in sufficient measure'.

With such strong views on partition, it might well have been expected that Gandhi would oppose the Mountbatten Plan. The Viceroy had indeed some anxiety on this score. Gandhi had no intention, however, of blocking a settlement which was accepted by leaders of the Congress and the League as well as by the British Government. At the meeting of the All-India Congress Committee which debated the Mountbatten Plan he made no secret of his own misgivings, but threw his weight in favour of its acceptance. By this act of self-abnegation he saved a split in Congress at a crucial moment, without compromising his own independence.

Partition having been decided upon, Gandhi's efforts were henceforth directed to mitigating its risks. He welcomed Jinnah's promise of equal rights and privileges to the Hindu minority in Pakistan, and urged the future Indian Union, as 'the major partner', to set an example to its neighbour in treating the minorities not justly but generously.

A becoming pageantry was to mark the transfer of power from Britain to India on August 15, 1947, but Gandhi was in no mood to think of bands and banners. The day for which he had longed and laboured had come, but he felt no elation. Not only was India's freedom being ushered in at the cost of her unity, but large sections of the population were uneasy about their future.

Early in August, after a brief visit to Kashmir, Gandhi passed through West Punjab and saw the havoc which the recent disturbances in that province had wrought; then he left for East Bengal, where the Hindus of Noakhali feared a fresh wave of disturbances after the establishment of Pakistan.

On arrival at Calcutta he found the town in the grip of communal lawlessness, which had been its lot for a year. With the exit of the Muslim League ministry and the transfer of the majority of Muslim officials and police to Pakistan, the tables had, however, been turned. It seemed as if the Hindus of Calcutta were determined to pay off old scores. Suhrawardy, now no longer Premier, and therefore somewhat chastened, met Gandhi and urged him to pacify Calcutta before proceeding to Noakhali. Gandhi agreed on condition that Suhrawardy would stay with him under the same roof in Calcutta and also use his influence with Muslim opinion in East Bengal to protect the Hindu minority. The Mahatma's choice fell upon a Muslim workman's house in Belighata, a part of the town which was considered unsafe for Muslims. Hardly had he moved into his new quarters when, on August 13th, a group of young Hindus staged a demonstration against his peace mission. He explained to them how he had been trying to end the fratricidal strife, and how hate and violence would lead them nowhere. His words fell like gentle rain on parched earth, and the young men returned to their homes converted. Calcutta was transformed overnight. Rioting ceased. On August 14th, the eve of independence was jointly celebrated by the two communities. Hindus and Muslims collected in the streets, danced and sang together. The incubus which had pressed down upon the heart of the town since August 1946 was suddenly lifted. On Id day Hindus exchanged greetings and gifts with Muslims. The scenes were reminiscent of the halcyon days of the Khilafat movement in 1920-2. Three to four hundred thousand people attended Gandhi's prayer meetings, where the flags of India and Pakistan flew together. Gandhi was pleased. 'We have drunk the poison of hatred,' he said, 'and so this nectar of fraternization tastes all the sweeter.'

This cordiality had hardly lasted for a fortnight when the news of the massacres and the migrations from the Punjab caused a fresh flare-up. A Hindu mob raided Gandhi's residence in Belighata on the night of August 31st; it was angry, abusive, violent; it smashed the windows and forced its way into the house. The Mahatma's words were drowned in a violent din; a brick flew past him; a *lathi* blow just missed him. Concurrently Calcutta relapsed into rioting.

This was a serious set-back to Gandhi's efforts for peace. His answer was the announcement of a fast from September 1st, to be broken only when peace returned to the town. 'What my word in person could not do,' he said, 'my fast may.' The announcement electrified Calcutta; the Muslims were moved, the Hindus shamed. Not even the hooligans of Calcutta could bear the thought of having his blood on their conscience; truck-loads of contraband arms were voluntarily surrendered by the communal underground. The leaders of all communities pledged themselves to peace and begged Gandhi to break the fast. Gandhi consented, but with the warning that if the pledge was not honoured he would embark on an irrevocable fast.

The Calcutta fast was universally acclaimed as a miracle; in the oft-quoted words of the correspondent of the London *Times*, it did what several divisions of troops could not have done. Henceforth Calcutta and Bengal were to remain calm; the fever of communal strife had subsided.

Immediately, Gandhi felt free to turn to the Punjab. In a sense the flare-up in that Province in the middle of August 1947 was only a continuation of the earlier riots in March 1947; the villages and the towns of the Punjab, seized with fantastic hopes or strange fears, had been dreading and at the same time preparing for a battle of the barricades. The administrative paralysis caused by the reshuffling of cadres on a communal basis, and the infiltration of communalism into the police and military had, by the end of August, led to a situation in which it was impossible for the Hindus to stay in West Punjab and Muslims to stay in East Punjab.

The sum of human misery involved in the movement of five million Hindus and Sikhs from West Punjab to East Punjab, and in the movement of an equal number of Muslims in the opposite direction was appalling. The danger, however, was that as the refugees arrived at their destinations with their tales of woe, violence might spread. This is indeed what happened in Delhi in the first week of September. Gandhi found the capital of India paralysed by one of the worst communal riots in its long history. He felt there was no point in his proceeding to the Punjab when Delhi was aflame. The Government had taken prompt and energetic action. But Gandhi was not content with a peace imposed by the police and the military; violence had to be purged from the hearts of the people. It was an uphill task.

The town had a number of refugee camps, some of which housed Hindus and Sikhs from West Pakistan, while others sheltered Muslims fleeing from Delhi for a passage across the border. The Hindu and Sikh refugees were in a difficult mood. Many of them, uprooted from their homes, lands and occupations, were going through unfamiliar pangs of poverty; some had been bereaved in the riots and all were bitter. They were anxious to wedge their way into the economy of Delhi; their eyes were riveted on Muslim houses and shops to replace those they had left behind in Pakistan. They could not understand the Mahatma's advice to 'forget and forgive' and to bear no malice in their hearts for those at whose hands they had suffered. They even blamed him for the division of India; his non-violence, they said, had been outclassed by violence. When he suggested that one day they would return to their homes in Pakistan, they smiled incredulously: he had not seen what they had seen; he had not suffered as they had suffered. He wore himself out in an effort to re-educate the people of Delhi; he heard grievances, suggested solutions, encouraged or admonished his numerous interviewers, visited refugee camps, remained in touch with local officials. It was an exhausting and sometimes a heart-breaking routine.

Gandhi had a half-serious and half-humorous way of saying that he aspired to live for 125 years, which, according to Hindu tradition, was the full span of human life. He was so unhappy, however, at the communal riots which began with the 'Great Calcutta Killing' that he repeated time and again that he did not want to 'be a living witness of the fratricidal strife'. Congratulated on his birthday he asked, 'Where do congratulations come in? Would condolences be not more appropriate?'

One wonders whether he had a presentiment of an early end, or whether these remarks were no more than occasional glimpses of the torture of mind and spirit which he suffered during this period. 'Life and death' he once described as 'the faces of the same coin'. He spoke of death as an 'incomparable friend'. There were several occasions when his life had hung by the slenderest thread. He was only twenty-seven when he was nearly lynched in the streets of Durban; eleven years later he was belaboured in Johannesburg by a rugged compatriot; in 1924 a bomb narrowly missed him while he was on his way to the Poona municipal hall. Several of his fasts brought him to the verge of a collapse; in at least two of them his survival seemed a miracle. As a soldier of non-violence, he had probably run more hazards than many a general had done on the battlefield.

On January 13, 1948 he began a fast. 'My greatest fast,' he wrote to his English disciple, Mirabehn. It was also to be his last. The fast was not to be broken until Delhi became peaceful. The town was ostensibly quiet; thanks to the stern measures taken by the Government, the killings had stopped. But the peace for which Gandhi had been working for four and a half months was not 'the peace of the grave', but a peace symbolizing the reunion of hearts. Of the latter there was little sign. Muslims did not dare move about freely in the town; reports reached the Mahatma that the refugees from West Pakistan were applying subtle methods to oust local Muslims from their shops and houses. The argument that Hindus and Sikhs were equally unsafe throughout the whole of West Pakistan struck him as irrelevant.

The fast had a refreshing impact on Pakistan, where it punctured the subtle web of propaganda which for ten years had represented Gandhi as an enemy of Islam. In India there was an emotional shake-up. The fast compelled people to think afresh on the problem on the solution of which he had staked his life. There was a sense of urgency; something had to be done quickly to create conditions in which he could end his fast. The Government of India paid out to Pakistan, at his instance, and as a gesture of goodwill, Rs. 55 crores (£44 million), which were due as part of united India's assets but had been withheld on account of the conflict in Kashmir. On January 18, 1948 representatives of various communities and parties in Delhi signed a pledge in Gandhi's presence that they would guarantee peace in Delhi.

After this fast the tide of communal violence showed definite signs of ebbing. Gandhi felt freer to make his plans for the future. He had promised the refugees from West Pakistan that he would not rest until every family had been rehabilitated in its native town or village. But he felt he could not go to Pakistan without the permission of the Government of that country. Meanwhile, he thought of returning to his *Ashram* at Sevagram. For several months almost all his time had been taken up by the communal problem. However acute this problem was, in a wider perspective it was only a red herring across the path of the country's onward march. The real problems of India, the social and economic uplift of her people, had never been absent from his mind. He thought of the tasks ahead. Constitution-making would soon be over. He had no thought of entering the Government or active politics in independent India, but he could do his bit to initiate new channels for constructive work. He discussed the possibility of unifying all the constructive organizations for the realization of the non-violent order which was their common aim.

Political freedom having become a fact, Gandhi's mind was switching more and more on to social and economic reform, and to the refurbishing of his non-violent technique.

However, he was destined neither to go to Pakistan nor to pick up the threads of his constructive programme. The first warning came on the evening of January 20th, when a bomb exploded in Birla House a few feet from where he was addressing his prayer meeting. He took no notice of the explosion. Next day he referred to the congratulations which he had received for remaining unruffled after the explosion. He would deserve them, he said, 'if I fall as a result of such an explosion and yet retain a smile on my face and no malice against the assailant'. He described the bomb-thrower as a 'misguided youth' and advised the police not to 'molest' him but to convert him with persuasion and affection. Madan Lal, a refugee from the Punjab who had been arrested, was in fact a member of a gang which had plotted Ghandi's death. These highly-strung young men saw Hinduism menaced by Islam from without and by Gandhi from within. When Madan Lal missed his aim, a fellow conspirator, Nathuram Godse, a young journalist from Poona, came to Delhi. With a pistol in his pocket he hovered round Birla House, where Gandhi stayed and held his prayer meeting.

Vaguely suspecting a conspiracy, the local authorities had increased their vigilance. Gandhi, however, would not permit the police to search those who came to attend his prayer meetings. 'If I have to die,' he told the police officers, 'I should die at the prayer meeting. You are wrong in believing that you can protect me from harm. God is my protector.' On the evening of January 30th he left his room in Birla House for the prayer ground. It was only two minutes' walk, but he was a little late that day, having been detained in a meeting with Sardar Patel. With his forearms on the shoulders of his grandnieces, Ava and Manu—walking-sticks as he called them—he walked briskly. As he approached the prayer ground the congregation of five hundred made a passage for him; many rose, some bowed low in reverence. He said he was sorry for being late, lifted his hands and joined them in a *namaskar* (salutation). Just at that moment Godse edged forward through the crowd, bent low as if to prostrate himself at the Mahatma's feet, whipped out his pistol and fired three shots in quick succession. Gandhi fell instantly with the words '*He Rama*' (Oh, God).

It was a strange irony that the apostle of non-violence should have met a violent end. The dark forces of hate seemed to have won; but theirs was a pyrrhic victory. The bullets which passed through Gandhi's chest reverberated in millions of hearts. The very wickedness of the crime exposed, as if in a flash of lightning, the fatuity and futility of communal fanaticism. The flames which reduced the Mahatma's body to ashes on the banks of the Yamuna on the evening of January 31, 1948, proved to be the last flicker of that conflagration which had enveloped the Indo-Pakistan sub-continent since August 1946. Gandhi had fought this fire with all his strength while he lived. His death was finally to quench it.

# Epilogue

THOUGH his role in the political liberation of India inevitably loomed large in the eyes of the world, the mainspring of Gandhi's life lay not in politics but in religion. 'What I want to achieve,' he wrote in his autobiography, 'what I have been striving and pining to achieve these thirty years—is to see God face to face, to attain *moksha*. I live and move and have my being in pursuit of this goal.' His deepest strivings were spiritual. Finding him in a political deputation, Montagu, the Secretary of State for India, had exclaimed, 'How have you, a social reformer, found your way into this crowd?'

Gandhi explained that participation in politics was only an extension of his social activity: 'I could not be leading a religious life unless I identified myself with the whole of mankind, and that I could not do so unless I took part in politics. The whole gamut of man's activities today constitutes an indivisible whole. You cannot divide social, economic, and purely religious work into watertight compartments.' He did not know, he said, any religion apart from human activity; the spiritual law did not work in a field of its own but expressed itself through the ordinary activities of life. To be truly religious one did not have to retire to the Himalayas nor shrink into the security of the home or a sect.

The dissociation between politics and religion, between statecraft and ethics has lasted so long, however, that neat minds revolt against any mixture of the two. Truth, charity, and love are considered virtues applicable only in the domestic and social spheres. In politics expediency seems to be the prime mover. Gandhi's whole career was a protest against this double morality. He did not divorce the sacred and the secular. His interest in politics derived from the fact that he developed a technique—Satyagraha—which sought to introduce the spirit of religion into politics. The question was often asked by western observers whether Gandhi was a saint or a politician; he was a saint who did not cease to be one when he entered politics. Gandhi himself considered the word saint too sacred to be applied to him. He was 'a humble seeker after truth', who had caught 'only the faintest glimmer of that mighty effulgence'. He made no claims to infallibility, and let all the world know when he was groping in the dark. If he thought or spoke of himself as if he were an instrument of God, it was not as a chosen instrument with a special revelation of God's will. 'My firm belief is,' he said, 'that He reveals himself to every human being, but we shut our ears to the still small voice within.'

His humility was not a cultivated virtue, but sprang from a ceaseless struggle for self-mastery in which he remained engaged from his childhood till the last day of his life. 'For him,' wrote his secretary Mahadev Desai, 'the struggle with the opponent within is keener than with the opponent without.' He described himself as an average man with less than an average ability. 'I admit,' he remarked, 'that I am not sharp intellectually. But I don't mind. There is a limit to the development of the intellect but none to that of the heart.'

Since he was continually elaborating his ideas on every subject, it was easy to confront him with his own earlier pronouncements on caste, machinery or *khadi*, and point out the discrepancies. In the glare of the ruthless publicity in which he lived, every one of his gestures and words was public property, but he willingly shared with the world even an ignoble thought if it happened in a dream to flash across his mind. What he wrote of Tolstoy is equally true of him: 'Tolstoy's so-called inconsistencies were a sign of his development and passionate regard for truth. He often seemed inconsistent because he was continually outgrowing his own doctrines. His failures were public; his struggles and triumphs private.'

Rabindranath Tagore once aptly described Gandhi as essentially 'a lover of men and not of ideas'. Though he loved to reduce all problems to his moral algebra, Gandhi did not ram his opinions down anybody's throat. 'Never take anything for gospel truth,' he warned, 'even if it comes from a Mahatma.' *Hind Swaraj*, his first political testament, included a scathing attack on modern civilization and all its appurtenances of schools, railways and hospitals, but Gandhi no more tried to foist this philosophy on his followers than to compel them to adopt the loin-cloth.

Gandhi devoted the best part of his life to one crucial problem: how to perfect and extend *ahimsa* (non-violence) in human relationships. For him, the validity of non-violence was independent of his own success or failure. His criticisms of Western materialism and militarism in *Hind Swaraj* were made five years before the outbreak of the First World War, when Europe was at the zenith of its prestige and power. These criticisms may have appeared quixotic fifty years ago; today, as the world trembles on the brink of a Third World War, they seem prophetic. By spurning material progress at the cost of moral values, and by irrevocably renouncing violence, Gandhi took a line in direct opposition to the two dominant ideologies of the twentieth century, capitalism and communism. He visualized and worked for a society which would provide for the essential needs of the community (and no more), and in which the decentralization of economic and political structures would minimize the incentives for exploitation within and conflict without. Such a society could, he believed, dispense with the coercive apparatus of the modern state, and depend upon non-violent techniques not only to maintain order but to protect itself against external aggression.

It is difficult to say whether Gandhi's dream will come true. Nations, like individuals, are tempted to continue along the beaten path, even though it may end in a blind alley. Gandhi knew the difficulties of translating his non-violent dream into the world of reality. But he refused to compromise on what he held to be the fundamentals. To the last he affirmed that even good ends do not justify dubious means; that our real enemies are our own fears, greeds and egotisms; that we must change ourselves before we can change others; that the laws of the family, of truth and love and charity, are applicable to groups, communities and nations; and above all, that 'non-violence is the law of our species, as violence is the law of the brute.' To those who are charged with the destinies of nations, all this may sound a very desirable but a very distant ideal. Yet, in the thermo-nuclear age, if civilization is not to disintegrate into a mass of torn flesh and molten metal, the premises of Gandhi have an immediate relevance.

# INDEX